ORDNANCE SURVEY MEMOIRS OF IRELAND

Volume Thirty-Eight

PARISHES OF COUNTY DONEGAL I
1833–5

First published 1997
Reprinted 1999
The Institute of Irish Studies,
The Queen's University of Belfast,
Belfast
In association with
The Royal Irish Academy,
Dawson Street,
Dublin.

Reprinted 2021 by Ulster Historical Foundation

Grateful acknowledgement is made to the Economic and Social Research Council and the Department of Education for Northern Ireland for their financial assistance at different stages of this publication programme.

We would also like to thank the office of the Taoiseach and the Department of Education in Ireland for contributing towards the costs of this volume.

Copyright 1997.

All rights reserved. No part of this publication may be produced, stored in a retrieval system Or transmitted, in any form or by any means, electronic, mechanical, photocopying, recording or Otherwise, without the prior permission of the publisher.

British Library Cataloguing-in-Publication Data.
A catalogue record for this book is available from the British Library.

Paperback ISBN 13: 978-0-85389-564-0
Hardback ISBN 13: 978-0-85389-565-7

Printed in Ireland by SPRINT-print Ltd.

Ordnance Survey Memoirs of Ireland
VOLUME THIRTY-EIGHT

Parishes of County Donegal I
1833–5

North-East Donegal

Edited by Angélique Day and Patrick McWilliams

The Institute of Irish Studies
in association with
The Royal Irish Academy

EDITORIAL BOARD

Angélique Day (General Editor)
Patrick S. McWilliams (Executive Editor)
Dr B.M. Walker (Publishing Director)
Professor R.H. Buchanan

CONTENTS

	Page
Introduction	ix
Brief history of the Irish Ordnance Survey and Memoirs	ix
Definition of terms used	x
Note on Memoirs of County Donegal	x

Parishes in County Donegal

Clondavaddog	1
Clonmany	12
Culdaff	21
Desertegney	24
Donagh	31
Killygarvan	36
Kilmacrenan	50
Mevagh	54
Mintiaghs (Bar of Inch)	64
Moville	68
Muff	80
Tullyaughnish	84
Lough Swilly (with Burt and Inch)	98
Miscellaneous Papers	151

List of selected maps and drawings

County Donegal, with parish boundaries	vi
County Donegal, 1837, by Samuel Lewis	viii
Fanad lighthouse	2
Carrickabrackey Castle	15

List of O.S. maps, 1830s

Buncrana	23
Moville	69
Kilmacrenan	51
Ramelton	85
Rathmullan	37
West Town, Tory Island	125

Ordnance Survey Memoirs

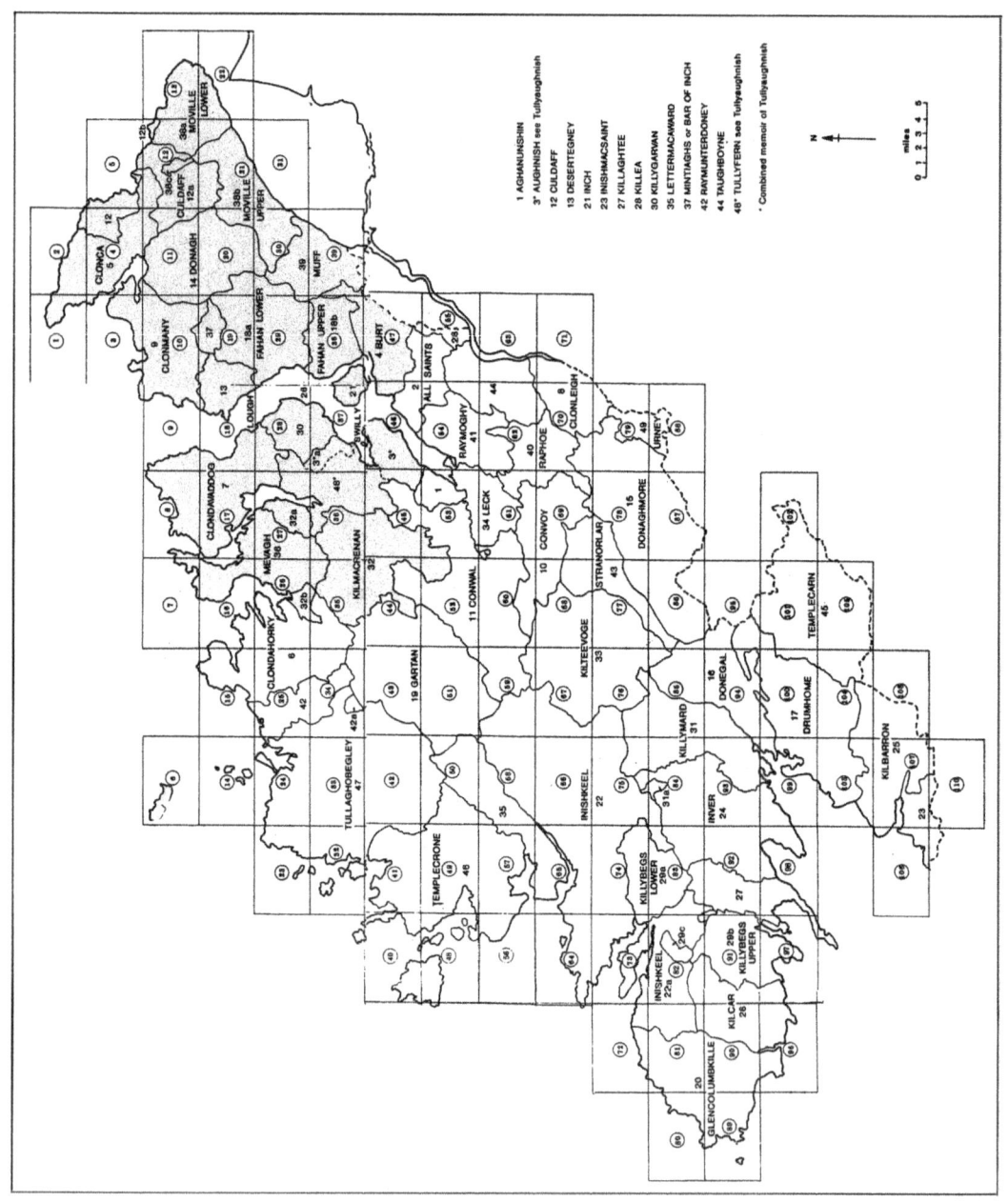

ACKNOWLEDGEMENTS

During the course of the transcription and publication project many have advised and encouraged us in this gigantic task. Thanks must first be given to the Royal Irish Academy which has made available to us the original manuscripts. We are also greatly indebted to Librarian Siobhán O'Rafferty and her staff for their continuing help in deciphering indistinct passages of manuscript.

We should like to acknowledge the following individuals for their special contributions. Dr Brian Trainor led the way with his edition of the Antrim Memoir and provided vital help on the steering committee. Dr Ann Hamlin and the Department of Environment have also provided valuable support, especially during the latter part of the project. Professor R.H. Buchanan's unfailing encouragement has been an inspiration to us. Without Dr Kieran Devine the initial stages of the transcription and the computerising work would never have been completed successfully: the project owes a great deal to his constant help and advice. Dr Kay Muhr's contribution to the work of the project is appreciated, as is that of former editor Nóirín Dobson. Mr W.C. Kerr's interest and expertise have been invaluable. Professor Anne Crookshank and Dr Edward McParland were most generous with practical help and advice concerning the drawings amongst the Memoir manuscripts.

We would like to thank the Director of the Ordnance Survey, Dublin and the keepers of the fireproof store, among them Leonard Hines. Finally, all students of the nineteenth-century Ordnance Survey of Ireland owe a great deal to the pioneering work of Professor J.H. Andrews, and his kind help in the first days of the project is gratefully recorded.

For his assistance in obtaining the illustration on the front cover, we are indebted to Queen's University Arts Librarian Michael Smallman. Special mention must be made of Colán MacArthur's kind help with the Memoirs. We are grateful to F.E. Hart for his suggestions. We would also like to thank Liam Ronayne, the Donegal County Librarian, for his support and interest.

The essential task of inputting the texts from audio tapes was done by Miss Eileen Kingan, Mrs Christine Robertson, Miss Eilis Smyth, Miss Lynn Murray and, most importantly, Miss Maureen Carr.

We are grateful to the Linen Hall Library for lending us their copies of the first edition 6" Ordnance Survey maps: also to Ms Maura Pringle of QUB Cartography Department for the index maps showing the parish boundaries. For providing financial assistance at crucial times for the maintenance of the project, we would like to take this opportunity of thanking the trustees of the Esme Mitchell trust and The Public Record Office of Northern Ireland.

Left:
Map of parishes of County Donegal. The area described in this volume, the parishes of North-East Donegal, has been shaded to highlight its location. The square grids represent the 1830s 6" Ordnance Survey maps. The encircled numbers relate to the map numbers as presented in the bound volumes of maps for the county. The parishes have been numbered in all cases and named in full where possible, but if this has not been possible a key is provided.

The following parishes have no Memoir: Aghanunshin, Clonca, Clondahorky, Fahan Lower, Fahan Upper, Gartan, Inishmacsaint, Inver, Kilcar, Killaghtee, Killybegs Lower, Killybegs Upper, Lettermacaward, Raymunterdoney, Stranorlar, Templecrone.

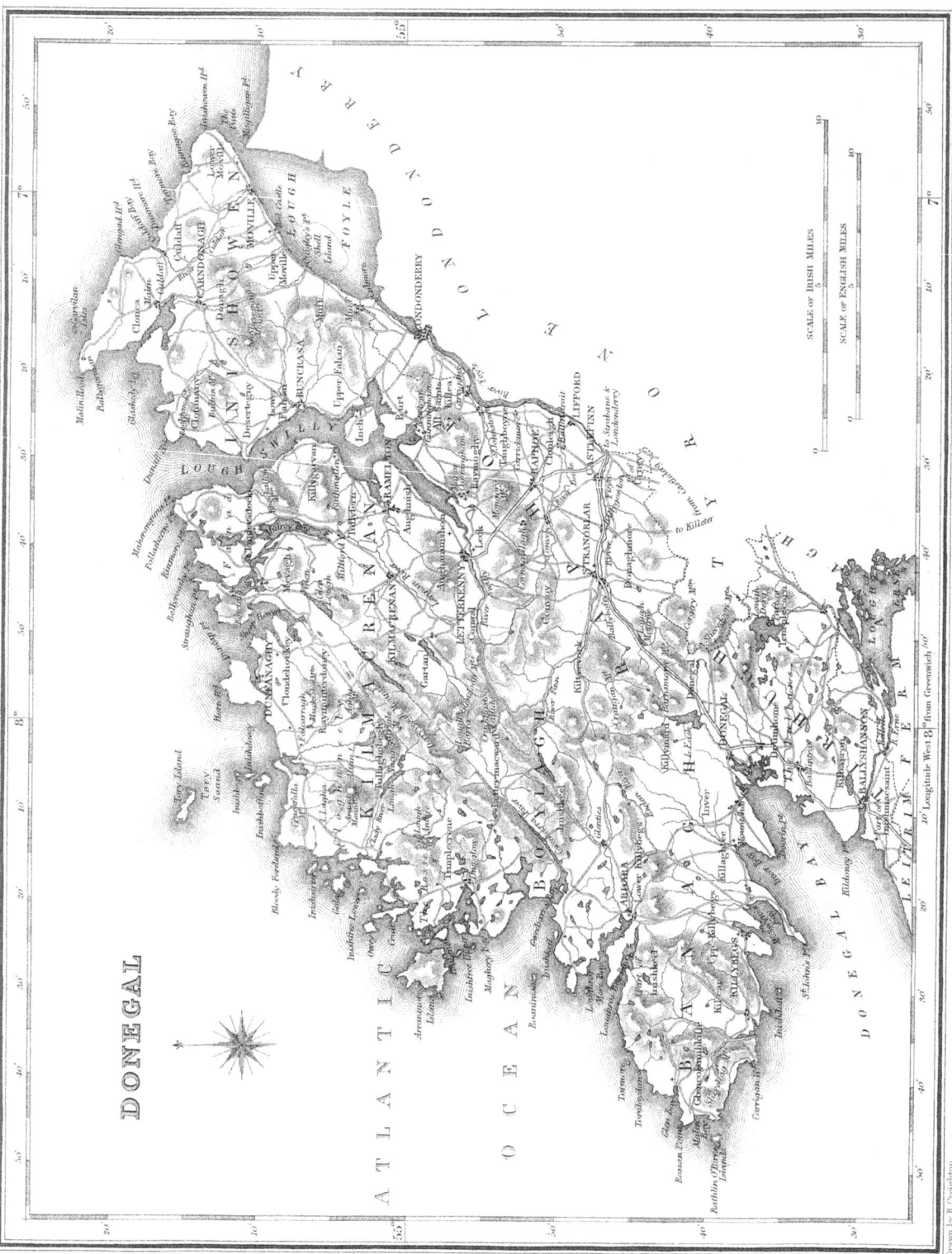

INTRODUCTION AND GUIDE TO THE PUBLICATION OF THE ORDNANCE SURVEY MEMOIRS

The following text of the Ordnance Survey Memoirs was first transcribed by a team working in the Institute of Irish Studies at The Queen's University of Belfast, on a computerised index of the material. For this publication programme the text has been further edited: spellings have been modernised in most cases, although where the original spelling was thought to be of any interest it has been retained and is indicated by angle brackets in the text. Variant spellings for townland and lesser place-names have been preserved, although parish and major place-names have been standardised and the original spelling given in angle brackets. Names of prominent people, for instance landlords, have been standardised where possible, but original spellings of names in lists of informants, emigration tables and on tombstones have been retained. We have not altered the Memoir writers' anglicisation of names and words in Irish.

Punctuation has been modernised and is the responsibility of the editors. Editorial additions are indicated by square brackets: a question mark before and after a word indicates a queried reading and tentatively inserted information respectively. Original drawings are referred to in the text, and some have been reproduced. Manuscript page references have been omitted from this series. Because of the huge variation in size of Memoirs for different counties, the following editorial policy has been adopted: where there are numerous duplicating and overlapping accounts, the most complete and finished account, normally the Memoir proper, has been presented, with additional unique information from other accounts like the Fair Sheets entered into a separate section, clearly titled and identified; where the Memoir material is less, nothing has been omitted. To achieve standard volume size, parishes have been associated on the basis of propinquity.

There are considerable differences in the volume of information recorded for different areas: counties Antrim and Londonderry are exceptionally well covered, while the other counties do not have quite the same detail. This series is the first systematic publication of the parish Memoirs, although individual parishes have been published by pioneering local history societies. The entire transcriptions of the Memoirs made in the course of the indexing project can be consulted in the Public Record Office of Northern Ireland and the library at the Queen's University of Belfast. The manuscripts of the Ordnance Survey Memoirs are in the Royal Irish Academy, Dublin.

Brief history of the Irish Ordnance Survey in the nineteenth century and the writing of the Ordnance Survey Memoirs.

In 1824 a House of Commons committee recommended a townland survey of Ireland with maps at the scale of 6," to facilitate a uniform valuation for local taxation. The Duke of Wellington, then prime minister, authorised this, the first Ordnance Survey of Ireland. The survey was directed by Colonel Thomas Colby, who had under his command officers of the Royal Engineers and three companies of sappers and miners. In addition to this, civil assistants were recruited to help with sketching, drawing and engraving of maps, and eventually, in the 1830s, the writing of the Memoirs.

The Memoirs were written descriptions intended to accompany the maps, containing information which could not be fitted on to them. Colonel Colby always considered additional information to be necessary to clarify place-names and other distinctive features of each parish; this was to be written up in reports by the officers. Much information about parishes resulted from research into place-names and was used in the writing of the Memoirs. The term "Memoir" comes from the abbreviation of the word "Aide-Memoire." It was also used in the 18th century to describe topographical descriptions accompanying maps.

In 1833 Colby's assistant, Lieutenant Thomas Larcom, developed the scope of the officers' reports by stipulating the headings or "Heads of Inquiry" under which information was to be reported, and including topics of social as well as economic interest. By this time civil assistants were writing some of the Memoirs under the supervision of the officers, as well as collecting information in the Fair Sheets.

The first "Memoirs" are officers' reports covering Antrim in 1830, and work continued on the Antrim parishes right through the decade, with special activity in 1838 and 1839. Counties Down and Tyrone were written up from 1833 to 1837, with both officers and civil assistants working on Memoirs. In Londonderry and Fermanagh research and writing started in 1834. Armagh was worked on in 1835, 1837 and 1838. Much labour was expended in the Londonderry parishes. The plans to publish the Memoirs commenced with the parish of Templemore, containing the city and liberties of Derry, which came out in 1837 after a great deal of expense and effort.

Between 1839 and 1840 the Memoir scheme collapsed. Sir Robert Peel's government could not countenance the expenditure of money and time on such an exercise; despite a parliamentary commission favouring the continuation of the writing of the Memoirs, the scheme was halted before the southern half of the country was covered. The manuscripts remained unpublished and most were removed to the Royal Irish Academy, Dublin from the Ordnance Survey, Phoenix Park. Other records of the Ordnance Survey, including some material from the Memoir scheme, have recently been transferred to the National Archives, Bishop Street, Dublin.

The Memoirs are a uniquely detailed source for the history of the northern half of Ireland immediately before the Great Famine. They document the landscape and situation, buildings and antiquities, land-holdings and population, employment and livelihood of the parishes. They act as a nineteenth-century Domesday book and are essential to the understanding of the cultural heritage of our communities. It is planned to produce a volume of evaluative essays to put the material in its full context, with information on other sources and on the writers of the Memoirs.

Definition of descriptive terms

Memoir (sometimes Statistical Memoir): an account of a parish written according to the prescribed form outlined in the instructions known as "Heads of Inquiry," and normally divided into three sections: Natural Features and History; Modern and Ancient Topography; Social and Productive Economy.

Fair Sheets: "information gathered for the Memoirs," an original title describing paragraphs of information following no particular order, often with marginal headings, signed and dated by the civil assistant responsible.

Statistical Remarks/Accounts: both titles are employed by the Engineer officers in their descriptions of the parish with marginal headings, often similar in layout to the Memoir.

Office Copies: these are copies of early drafts, generally officers' accounts and must have been made for office purposes.

Ordnance Survey Memoirs for County Donegal

This volume, the thirty-eighth in the series and the first of two for county Donegal, contains the Memoirs for 14 parishes in Inishowen and north east Donegal, as well as an account of Lough Swilly and adjacent coastlines. There are 2 types of account: the statistical reports written by young lieutenants of the Royal Engineers who were mapping the parishes, namely William Lancey and W. Delves Broughton, dating between 1833 and 1835; and replies to queries sent out by the North West Society in the 1820s, written by a variety of local residents with farming and clerical backgrounds. These include the author of the Lough Swilly account, who was probably one of the Montgomerys of Moville. This ambitious work was written for the North West Society and the description of the parishes of Burt and Inch appended to the end follows the familiar form.

Our evidence for authorship comes in a letter from W. Stokes (possibly the Dr Stokes referred to in the Lough Swilly account) written in 1823 to James Sinclair of Holyhill, near Strabane, a gentleman of the North West Society. This gives the purpose behind the report as recommending sites for safe harbours. There was also a copy of part of this account of Lough Swilly, and of Burt and Inch, in the papers at Phoenix Park now housed in the National Archives, Bishop Street, Dublin, and the latter account was credited to Mr Montgomery.

During the course of the long and fascinating description of the features and maritime riches of Lough Swilly, Lough Foyle, Mulroy and the coastline of the north west, it is clear that several people were involved in its compilation, including pilots and sailors like Captain Smyth of Rathmullan, Sam Craig of Aughnish, Charles Williams of Drumbear on Mulroy and James Meenan and 2 other Tory islanders, as well as farmers like Thomas Anderson of Cloghglass on Inch Island, who contributed to the Burt and Inch report.

The editors have been particularly concerned to present the original order of the account, despite its meandering up and down the coast, and for this reason include the description of Burt and Inch where originally located, not in parish order. We have also retained the many variant spellings of the different marine features and townland names in this account and trust that this will not lead to charges of inconsistency, as the proliferation of such variants indicates the rich linguistic heritage of the region. This account is of interest in its use of the English language as well as for place-names, for instance, the use of "throughother" as a term in textiles.

Besides providing a different chronological dimension, the replies to queries from the North West Society offer a different perspective to those reports of the map-making Royal Engineers. Particularly unusual is that by the Presbyterian minister for Donagh, the Revd Rogers, who could probably understand the Irish language because he uses Irish script.

The military men had a good appreciation of the flora and fauna of the region, and the list of birds with their Latin and common names (from the miscellaneous papers) is probably their work. They also provide some interesting detail about the fishing industry, comments on agriculture and, despite their outsider status, some good observations on social life.

The Memoir for Templemore has great relevance for this part of Donegal and contains descriptions of the magnificent Grianan of Aileach site just above Burt, surely a treasure in Donegal's crown not Derry's; and as the economy of Donegal was so intimately linked with the port and markets of Derry city, this Memoir provides an important part of the picture of how many Donegal households achieved their livelihood. Inishowen parishes have had centuries-old connections with parishes on the other side of Lough Foyle, for instance, Magilligan published in volume 11 of the series, and readers will find such Memoirs useful in complementing the information from those in this volume.

Readers will notice that both forms of spelling Ramelton and Rathmelton are to be found, the first in the 1820s account of Lough Swilly which is by a local (Inishowen) man, and the latter in the account by Lancey which is to be found on the contemporary maps. Otherwise spellings of major place and parish names follow those found in *Donegal History and society*, eds William Nolan, Liam Ronayne, Mairead Dunlevy (Geographical Publications, 1995). As with previous volumes, variant spellings are given in angle brackets, although townland names are left as written by the author of each account; this volume is notable for the number of variant spellings, particularly around Muff.

The above volume, together with the *Archaeological survey of Donegal* by Brian Lacey et al. (Donegal County Council, 1983), is essential reading for anyone interested in the history and landscape of Donegal. *The Heritage of Inishowen* by M.R. Colhoun (North West Archaeological Society, 1995), is a welcome addition to the archaeology, history and folklore of that area. The synopses of family histories, as for instance the Hart family, offered by the PRONI in their calendars of estate papers are well worth consulting. Articles in the Donegal Historical Society Annual on prominent Donegal individuals and families are also recommended.

Donegal and its portrayal through the Ordnance Survey of the early nineteenth century has been brought to the attention of the public more than any other county in Ireland through Brian Friel's play *Translations* (Faber, 1981), which is set in "fictional" Ballybeg, county Donegal, in 1833. The debate arising out of this play raises interesting issues about the interpretation of historical events (see J.H. Andrews' "Notes for a Future Edition of Brian Friel's *Translations*" in *The Irish review* (no.13, winter 1992/93). The view of Donegal presented by these Memoirs has added value when this background is taken into account.

Drawings in the Memoir papers are listed below and are cross-referenced in the text; some are illustrated. The manuscript material is to be found in Boxes 21 and 22 of the Royal Irish Academy's collection of Ordnance Survey Memoirs, and section references are given beside each parish below in their printed order.

Clondavaddog	Box 21 II 1-2
Clonmany	Box 21 IV 1
Culdaff	Box 22 XII [2]
Desertegney	Box 21 VII 1
Donagh	Box 21 VIII 1-2
Killygarvan	Box 22 XVII 1
Kilmacrenan	Box 22 XIX 1
Mevagh	Box 22 I 1
Mintiaghs	Box 22 II 1
Moville	Box 22 III 1, 2, 4, 3
Muff	Box 22 IIIa 1
Tullyaughnish	Box 22 X 1
Lough Swilly (including Burt and Inch)	Box 22 VII 1-10, Box 22 XII [4]
Miscellaneous	Box 22 XII [4]

Drawings

[By Lieutenant W. Lancey unless stated].

Clondavaddog (section 1):

Fanad lighthouse, view looking north, with dimensions [illustrated].

Ruins of Moress Castle ruins, with dimensions.

Sculpted head of St Vaddock in Rosnakill churchyard, with dimensions.

Giant's grave in Ballyhurk, with dimensions.

Standing stones in Ballyhernan.

Parishes of County Donegal

Clonmany (section 1):

Tomb in Binnion graveyard.

Carrickabrackey Castle, view looking north [illustrated].

Detail of loophole in castle.

Desertegney (section 1):

Plan of Cloghogle at Munniaghs, with annotations.

Giant's grave at Munniaghs.

Killygarvan (section 1):

Giant's grave in Upper Drumhallagh, ground plan; view of stones with key.

Giant's bed in Upper Creavary.

Ruins of Carmelite priory in Rathmullan: doorway with dimensions; holy water stoup and 3 sections of plaster mouldings.

Sculpted stone in wall, Rathmullan, with dimensions.

Arms of McSwine family over doorway in Rathmullan ruins.

View of Rathmullan ruins from the sea, drawn to scale; east view of part of ruins, west and ground entrance of ruins.

Killygarvan old church, ground plan with orientation and dimensions; view of west and east end with dimensions; south wall with dimensions of door and window openings, north and back wall with dimensions.

Killygarvan church looking north, by A. Calder.

Arms of McSwine in wall of Killygarvan old church.

Mevagh (section 1):

Old parish church of Mevagh, with dimensions.

Ruins of Rosapenna House, with dimensions.

Melmore tower, with dimensions.

Shuggling Stone Lackagh bridge, view from south, 2 section drawings.

Shuggling Stone, vertical and longitudinal sections with annotations.

Rocking Stone from Island Magee, county Antrim, 2 sections with annotations and dimensions.

Tullyaughnish (section 1):

Ruins of Killydonnell Abbey, with dimensions.

Window at Killydonnell Abbey.

Moulding at Killydonnell Abbey.

Ruins of old castle in Rathmelton, with dimensions.

Ground plan of Rathmelton showing situation of castle, between shore and Castle Street.

Old tower of Fort Stewart, with dimensions.

Cromlech near roads in Gortnaverne.

Trumpadisha Stone.

Parish of Clondavaddog, County Donegal

Statistical Report by Lieutenant W. Lancey,
April 1835

GEOGRAPHY OR NATURAL STATE

Name

In the map, said to be Ptolemy's, attached to [blank's] work on the *Bardic history of Ireland*, this district is called Fanait. In *Collectana Sacra* by Revd Dr Doyle, the Roman Catholic Bishop of Raphoe (1788), it is said that St Moadog (Mhoidog) was patron saint of the peninsula of Fanad <Fannet>.

The name of this parish is Clondavaddog <Clondevaddock> but properly Cluain-ne-mhoiadog. Cluain signifies "deception" and it is from this idea: certain select tracts of land, commonly the most fertile soil being kept for meadow or other uses from cattle or common pasturage, were called "cluain," from deceiving the cattle which are let into it when the crop is cut down and carried away.

"Some of the late posterity of Suibhne were in later times proprietors of large districts in the county Donegal called Fanit, in Irish Fanonuid, which signifies "under bog." Suibhne was afterwards corrupted into McSwine or McSweeny." Some say Fanad means Fahan-art "at the valley," others that Clondavaddog is "the plover's feeding ground," but the most probable meaning of Clondavaddog is Cluain-na-mhoidog or waddog, "the valley of St Waddock," distinguished from Cluainnamanach or Clonmany on the opposite entrance of Lough Swilly.

Locality

This interesting and highly picturesque district lies on the left bank of Lough Swilly at its confluence with the Atlantic Ocean, by whose waves its shores are washed to the entrance of Mulroy bay which embraces it in its winding and beautiful course to the mearing of Tullyaughnish, which parish runs along its southern gorge for about 4 and a half miles.

This peninsula is about 10 miles in length and 7 miles in breadth in its widest part. It lies in the north east part of the barony of Kilmacrenan, in the county of Donegal, diocese of Raphoe and north west circuit, and contains 26,255 acres, 15,467 acres of which are cultivated, 10,502 uncultivated and 286 are water.

The parish paid county cess in 1829 920 pounds 17s 10d; in 1830 591 pounds 8s 7d ha'penny; in 1831 675 pounds 13s 6d; in 1832 903 pounds 5s 7d ha'penny; in 1833 829 pounds 19s 7d ha'penny; in 1834 827 pounds 1s 2d.

NATURAL FEATURES

Hills

The principal range of hills is that of Knockalla, composed of quartz rock, and is evidently a continuation of Urris on the opposite coast of Lough Swilly. This range is so abrupt on the east shore that no road has been attempted to be made over it. North of Knockalla is a low undulating country composed of quartz rock and limestone, succeeded by 2 chains of quartz hills divided by the waters of Fanad and Loughs Kindrum and Kinnylough. These ranges are traversed by green stone dykes and run, together with Knockalla, in the usual direction in the barony from north east to south west.

Knockalla is 1,196 feet high, the elevation of the valley to the north of it about 100 feet, and the chief eminences north of this are Lurgologhan and Kindrum, and Murrian, running south west to north east, the highest, being 751 feet.

Lakes

Lough Swilly, which has so frequently been referred to in the Memoirs of the other parishes that there is little here to be added to its description. The Swilly rock, on which the *Saldanha* frigate was lost, lies on the east coast of Fanad and the greater part of the parish lies without the Martello towers erected for the defence of the lough. In the war it was not unusual to see 6 lines of battleships in the harbour. [Crossed out: There are 44 loughs registered for content in the parish, the largest of which are Kinnylough, 182 acres, Kindrum, 155 acres and Shannagh, 71 acres].

Mulroy Bay

This bay washes all the western shore of Fanad and is remarkable for its circuitous courses, its general direction being south and south east. It is 1 and a quarter miles across at its entrance. At 8 miles from the ocean it passes through the narrow channel of the Hassans and spreads itself for

Fanad lighthouse

1 mile in breadth, flowing to the north and south. This return to the north averages 1,760 feet in breadth for 2 miles, is again contracted to [blank] feet at Moress ferry, whose swelling at [blank] feet peninsulates Moress, is studded with islands and runs to within 1 and an eighth miles of the ocean, forming the north west part of the parish into a large peninsula which is known by the name of "between the waters."

The bay runs in a fine sheet of water from the Hassans to Cratlagh in Tullyaughnish and is navigable for vessels of 100 tons.

4 principal loughs lie north east of the head of the waters of Fanad, between it and the ocean. The first, called Kindrum, contains 155 acres and is only 460 feet from the head of the waters, and contains fine trout. The second, called Kinnylough, contains 182 acres and is 660 feet from the first and 890 feet south of the ocean, between which and its shores is a tract of barren land.

This lough has 14 islands of low elevation (the highest is 64 feet), on 2 of which the ruins of stillhouses exist. The third is separated from the second by a space of sand of 528 feet; its name is Magherydrummon and contains 24 acres but no islands. The fourth is 1,300 feet to the north east of this, is known by the name of Shanagh and contains 71 acres and is 30 (?) feet deep.

Kindrum and Kinnalough are shallow: in many places their surfaces are covered with reeds. Black granite is found to the north of these loughs.

Table of Loughs

Ballyforiskey, 4 acres 2 roods 25 perches.
   Sessagh, 1 acre 22 perches.
   Blind lough, 1 rood.
   Runbuoy lough, 28 acres 2 roods 39 perches.
   Upper Tallanees lough, 4 acres 1 rood.
   Kindrum lough, 155 acres 6 perches.
   Lower Tallanees lough, 12 acres 3 roods 14 perches.
   Lough Beg, 1 acre 6 perches.
   Lough Sobin, 1 acre.
   Lough Nagleia, 22 acres 1 rood 29 perches.
   Gortnaglin lough, 2 roods 10 perches.
   Gortnatra lough, 4 acres 1 rood 25 perches.
   Lough Dugh, 1 acre 1 rood 22 perches.
   Lough Nagreen, 8 acres 1 rood 27 perches.
   Washing lough, 12 acres 2 roods 30 perches.
   Lough Beg in Glinsk, 1 rood 36 perches.
   Lough Naparte, 6 acres 5 perches.

Lough Sallagh, 2 acres 9 perches.
Ballyhurk lough, 11 acres 1 rood 26 perches.
Lough Beg in Meenagh, 1 rood 29 perches.
The Loughan in Leatbeg, 3 roods 38 perches.
Lough Dugh, 1 acre 35 perches.
Kinny lough, 182 acres 1 rood 7 perches.
Maghrydrummon lough, 24 acres 13 perches.
Lough Shannagh, 11 acres 2 roods 16 perches.
Thrushnahan lough, 13 acres 38 perches.
Inish Cardigh lough, 3 acres 1 rood 21 perches.
Dubhleach lough, 2 acres 25 perches.
Ballymagahy lough, 12 acres 4 perches.
Bran lough, 3 acres 1 rood 36 perches.
Fanny lough, 32 acres 3 perches.
Mill Pond, 2 roods 7 perches.
Lough Sallagh, 2 roods 37 perches.
Lough Diora, 5 acres 3 roods 12 perches.
Lough Finahan, 6 acres 3 roods.
Lough Beg, 3 roods 23 perches.
Lough Goragh, 5 acres 2 roods 28 perches.
Lough Cloghmore, 6 acres 2 roods 32 perches.
In Ballure, Lough Hannae, 5 acres 1 rood 32 perches; Lough Lane, 2 acres 1 rood 30 perches.
Ballynashanagh lough, 2 acres 3 roods 2 perches.
On mearing of Lower Drumfad, 1 acre 17 perches.
On mearing of Upper Drumfad, 4 acres 2 roods 4 perches.
Lough in Torledon, 2 acres 2 roods 29 perches.

Rivers

There are no rivers in the parish and not many brooks or rivulets of consequence. The largest is that draining Glenvagh, south of Knockalla, which rises in Muntccimlin on the southern mearing of the parish and runs over a rocky bed to the north east for 3 and a half miles, and empties itself to Lough Swilly in Binnington. The source of this stream is about 700 feet high. The tide river at Ballykinard is the next in consequence and is too small to require any particular description.

Bogs

Bogs are becoming scarce; their general height above the sea is 350 feet. Considerable quantities of fir timber with some oak are found in the turf banks and much was obtained from Tamney <Tamny> lough about 3 years ago, when it was partially drained. These trees appear to have been blown down by the violence of the north west gales and in some cases have suffered from fire. Some of the tenants have purchased the fuel, the expense of which varies from 2s 6d to 5s a dark.

Umricam and Shedogh get theirs from Rosguill and boat it across the Hassans.

Woods

There are no natural woods now in Fanad, but from the remains found in the bogs there is little doubt it was a woodland district. Glinsk exhibits partial traces of natural woods.

Coast

In Runbuoy bay the surf rolls in in a most magnificent manner. When the ocean is a perfect calm the seas, from 4 to 7 feet high and no less than half a mile in length, move in one green unbroken mass to the strand and, falling over, dash in endless succession against a beach whose substratum is granite. At the right and left the low granite headlands of Rushmore and Runbuoy are covered with surf, and hence to the lighthouse at the confluence of Lough Swilly no vessel can find shelter. In the lough, however, all the British fleet might ride in security and, although the coast of Fanad is bold and rocky, numerous landing places are met with, that of Ballymastocker bay being frequently impracticable from the surf.

The only danger in the navigation of Lough Swilly is the reef near its entrance, for large vessels with loss of both anchor and cables could be beached in security south of Rathmullan. Runbuoy has been alluded to in the Memoirs of Tullyaughnish and Mevagh. Large vessels can take temporary shelter at its mouth, but vessels even of 100 tons require skilful pilots to anchor them in security.

The direction of the coast runs to every point of the compass, that of Lough Swilly being from north east to north for 10 miles, that of the ocean west, south west and sweeping round to the south west to the headland of Runbuoy for 7 miles. The coast of Mulroy runs in every direction, the general line being to the south and south east for 30 miles, being a total of 47 miles of sea-coast. The scenery is equally varied: the coast of the lough is rough and rocky, and bold with small sandy bays. The ocean for a considerable space is a low tract of sand.

The entrance to Mulroy is low rocks and sand at Doaghmore, which is succeeded by rough hills running down to the water. From Leatbeg to Umricam and Moress the shores are bold but are not rough; Lurgacloughan and "round the waters" to Fanad the coast is rocky and barren. South of Moress it is low, accessible and cultivated, having the high road into the parish along a considerable part of its margin. Fine caves exist on the coast of Lough Swilly, at Doaghbeg and Mulled, and in Magherywarden at Knockalla.

The climate is moist but healthy.

NATURAL HISTORY

Zoology

Cod, haddock, ling, turbot, flounder, sole <soal> found in Lough Swilly and the banks of Tory and Malin Head. Herrings are taken on the coast and in the lough. Glassons, sprats, oysters and scallops are obtained in Mulroy. Lobsters at Glinsk and all the deep-sea fish at its mouth. Seals are not uncommon but are seldom taken. Eagles, hawks, shaggs, gulls, cormorants, water hens, wild pigeons in the caves at Knockalla. Foxes, badgers, rats, rabbits, hares etc. are common.

Eagles build in Binalan and are not numerous. I saw at Crockglass a bird hovering over and descending in the hills which I took to be an eagle. A country lad called it a kite, but I was informed by others that eagles from Binalan are frequent on this hill.

Geology

This is a primitive district composed of black granite, quartz rock, talc slate, blue limestone and dykes of porphyritic greenstone. The granite lies on the north coast. Quartz is the prevailing rock and the limestone occupies Springfield, Tamney, Ballyhernan, Fanavuntly, Toame, Tullnadall, Laddin, Lurgaloghan, Gortnatra, Fallanees, Tullyconnell, Upper and Lower Currin, Ballywhil?

The general direction of the hills, valleys and loughs is from north east to south west and the same connection between the dykes and loughs described in Tullyaughnish was observed in Tamney and the shore of Mulroy at Crohan Island, Upper Carlan and Rosnakill. Good specimens of small quartz crystal is observed in Knockalla.

MODERN TOPOGRAPHY

Towns

The first Monday of the month a market is held at Rosnakill, but Tamney is the chief village of Fanad, although not the largest. It consists of a few good whitewashed houses of 2-storeys high, has a post office and police station but no market.

Doaghbeg is the chief Roman Catholic village, Glinsk the chief Protestant one. The villages of Leatbeg and those near the lighthouse are large but there is nothing remarkable in this except their number and position.

Public Buildings

Rosnakill church is said to be built on the ruins of the ancient church. A legend states "the people, anxious to build a place of worship, commenced in an adjoining hill but their daily labours were destroyed in the night by unknown hands, when St Waddock arrived with the first ass seen in Fanad.

He informed them if they would lade the panniers with stones, his ass would take them to the proper place for the erection of the church. The ass cantered away to a rocky spot and, lying down, deposited his burden. The church of Rosnakill was erected on the site of which the more modern building stands. It was rebuilt in 1785 by subscription, cost [blank] and can contain 250 persons, 80 sittings being in the gallery.

The Roman Catholic chapel at Massmount, half a mile north of Tamney, is well situated on the shore of Mulroy. It is a modern building 20 feet by 150 feet, erected by subscription in [?] 1785 by Revd J. Friel, parish priest, cost 250 pounds; has a gallery and can hold 380 persons. The ground was given by Mr Patton at a peppercorn rent.

Mass is said in 2 other places in Fanad, one in an unfinished mass-house in the townland of Vanavoulty, and in Glenvagh (district south of Knockalla) and in an unused house. Mass is said in these detached houses every alternate Sunday.

There is no Presbyterian place of worship in Fanad. That of Carrowkeele in the adjoining parish is frequented by the Scotch Church.

Lighthouse

The lighthouse at the entrance of Lough Swilly stands on a projecting rock and is 108 feet above the sea. It was commenced in 1815 and completed in 2 years by the Commissioners of the Ballast Board. It is of granite and was sent from the North Hall, Dublin, ready prepared. There are 9 stationary lights, 4 red and 5 white.

The building is 31 feet high. Its erection was superintended by Mr Carpenter of Dublin and cost about 2,000 pounds. [Drawing of lighthouse, with 3 windows, dimensions 31 feet high, 11 feet at the base].

Knockalla Battery

The battery lies under Knockalla mountain and, with the fort of Dunree, defends the entrance of the lough. It is armed with 7 French 42-pounders on the lower battery, taken out of *La Hoche*, now the *Donegal*, with 2 24-pounders on the upper battery which is 38 feet higher, and one 24 feet under on a Martello tower to the land, commanding the whole. Barracks and officers' quarters are within the fort for 2 companies of infantry and 1 of artillery; see Dunree Fort in Desertegney Memoir.

Gentlemen's Seats

Greenfort, the residence of Captain Barton, stands in Ballymastocker bay and commands a beautiful view of Lough Swilly and the opposite mountain of Urris. The house is a modern whitewashed building and stands in about 60 acres of ornamental ground having a garden and orchard.

Springfield is a building of 2-storeys high. It was erected about 100 years ago by Mr Patton and cost [blank].

The Glebe House was built in 1795 at an expense of 1,400 pounds, to which the Board of First Fruits gave 100 pounds. It is a tolerably good house and pleasantly situated.

Bleach Greens

There is no bleach green at present in Fanad: Rockvale on the north bank of Kindrum lough was formerly a bleaching establishment.

Mills

The mills in this district are not numerous and of the most common kind; their wheels are usually overshot, 10 feet in diameter by 24 inches in breadth.

There are corn mills at Torledon, Ballycallan, Rahaggory, Ballyheeran, Kindrum, Ballymagahy South and 1 flax mill at Springfield.

There is a tuck mill in Kindrum. The district manufacture is Waterloo blue cloth for common use.

Communications

The only road from Rathmelton to Fanad passes along the shore of Mulroy bay, and is a good line and well kept up as far as Tamney and Captain Babington's. All the other roads in the parish are indifferent: most of them very bad and some of the country communications execrable. The county pays the expenses of the repair. There are no bridges worthy of notice and, except by the first road noticed above, the trade of the district is necessarily restricted to horse carriage.

The road to Rosguill passes from Tamney by Moress ferry, at which boats are provided, the charge for a man and horse being 6d. After passing this you are obliged to cross a second ferry called Rawri's before you arrive in Rosguill.

ANCIENT TOPOGRAPHY

Moress Castle

[Drawing of castle, 38 feet high, by 24 feet 6 inches and 21 feet].

The only ruin in Fanad <Fannaught> is that of Moress Castle, which stands on a small island in Mulroy bay, a little south of the landing place at Moress ferry. An angle from its walls only now remains. It is said to have been one of the strongholds of McSwine, and from its position was not likely to have been taken by the coupdemain.

Ecclesiastical Remains

The following sketch exhibits the head of St Vaddock built up in the wall of Rosnakill churchyard: [drawing of sculptured head, 2 feet 6 inches high by 1 foot 6 inches wide].

In Lower Ballyhernan may be seen, in a limestone wall, part of the gable of a church erected by subscription 100 years ago during Mr Johnston's incumbency. The roof having fallen in about 55 years since, and the building suffered to decay, its materials were by the country people appropriated to their own uses.

Thuras-na-vadock: in Doaghmore is an ancient graveyard and holy well much resorted to by the inhabitants. The priests prohibited annual stations at it about 30 years ago and it is said that the parish derives its name from it.

Thuris-a-derg on the west slope of Cnoc Glass is frequented for prayer. There are about 16 small stones about 1 foot high, with a rudely cut cross on each, placed round the well. These are quite modern. I spoke to the individual whose zeal erected them.

There is an old graveyard a mile west of the lighthouse in the townland of Ballure called Relunapatha, and near to it St Patrick's Well. The pigs honour this ground so much that, although frequently seen running through it, they are never known to root up its surface.

Stations are held at the ruins in Carryblagh.

Giant's Grave

[Drawing with dimensions]. The giant's grave in Ballyhurk consists of 2 stones standing erect, the other lying flat similar to the gravestones. They are 5 foot long by 3 feet broad and 6 inches thick.

Standing Stones and Forts

The 2 standing stones at Ballyhernan [drawing] stand east and west and on the top of the hill. The largest is 6 feet high and 1 foot broad on the north, 1 foot 2 inches on the east, 8 inches on the south and 1 foot 2 inches on the west side. The small stone is 3 feet high by 1 foot square, and they stand 6 feet apart.

There are also standing stones at Torledon, Fallanees, Ballyhurk, Ballyforiskey, Lower Drumfad; and Danes' forts in the townlands of Aughadrenna, Lower Ballymagoan, Cashel Glebe, Glinsk, Lurgaloghan, Doocarrick, Umricam, 2 in Gortnataragh, Kinnylough, Crohan and Moress.

Castle

There is the foundation of an old castle in Doaghrahin, the history of which I could not obtain.

MODERN TOPOGRAPHY

General Appearance and Scenery

The entrance into Fanad from Milford by the bank of Mulroy is considered in the country to be a sight worthy of going many miles to see. Descending a small hill the waters of the bay, studded with islands, enter suddenly into the landscape already extensive and interesting, the eye being arrested by Lough Salt immediately before you usually capped with clouds. The road winds along the shore of the bay with bold high crags, on the right the bay opening and the distant hills of Rosguill and Fanad closing the view.

But this entrance is not to be compared to that from Glenvagh, where you stand on the summit level of the road and behold decidedly a most magnificent mountain view before you; and at your feet, after many bold and craggy descents, lie the placid waters of Mulroy with Lough Salt on your left, Errigal <Arrigle>, Muckish, Horn Head and Granra in the distance, with the rough bold hill of Knockalla close on your right, the ocean backing the extreme distance behind.

To the east, over the valley of Glenvagh through which the road passes, is seen Lough Swilly and the high hills of Inishowen.

It would take too much space to attempt to enumerate the many fine landscapes to be met with in Fanad. One of the most worthy of note is at the turn of the road near Crohan Island, where the islands on Mulroy and the adjacent rough rocks' heights are strikingly contrasted. The road from Tamney to Rosguill is highly picturesque. The sea views on the coast, the descent to Kinnalough, with its extensive waters separated from the ocean by a belt of bright sand with rough rocky hills on every side, are not among the least of the beauties of this district. Unfortunately trees are scarcely to be seen.

SOCIAL ECONOMY

Early Improvements

I have no information respecting the early inhabitants of this district. It belonged to McSwine and was confiscated in Elizabeth's time, but to whom it was given I am not aware. Its extensive seacoast and its peninsulated character must have always made it a place of strength to its inhabitants.

Considerable improvements are now being made by Mr Norman of Fahan in this as well as his Inishowen property. The villagers are no longer suffered to congregate in a gaggle of dirty houses, but each farmer has a new house in his land to which Mr Norman handsomely contributed, and the holdings are fenced in. There are neither counties, farming societies or anything to excite an agricultural interest, and the nearest market, Rathmelton, is 16 miles from the northern coast of the parish.

Obstructions to Improvement

Run and dale keeps down the fences in Clondavaddog. Hundreds of acres may be seen without an attempt at an enclosure and it is, without exception, the worst fenced district I have yet met with.

Local Government

There is no magistrate residing in the parish. 4 police, an officers' detachment of 11 men belonging to the revenue, a coastguard station of 5 men and 2 boats at Crawris, with a detachment of artillery consisting of 6 men and a marked gunner, are stationed at the Knockalla tower.

Petty sessions are held in Rathmelton and Rathmullan every 14 days(?); the crimes are those of an usual nature. Illicit whiskey is increasing but smuggling is unknown.

Dispensaries

A dispensary and medical man are established in

the parish. He attends 1 day in the week in Rathmullan and receives 100 pounds a year for both parishes. The usual complaints are [blank].

Table of Schools

The pupils in the following schools are taught to read the Scriptures, which must invariably lead to a perceptible improvement in their moral habits.

Tamney parish school, 68 Protestants, 39 Catholics, 58 males, 49 females, total 107, established before 1825.

Drumfad, 78 Protestants, 66 Catholics, 84 males, 60 females, total 144, established in 1832.

Glenfanet (?), 54 Protestants, 27 Catholics, 53 males, 28 females, total 81, established before 1825.

Minniagh, 11 Protestants, 53 Catholics, 41 males, 23 females, total 64, established before 1825.

Leatbeg, 35 Protestants, 15 Catholics, 31 males, 19 females, total 50, established before 1825.

Sunday Schools

Tamney, 43 Protestants, 31 Catholics, 32 males, 42 females, total 74, established before 1825.

Kindrum, Ballyness, Gortnachor and Ballynalosht: [blank].

Poor

The numbers in the poor lists are about 90 but there are few mendicants belonging to the parish. Numbers resort to it as it has the character of being a good potato country, a lending fund, a religious lending library and temperance society as supported by the curate, the former having a capital of 120 pounds always floating in the parish.

The church collection is about 7 pounds per annum, usually laid out in clothing for the destitute. The townland of Drumany was purchased for the poor of this parish by money left by the rector Johnston about 100 years ago, to which a sum was added by Dr Bedford. Drumany is bishop's land; its rent is 15 pounds held in trust and renewed by the incumbent of the parish, and is reserved by will for Protestant widows only.

Religion

There are belonging to the Church Establishment 1,211 souls, 540 Presbyterians and 7,755 Roman Catholics, making the population 9,506. It was 8,486 in 1821 and consisted of 1,519 families.

The rector of the parish, Mr Maturin, receives [blank] tythe. The priests receive from each family 2s a year, 1 stook of barley and 1 hank of yarn, besides dues at christenings, marriages, deaths etc.

Habits of the People

The cottages are for the most part coarsely and rudely built, with little whitewash and plenty of straw ropes to tether down the roofs. They are all of stone with glass windows, generally 1-storey high, with 2 rooms in a filthy state; Tamney and Rosnakill are the chief exceptions.

The food of the peasantry is principally potatoes which, from the abundance of seaweed used in their culture, are early and abundant. Turf is used for fuel, the bog timber being more usually devoted to the purpose of building.

The women wear red cloaks and the men Waterloo blue cloth. Many of the people live to 70 or 80, no man in Fanad ever having been known to have had the gout, and they boast that none of the clan were ever hanged. The usual number in the families may be taken at 5 without a decimal.

They have no amusements or patrons' days. Malin and Doon Wells supply the superstitious with places of pilgrimage. Bealtinne is kept up and an immense weight of ignorance prevails among the mass of the people.

Emigration: a few emigrated to England and Scotland for harvest.

Remarkable Events

In March 1797, previous to the last rebellion, Dr Hamilton, rector of the parish (author of the *Guide to the Causeway*), was murdered in a most barbarous manner in Sharon, the glebe of Rye in the Lagan.

On the evening of the 5th November 1811 the *Saldanha* frigate, the Honourable Captain Pakenham, was lost on the Swilly rock and 350 souls perished. The night was very rough, with a north west gale and snow. She was seen by her light coming into Lough Swilly at 8 p.m., shortly after which the wind changed to south east and she was immediately on a lea shore when, it is supposed, on working to windward she struck and went to pieces. At 11 p.m. her wreck in 2 parts drifted into Ballymastocker bay.

Many bodies were on the wreck and one sailor made his way on shore, and might easily have been saved had not the adjacent country people proceeded to plunder the vessel. He was neglected till the morning when, a guard having been put on the wreck, he was placed before a large fire in his wet clothes and filled with rum, an abundance of which came on shore. In a short time he died without having given any satisfactory account of the accident.

Part of the *Saldanha's* rudder chain was found on the Swilly rock and about 100 bodies were picked up. This account was given by one of the coastguards at Crawris who had been employed in guarding the wreck, he being at that time in the revenue stationed at Rathmullan.

Productive Economy

Manufacturing

The linen trade here as elsewhere, is rapidly on the decline. Coarse wrappers are those most usually made and are sold in Rathmullan. Druggets, blankets and stockings are made for home use.

Fairs and Markets

There is a monthly fair at Rossnakill but Rathmelton fair is the general market of Fanad <Fannaight>.

Rural Economy

The name of the persons to whom the townlands belong will be found in the Name Book but upwards of one-half the parish belongs to Lord Leitrim. Captain Babington and Mr Patton are the only residents.

Size of Holdings

The usual size of the holdings is about 4 Cunningham acres and grazing for 4 cows, and lets for about 12s 6d an acre, the annual rent of the parish being about 7,000 pounds. The lands are not subject to any taxes besides tithes and the county cess.

Some of the farmers are respectable yeomen, a few are independent but the mass of the people are farming for existence only. The farmhouses near Tamney and Rosnakill are good but generally they are of the usual mean and dirty appearance. There are no farms as examples to the people.

Seaweed is the chief manure and produces early potatoes. Farmyard compost and a little lime are added by those who have them.

No improved instruments are used beyond a few iron ploughs. Horses' backs are the chief means of transport.

Crops

The rotation of crops is of the commonest kind, viz. potatoes, barley, oats, flax and *weeds*. About quarter or half of the farms, according to their size, is under potatoes; average produce of oats is 90 stones and barley 126 stones. The Scotch are valued at 5 and 6 pounds.

Grazing and Wages

No farms are used exclusively for grazing. There are plenty of sheep in the parish and there being few fences, three-fourths of the district may be said to be a sheep-walk as they run wild over everything.

Irrigation is not practised.

Farm servants receive 2 pounds to 2 pounds 10s and women obliged to work 2 quarters in the farm, only 20s each half-year.

Livestock

There are very few good cattle, but good ponies, either from Raghery or bred from that stock, with plenty of asses, pigs and poultry, comprise the stock of Fanad. Captain Babington stall-feeds on a very limited scale. A pony can be bought from 4 to 10 pounds, a good ass 15s to 25s and cattle from 3 pounds 10s to 5 pounds a head.

Uses made of the Bogs

The bogs are grazed usually in the summertime. The timber is used for building. The people have not the unlimited use of the bogs for cutting and the southern part of the land between the waters is supplied from Rosguill.

Drainage

This is seldom practised. The farmers adjacent to Tamney lough about 3 years ago opened drains and let off a considerable quantity of water, and obtained some land with several pieces of good timber found in the bed of the lake.

Nothing like systematic drainage is carried on: an attempt has lately been made to embank a piece of Mulroy at Moress but is hitherto quite a failure.

Planting

Nothing of this nature is attempted. The north west wind prevails and would be rendered less destructive if the country were sheltered with trees. Planting might be advantageously employed as means of ornament and profit, many districts being quite unfitted for any other purpose. The bogs supply the country with timber for cabin purposes.

Parish of Clondavaddog

Sea-Coast

Kelp is made on the ocean coast and turned to considerable profit. The townland of Bally-oriskey, the rent of which is 140 pounds per annum, sold last season no less than 55 tons of kelp at 3 pound per ton to Mr Shields of Ballyhernan, who exported it to Scotland. The other towns along Runbuoy bay disposed of 14 tons, from Runmore to the lighthouse 60 tons, 1 boat on this shore being used expressly for collecting seaweed.

In the fall of the year, and during the storms of winter, the people employ themselves in gathering the long tangles thrown up by the sea. The stems are saved and piled in stacks of considerable size to dry. In the spring fresh weed is collected and, when partially dry, is thrown on the fires previously made with the prepared tangles.

Fishing

There are about 50 boats in Lough Swilly from the lighthouse to Runmore; to the west the people have 10 or 12 and 20 corrachs; in Runbuoy bay, Ballyoriskey has 5 boats and 37 corrachs; from the lighthouse to the Hassans in Mulroy 30 boats; from the Hassans to Tullyaughnish about 8.

No corrachs are used in Lough Swilly or Mulroy. All the boats in the former have from 5 to 7 nets and about one-half of those between Ballyoriskey and the Hassans. Those on the ocean are all supplied with nets, the kelp boats mentioned above excepted.

The 5 boats of Ballyoriskey carry 12, 10, 8, 6 and 5 herring nets. The sea is about 6 fathoms deep and the nets from 18 to 21 fathoms long, of 5 score meshes, each mesh being about 1 and a half inches, making the net from 3 to 4 fathoms deep. The usual number of nets carried by the other boats varies from 5 to 7.

The herring season commences about [blank] and ends [blank]. This once beautiful supply of providence has now nearly ceased on the north west of Ireland. I have never heard any good reason given for the few shoals of fish that are seen on the shores but I suspect, as the drifting of the sand and the destruction of the fishing took place about the same time, that their haunts were then destroyed and they have sought other places to deposit their spawn; see Memoir of Mevagh.

30,000, 40,000 to 60,000 a night are considered to be a very large take, but seldom such success is met with. They are sold from 1s to 3s a hundred, according to the supply in the market; none are exported.

The corrachs are employed in deep-sea fishing along the coast. Few fish are taken in Mulroy and this article of profit is not sent to any market but is entirely used by the inhabitants.

There are no salmon weirs in Fanad.

Remarks on Cultivation

The soil of Clondavaddog is bad and very little good ground is met with, that lying between Knockalla and Crohan, some of it on a limestone bottom, being the best, from the quantity of seaweed on so extensive a coast.

Potatoes are raised in great abundance and, like those of Clonmany and the bottom of Rosguill, are celebrated for being good and early. Some portions of the parish are, from the frequency of the granite rocks on the surface, cultivated with the spade. No hopes of any great improvement can be looked for until run and dale ceases. The people by this vicious system are congregated in thick villages and the country left entirely without fences.

The highest point to which cultivation has been carried to is in Torledon, 400 feet. The north west wind is that most feared by the farmers. Limestone, although superabundant, is seldom used and would be profitable to seaweed which also abounds. The streams for machinery scarcely exist, nor is there anything to encourage its erection. The product of the sea is partially neglected but not that of the coast.

The roads and communications are generally *very* bad.

DIVISIONS

Divisions and Townlands

Glenvagh is that part of the parish which lies in the valley south of Knockalla, on the coast of Lough Swilly. The lower or northern part is called the bottom. It is an undefined line from Doaghmore on the west to the head of Mulroy by Kindrum and thence to Doaghbeg on Lough Swilly.

Townlands: this information will be found in the Name Books [signed] William Lancey, 23rd April 1835.

MEMOIR WRITING

Letter concerning Population

On His Majesty's Service, William Lancey Esquire, Royal Engineers, Donegal. You are requested to attach this to the Memoir of Clondavaddog: it was overlooked, [signed] W. Lancey, Lieutenant Royal Engineers, 2nd May; [to] Lieutenant Larcom.

Fanet, 16th March 1835.

My Dear Sir,

In giving you the number of families and individuals belonging to the Established Church in the parish of Clondavaddog, I stated it to be 192 families, 968 individuals. Having been lately called on to make a census for 1834 for the population commissioner, I find the return I gave you was incorrect and I wish, if not too late for your report, to correct my mistake. I find the numbers to stand thus: 231 families containing 1,214 individuals. The enumerator's book gives 1,211 Church people, 569 Presbyterians, 28 unknown and 7,784 Roman Catholics, total 9,595.

I am, my Dear Sir, very truly yours, Henry Carre.

Replies by Reverend Henry Maturin to Queries of North West Farming Society, July 1825

NATURAL FEATURES AND PRODUCTIVE ECONOMY

Description of Parish

This parish is nearly a peninsula, being bounded by the sea on 3 sides, on the north by the Atlantic, on the west by Mulroy and on the east by Lough Swilly, and on the south by an imaginary line about 3 miles long connecting these 2 inlets of the sea.

Its greatest length is more than 6 miles and its greatest breadth more than 4, containing about 24 square miles or about 15,000 acres. Within this area is included 60 quarterlands or townlands and a population, according to the census taken in 1821, of 1,519 families and 8,480 inhabitants. A considerable portion of the land consists of mountains, moors and bogs.

Surface

The mountains do not rise to a remarkable height and are masses of rocks of the siliceous kind covered with a thin vegetable surface which does not, however, conceal their rugged summits. These mountainous tracts are the common pasture-ground for each townland and, between heather and grass, will feed cows at the rate of 1 to 4 acres. The whinstone occurs most frequently, yet some tracts of limestone are also to be found.

The highest ground in this parish is part of a mountainous range called Knockalla near to Lough Swilly, which stands at its greatest elevation 1,120 feet above the level of the sea.

The arable ground is generally a light shallow loam without fences or trees and is usually cropped on the following order: 1 potatoes, 2 barley, 3 oats, 4 oats, 5 flax, 6 oats. This rotation takes place in land of the best quality, but in the second and third-rate lands the fourth crop is omitted in one tract called the bottom along the shore of the Atlantic, where seaweed is the usual manure.

They generally take but one crop after potatoes; that crop is barley. Their land, they say, does not answer for oats and flax, and this defect they attribute to the constant use of sea manure. This tract contains about one-third of the parish.

Glenvar

Another tract of the parish called Glenvar, between Knockalla and Lough Swilly, is also distinguished by only one crop after potatoes namely oats, the mossy nature of the ground, I believe, rendering it unfit for barley and flax. The land when exhausted is in some instances sown with grey peas and thus made to produce another crop of oats.

SOCIAL ECONOMY

Valuation and Rents

The rent of the parish may be estimated at 7,000 pounds yearly, the county cess at 700 pounds and the composition for the tithes under the late act of parliament is 501 pounds 17s 6d per annum. Rents in general are moderate and the condition of the people comparatively comfortable, that is, if compared with the state of the peasantry in the south of Ireland.

Yet the small holdings into which the land is subdivided are in many cases barely sufficient to supply the family with necessaries, and the various charges on the land cannot be answered without reducing diet and clothing to their very lowest state. The want of decent clothes, I am sorry to say, is a very prevalent cause of absence at public worship.

Illicit Distillation

But the great source of disorder and distress is the practice of illicit distillation, which is carried on in every part of this parish. Could it be totally suppressed and a market opened for barley and other grain, the condition of the people would be greatly improved.

Parish of Clondavaddog

Schools

We have 6 schools in the parish and parents manifest a strong desire to give some degree of education to their children; but by the influence of the priests, Popish children have been generally withdrawn from Protestant schools and very little has been done to provide schools for them.

Emigration

The emigration which takes place every year to America, Scotland and England makes young men desirous of some schooling before they go abroad. [Signed] Henry Maturin, Fannet Glebe, 12th July 1825.

Parish of Clonmany, County Donegal

Statistical Report by Lieutenant W. Lancey, May 1834

NATURAL STATE

Name

The usual method of spelling the name of this parish is Clonmany. It is pronounced as it is written and means "the fertile valley of the monk," from cluan "a fertile valley" and mannach "a monk." Its fruitfulness and locality, combined with the supposed site of a monastery, fully support this derivation.

Locality

It is situated on the right bank of Lough Swilly and the coast of the Atlantic Ocean, and is surrounded by the parishes of Donagh, Mintiaghs and Desertegney in the barony of Inishowen, diocese of Derry and county of Donegal. Its extreme length is 8 and three-quarters miles and breadth 7; it contains 23,379 acres, about 6,500 of which are cultivated, 16,722 acres uncultivated and 157 acres of water. &Natural Features

Hills

The principal range of hills rises from the bank of Lough Swilly and is composed of Urris, Mamore, Little Slieve Kerryna, Rathlinmore, Rathlinbeg and Straid, which stretch towards the north east and terminate abruptly in the plain west of the parish church. The second range is formed by Clonmany glebe in Ruskey, Bulbon and Altihallan bounding the southern side of the parish; extreme pole or Little Slieve Snaght, Bannin, Donagh rock and Drummineagh are a part of the Slieve Snaght range lying in the south east corner; and the Tulnabratley hills on the north bank of Strabraga bay are the commencement of high ground extending into Donagh.

Of these hills, Urris, 1,379 feet, Bulbon, 1,628 feet, Rathlinmore, 1,656 feet are the highest; Tulnabratley, 946 feet from the north side of Strabraga bay; and towards the south Little Slieve Snaght, 1,193 feet and the Bannin, 1,044 feet, Drummineagh, 715 and Donagh rock, 507 feet above the level of the sea.

Loughs

Loughs Crun and Fad on the north side of Urris mountain are of small extent, the former 2 and a half acres, the latter 3. They are 900 and 977 feet above the sea. Lough Crun discharges itself into Lough Swilly by a small stream 56 chains in length.

The principal lakes are Lough Fad and Lough Norein in the townland of Mindoran. Lough Fad is 102 acres in extent and 410 feet above the sea. Its reputed depth is about 25 feet. It contains 1 small island not more than a square chain in extent. Lough Norein contains [blank] acres and is divided into 2 unequal shares, 490 acres to Clonmany and [blank] to Mintiaghs. There are 2 small islands about half an acre each and the mearing runs through the southern one. The lough is about the same depth as Lough Fad and is 498 feet above the sea.

The loughs in Kennaght are of no importance. They are sometimes nearly dry and are of little depth. The larger one is 5 acres, the other 1 acre.

Rivers

The principal river, called Clonmany, is that which rises in the Mintiaghs and enters the parish at the mearing of Altahalla and Mindoran. Its general direction is to the north and it flows between the church and chapel near the middle of the parish, and empties itself into the ocean to the west of Binnion <Binion> about 7 and a quarter miles from its source in Mintiaghs. Its general depth is only a few inches but towards its mouth it is about 2 or 3 feet and its breadth 50 or 40 feet. At the mearing of Cleagh and Cloontagh the river receives a stream flowing from a swamp in the south end of Cloontagh and flows through it for 3 and a half miles, receiving several smaller rills of water in its course. The swamp is 667 feet high.

The next principal stream that falls into the Clonmany river is at the Gort and drains the mountain district of Straid and Addemill for 4 miles, rising in the ridge south of the Foxes rock, 850 feet above the sea.

There are many smaller rills of water draining the parish but none of any consequence. The waters of Clonmany are not in sufficient quantity to be well calculated for machinery, nor is their velocity great.

The Clonmany river overflows about Lammas near its junction with the ocean, where the land is very flat and does considerable damage. Common drains are the only method used to carry off the floods and, as the mouth of the stream is

Bogs

The mountains generally have very little bog on them fit for fuel except in Mindoran and Cloontaghs. In the former it is 4 feet deep, in the latter sometimes 15 feet. Their extent may be estimated at [blank] acres and are about 670 feet above the sea. Fir and oak trees are generally found and in a bog in Ballyliffin 2 or 3 distinct layers have been observed, the large roots of some placed over the trunks of others; no stumps were observed in an erect position nor do the bogs contain islands of gravel.

Woods

There are no woods at present, but in Urrismanagh tradition states that one existed on the side of the mountain.

Coast

There are no ports fit for anchorage except for small vessels for an occasional purpose, except Strabraga bay which is very shoal [shallow] and a great part of it left dry at low water. The only island is Glassheady (a green shade) about 7 and a half acres in extent and a mile west of the Isle of Doagh. It is an abrupt rocky spot celebrated for seals and seaweed.

The principal headlands are those of Urrismanagh, Dunaff, Binnion and Carrickabrackey Castle. There are no extensive caves. Boats can effect a landing on the sandy strand in Urrismanagh and to the south of Dunaff, in smooth weather from the north coast of Dunaff to Binnion, the coast being a round small boulder beach to the north part of Tullagh and then sand with a few rocks to Binnion.

From Binnion to the castle there is a fine level strand which is succeeded by steep shelving rocks. To the west of Dunmore there is a sandy beach and from thence to the entrance of the west branch of Strabraga bay boats can land at almost any point, and then no impediment presents itself to the junction of Donagh parish.

Strabraga bay is dry for a considerable extent and horses and cattle are constantly taken across it from Straas to the town of Malin.

The general direction of the coast of Lough Swilly is north from Desertegney to the ocean. It then turns east to the isthmus of Doaghs and runs north to Carrickabrackey Castle, when it sweeps round to the south east and west, forming the west and north banks of Strabraga bay, and then to the east to the parish of Donagh. The appearance of the coast is not striking except at Urrismanagh, Dunaff and Binnion, which present fine precipices to the ocean; the rest is generally low.

There are no lighthouses or beacons in the parish.

Climate

The climate is moist. The harvest commences in August, potatoes in October and the mountain lands a little later.

NATURAL HISTORY

Botany

Stramomium, called thorn-apple, grows in the sands at Leenan and is used for smoking by asthmatic persons. It flowers in the end of August. Sampire is found on the rocks of Dunaff and is obtained by descending the rocks with ropes. It is used for pickles.

There are no woods in Clonmany but a few sycamore trees at Dresden.

Zoology

Red foxes, hedgehogs, water rats, otters, badgers, weasels, lizards, grouse, partridge, hares, rabbits, woodcocks, snipe, woodpigeon, rooks, crows and a few eagles in the inaccessible precipices. Seals, porpoises, cod, ling, salmon, mullet, white trout, turbot, plaice, flounders, soles ‹soals›, eels, skate, herrings; lobsters and crab abound; shrimps but no oysters; black trout in Loughs Norrin and Fad in the south east of the parish.

Geology

The range of Urris and Rathlinmore is chiefly quartz rock, Bulbon and Altihalla the same talc slate, Little Slieve Snaght talc slate, Bannon a porphyritic greenstone dyke, Dunaff Head red granite and quartz rock, Binnion quartz rock, Tonebratley talc slate, at the old castle a porphyritic greenstone dyke with quartz rock.

The whole parish is a primitive formation of granite, quartz rock and talc slate with greenstone dykes. On the coast of Tullagh, in Ballymacmurty, banks of indurated sand of a modern formation are now breaking up and flooding the adjacent country.

Modern Topography

Towns

There are no towns but a number of villages: Ballyliffin is the principal. It contains some houses of 2-storeys and appears to be an ancient place.

Public Buildings

The church was built by Dr Chichester about 50 years ago. The burial ground is still used by the Roman Catholics. It is supposed to be the site of an old monastery founded by Columbkill. This building could contain 250 people. It has neither bell or gallery and is of the plainest style with a square tower and low pinnacle.

The Roman Catholic chapel was built 20 years ago, enlarged in 1833 and has a gallery now erecting. It can hold 2,000 persons and was built by subscription.

Gentlemen's Seats

Dresden, the property of Captain Metcalf, situated in Straid, was built by Mr Clark 100 years ago.

Glen House, the residence of Mr M. Dougherty, in Straid, was rebuilt by Mr O'Donnell 30 years ago and cost 300 pounds.

Binnion, the residence of Mr Loughry, in the townland of Binnion, was built by Mr Venables 50 years ago.

Jermane, in the town of Straid, was built 20 years ago and cost 300 pounds.

Rockstown, the present residence of the coastguard, was built in [blank] by Mr Charleton.

The Glebe House in the Gort was built 15 years ago and cost Mr Dobbs, the rector, 600 pounds.

There is nothing remarkable in any of these houses. They are of the plainest kind. They tend to enliven the country: each has its gardens and a few fruit trees, and there is a rookery at Dresden.

Mills

There are 3 corn mills in the parish situated in Straid, Cleagh and Strass. They are overshot wheels of about 12 feet diameter and 2 in breadth. There are no disputes respecting water or fishing rights to prevent the erection of mills. There is also a tuck mill in Mindoran with an undershot wheel of about 10 feet by 2.

Roads

They are tolerably good. The main ones are from Carn and Buncrana. That through the Gap of Mamore is very steep and is so covered with loose stones that few persons would venture to ride down it. It is, however, a most convenient pass for the people of the west end of Clonmany, as there is no other spot over which a road could be carried. From the north side of the gap the road to the church is very good and the whole of the main and crossroads appear to be well laid out.

From the gap round by the coast and the church to the entrance of Mintiaghs the chief communication in the parish extends 11 and a half miles; the average breadth is 30 feet. It is made in the usual manner with broken stones at the expense of the county.

Bridges

There are few bridges. That near the church has 2 arches and is built of common stone. It is a modern erection and was paid for by the county. The depth of water does not exceed 9 inches in common occasions.

There is also a single arch across the stream near the tuck mill in Mindoran.

Ancient Topography

Ecclesiastical Remains

St Columbkill resided in Clonmany, according to the tradition of the people. The church is said to be built on the site of a monastery founded by the saint. The Roman Catholics continue to bury their dead in the churchyard and the tradition is borne out by an old tomb in the east of the building made of greenstone and of the precise appearance of those of St Columb's era in Iona.

Note: the people of Iona informed me that the greenstone slabs of which the tombs are made in that island were brought from Inishowen, and from what I have seen of the greenstone rock of Clonmany and that used in the tower of Magilligan brought from Inishowen, I think their tradition is founded on truth and there is no such greenstone in Iona.

Ruin

There is an ancient ruin in Binnion of which I have not yet been able to obtain any satisfactory information, the remains of a small burial ground (at present used only for children who die before baptism) having a stone cross of 4 feet 6 inches in height in its centre and the ruin of a round building (tower?) detached a few paces to the west. It has the reputation of being the oldest relict of

Parish of Clonmany

antiquity in the neighbourhood; merely the trace of the walls exists. The burial ground might or might not have been the interior of a large [building?].

Tombs

A modern tomb of 1720 is nearly defaced. Another of 1725, of the McNiel family, is in a good state of preservation. The arms are a bloody hand and a fish.

[Drawing of a tombstone showing mouldings in relief].

St Columb's Well

St Columb's Well in the west of the road in the Gap of Mamore is visited by the people on the 8th of June, but the practice is falling into decay.

Carrickabrackey Castle

Carrickabrackey Castle stands on a greenstone dyke in the north west point of the Isle of Doagh, 1 mile east of the island of Glassheady; is built of rough quartz rock of the same kind as the rocks within a few yards of it. It means "the prison of the rock," a most appropriate name. [View of Carrickabrackey Castle [from the?] south, showing 3 towers, a wall and outbuilding].

The principal and western tower is rectangular, the inside dimensions being 10 feet by 8 feet 6 inches. It consists of an upper floor supported by 3 beams, and a terrace with castellated walls above. Neither the floors or terraces in this or any of the towers at present exist. There is a door on the east side and one on the north now built up, a loophole on the south, the wall being 5 feet thick and the interior dimensions 3 feet 9 inches high by 3 feet 3 inches long, diminishing to a very small outlet. There were other loopholes which are now built up [drawing of loophole].

In the upper storey to the west a fireplace and chimney in the thickness of the wall, on the north a recess in the thickness of the wall, the interior wall being flush with the rest of the building, leaving a small doorway at the east end. This recess is sufficiently large for a person to sleep in (query was this the prisoner's cell?). On the south a recess in the wall supported by an elliptic arch 4 feet (?) in span.

The square tower is connected to a circular one standing at its south east corner, the communication from one to the other being protected by a wall in which, on the south side, is a door, the principal

Carrickabrackey Castle

entrance, which is 5 feet high. The door-posts are solid blocks of quartz rock about 14 inches thick. The door on the inside was fastened by 2 iron bolts that ran from right to left and a strong beam of timber, the groove for which still remains.

The door into the round tower is 3 feet wide by 2 feet 2 inches, its diameter 10 feet 6 inches, has 5 loopholes on the ground floor, had an upper storey and a castellated terrace, and protected by a flank defence, the south and east side of the square tower.

The trace of the foundation of a small building still exists to the north of these towers, doubtless once connected with them.

A round tower, now detached from the main body of the castle, stands a few yards to the south east, and a strong wall from it, embracing a small enclosure to the rocks on the sea-coast, completes this ruin.

The door of this tower is 3 feet 10 inches by 2 feet 1 inch. It has 5 loopholes on the upper floor and had a castellated terrace above. There are 6 loopholes below. The wall at the door is 2 feet 2 inches thick and 3 feet 3 inches at the loophole. They are 2 feet high by 2 feet 2 inches wide on the inside, terminating about 12 by 6 inches.

There is no legend connected with this castle except that it belonged to the O'Dogherty family. There is a landing place for boats to the west of the square tower, within a stone's throw of its battlements.

Forts

There are only 4 forts in the parish, one in Dunaff, one in Gaddyduff, one in Rusky and one in Rashary [Rashany].

Standing Stones

In Tullnabratly there are 3 remarkable stones called Granny's Bed, Macool's Bed and Darby's Bed; in Carrareagh there are cloghogle stones, and in Fugart 2 erect ones; in Maghernell 1 standing stone and 1 cloghogle stone. In Mindoran are standing stones, and north of the town of Ballyliffin there is a flat stone supported by 2 uprights and an erect stone at some distance to the west of them.

MODERN TOPOGRAPHY

General Appearance and Scenery

This parish combines great variety of scenery: mountains of quartz rock, whose summits are scarcely clothed with heather, rise abruptly from fertile and level lands of the richest cultivation to the height of 1,656 feet. In descending the Gap of Mamore, a pass of 800 feet above the sea, the rich land of Urrismanagh, backed by the low precipitous coast of Leanan, the fine granite promontory of Dunaff, separating Lough Swilly from the sea, and the low headlands of Tullagh with the Atlantic Ocean spread out beneath your feet and present a striking and no very ordinary landscape. The western coast of the lough at Fanad with Binnion and the fine promontory of Malin Head to the east contribute much to this varied and striking picture.

After descending the gap and passing along the sea-shore with Rathlinmore on your right, up on past the church, the mountain of Bulbon with Slieve Snaght and Bannion in the distance appear to advantage.

At the village of Ballyliffin a new landscape presents itself: beneath you lie the rich and flat lands of Ballyliffin and Tulnabratly, bounded by wild hills to the south and Strabraga <Strabrega> bay to the north. Beyond are the townlands of Carrickabrackly, Ballymeenaroarty with part of Carraghreagh and Legacurry in the Isle of Doagh, one desert of sand at the north west extremity of which stands the ruin of the castle. To the left is Glassheady <Glashady> Island and on the right in the distance Malin Head with its hall and village.

SOCIAL ECONOMY

Early Improvements

The proximity to the sea-shore, with fine level lands, were doubtless the principal causes of the parish being thickly inhabited. It is, with Donagh and Malin, the chief residence of the sept of O'Doherty. There are 166 families in the parish, 5 of whom only are Protestants; the rest are Roman Catholics; and about 700 families or 3,920 people bear the name of O'Doherty, usually called Dogherty. 3,305 of the inhabitants are males, 3,202 females, total 6,507 by the census of 1831.

Obstructions to Improvement

Run and dale prevails and, by the increased population, the farms are too much cut up. The people generally complain of high rents and the country is disturbed on this account.

Local Government

There is no magistrate in the parish, but a stipendiary magistrate resides at Carn. The present force of police is 7 and 1 officer, and 25 soldiers are detached from Derry in consequence of the disturbed state of the country. There are also an officer and 12 men of the revenue police and 1 officer and 5 of the coastguard. Petty sessions in Buncrana take cognizance of crimes committed in Clonmany.

Illicit distilling is on the decline and very little smuggling is going on at present.

Dispensaries

There are no dispensaries. The poor apply to Carn and Buncrana for medical relief.

Schools

There are no schools nor any public establishment. The people are anxious to have their children taught English, but schools are yet scarce; and the habits of the people have not been acted upon by education to any great extent.

[Table contains the following headings: name of townland, number of scholars subdivided by religion and sex, remarks].

Urris, 40 Catholics, 20 males, 20 females, total 40; 1d a week and 2 pounds 2s from Mrs Merrick.

Parish church, 6 Protestants, 44 Catholics, 25 males, 25 females, total 50; 2 pounds from rector and 1d per week.

Ballyliffin, 30 Catholics, 15 males, 15 females, total 30; 1d a week for each scholar.

Doaghs, 30 Catholics, 15 males, 15 females, total 30; 1d a week for each scholar.

The masters teach in cabins and alter their place of residence continually.

Poor

There are not many mendicants but many of the people are miserably poor; yet the population as a whole are tolerably well off. There are no charitable institutions for the poor, aged or infirm.

Religion

There are only 5 Protestant families and 1,161 Roman Catholics. The rector does not reside but keeps a resident curate. The living is under the composition at 410 pounds per annum with a glebe of 55 pounds. 3 priests officiate in the Roman Catholic chapel, who are paid by the customary offerings and dues.

Habits of the People

They are an industrious people for about 6 months in the year. The other 6 they do nothing except a few who occasionally fish. The cottages are dirty, built of stone with glass windows, 1-storey high with 1, 2 or 3 rooms, seldom whitewashed, with thatched roofs bound with straw ropes. Their food: potatoes, milk, meal, sea-wrack, shellfish, herring according to their circumstances. Turf and fir are used for fuel.

Their dress is good: the parish is celebrated for good home-made clothing.

They live from 60 to 80 but rarely to 100; the average number in a family 5; they marry at 19.

Amusements and Traditions

Cock-fighting, hurling and dancing are declining. The game of common is still practised. They frequent St Columb's Well at the Gap on the 8th of June and drive cattle into the sea, and on St John's Eve they light bonfires and drive cattle through them.

They cry at funerals but do not hire persons called "keenie." The priests are endeavouring to get rid of as many superstitions in Clonmany as possible.

Character of the People

In 1816 the inhabitants rescued a seizure from the revenue officers and confined them with a party of military, 40 in number, for 2 days at the house called Binnion, where they were relieved by a troop of dragoons and some infantry from Derry. They have often successfully attacked the soldiers on duty with the revenue in the Gap of Mamore and on one occasion shot one of them.

Emigration

About 40 persons are going to different parts of America this year.

About 50 families send some of their number to England and Scotland to harvest annually and the rest keep house and plant potatoes; some go to the looms.

Remarkable Events

Friar Dogherty, a poet, lived about 50 years ago at Carrickabrackey <Carrickbracky>, and Shane Dogherty, called Mac'avergy, born at Malin, lived in Clonmany about 70 years ago. Their poetry was never published.

PRODUCTIVE ECONOMY

Linen Trade

There are upwards of 100 looms for linen, blankets, flannel and druggets. Hand-spinning is general in the cottages. 1 lb. of flax is usually spun into 4 hanks of yarn and sells for 15d a spangle.

There is not much flax grown in the parish. Woollen cloths sell for 4s a yard, of very good quality, blankets 16s a pair and druggets used for petticoats, and waistcoats, red and blue narrow stripe, for 1s a yard. There are not 10 women in the parish who do not wear this article and it is very general among the men.

Fairs and Markets

The only fairs in Clonmany are held in Ballyliffin 4 times a year, principally for amusement and the sale of cattle. The first takes place on St Patrick's Day, the second on Midsummer Day, the third at Lammas (12th August) and the last at Hallowday, the 1st of November.

The markets of Derry, Carn and Buncrana are the outlets for the produce of this parish.

Proprietors

The principal proprietors under Lord Donegall, who is the chief landlord, are the Revd W.H. Harvey, whose lands are at present held by Mrs Merrick, viz. Urismana, Leenan, Dunaff, Letter, Kenaght, Tallagh, Cleagh and Altahalla.

The Dogherty family possess Straid, Anney, Ardagh, Lonebratly, Ballymacmurty and part of Ruskey.

Mr Loghery possesses Dunally; Archdeacon Torrens holds Magherymore; Miss Harvey, Cloontagh; Sir A. Chichester and the Revd S. Montgomery, each a part of Ballyliffin; Mr Curry, Straas and Rashany; Councillor Dobbs, Carra-reagh; Mr Cary, Fugart; Mr Harvey of Malin Hall, Legacurry and Carrickabracky and part of Ruskey; Adervil, Mindoran and Gaddyduff belong to the church.

Farms and Rents

The only residents are the Dogherty family and Mr Logherty [insert marginal note: Loughry <Loughrey>]. The chief agent Mr Dogherty is resident and receives 5% on the sums collected. The usual size of the holdings is from 5 to 12 acres. The largest farm is 50 acres, very few above 20 and only 1 freehold in the parish. There are few leases, none in Mrs Merrick's lands but she has promised not to alter the rents for 21 years (her lease having 26 years to run).

Information as to the average rent is very difficult to be obtained, as the tenants and agent differ materially on the subject. 3 acres of good land and grazing for 2 cows costs 4 pounds 16s a year and the tenant puts the whole rent on the arable and calls it 32s an acre; it is paid wholly in money. In Tullagh, where the crops are much exposed, a farm of 14 acres, 10 only of which is arable, is let for 36 pounds, as stated by the tenants.

The farmers are respectable but they work only for subsistence. There is no land let on the conacre and there are fewer enclosures in Clonmany than in any other parish I have seen. The arable land is too good to lose by enclosures and, as it is tilled in run and dale, it does not so much require it.

There are 3 large tracks of reclaimed bog, quite flat, without any fences, which produce superior crops. The boundaries in other parts of the parish are of stone. For many miles a bush is not to be seen.

The county cess and tithes are the only taxes, and the farm buildings are superior to the usual run. The tenants build and keep them in repair.

Manures

There are no farms kept for example. The best soil is reclaimed bog manured with seaweed, sand and compost. The former, being easily procured, is abundantly used and gives excellent crops. Boats are sent to the rocks left dry at low water and to Glassheady Isle for seaweed. Burning the soil except in reclaiming land does not exist.

Machinery

Iron ploughs are scarce, no threshing machines and few carts. In the west end of the parish the usual method of transporting produce is by horses. 2 baskets, whose bottoms swing upon hinges, are suspended on the back of a horse and used to carry manure from the farmyard to the fields.

Rotation of Crops

The rotation of crops is potatoes, oats, barley, flax and then again potatoes. 176 stone of seed are used on an acre, the produce of which varies from 20 to 60 sacks of 24 stone each, and sells from 2s 6d to 5s a sack in the latter part of the season. Oats require 24 stone to an acre and produce 120 stone in good and 76 in bad land, and sell for 7d per stone. Barley takes 16 stone an acre and produces 100 stone at from 7d to 9d a stone. Flax is sown at the rate of 32 gallons an acre and the produce will sell for 6 guineas on the ground.

No sum can be stated for the expense of carrying these commodities to market, except that a cart can be hired at 2s 6d a day, and the nearest markets are Carn and Buncrana, the one 7, the

Parish of Clonmany

other 10 miles from the middle of the parish. A few rabbit skins are procured at Leenan, which will sell at 2s a dozen.

Farming Methods

There are no farms devoted to grazing but there is more of this kind of farming carried on in Clootagh, Mundoran and Adervil than elsewhere. Scarcely any forced grass is planted. Common irrigation is practised but not extensively. The extreme barrenness of the mountains prevents grazing to any extent.

Farm servants receive 3 guineas for 6 months, women servants half that sum with board and lodging.

Cattle

A good Inishowen pony is sold for 12 pounds; the average price is 9 pounds. A good mountain sheep is worth 16s. The Irish breed of cattle still prevails and fetch 4 pounds 10s a head. Pigs cost from 12s to 20s and there is plenty of common poultry and some of the pheasant breed.

There are no jobbers of cattle or jockeys in Clonmany and green feeding is not practised. The average number of horses is 1 to a family. 1,166 cattle may be reckoned at a higher average.

Uses made of Bogs

The bogs are grazed and used for fuel. Charcoal is made only for the blacksmiths in the parish and the bog wood is burnt for fuel. A day's cutting of turf costs 7s.

Drainage and Planting

Drainage: this is carried on successfully whenever required, as the lands usually are well situated for drains cut through the turf.

There are few young trees in the parish and no plantations. When required, they are purchased in Derry. The only trees of any age are those at Dresden. In the rest of Clonmany there are fewer bushes than usual in the country.

Sea-Coast

The sea-coast is very little used for kelp at present, as it yields a better return when laid on the land for manure. It used to sell from 2s to 4s a cwt.

Fishing

There are about 55 men employed occasionally in fishing when they have nothing else to do or when shoals of herrings are known to be on the coast.

There are 8 boats between Urris and Dunaff. Each boat has 6 or 7 herring nets 17 fathoms long and 3 fathoms or 160 meshes deep. Between Dunaff and Binnion there are 3 boats. Only one has herring nets about 16 fathoms long and 160 meshes deep.

Between Binnion and Carrickabrackey Castle the people have 4 boats but no nets. There are about 12 boats in the Isle of Doagh used principally for bringing turf from Malin, as there is none in Doagh; these boats are seldom used in fishing. The boats of Clonmany are manned with 5 hands each and are the private property of the boatmen.

The sea and lough contain plenty of fish, enumerated under Zoology. The banks are in the neighbourhood of Malin. Fishing with nets is the most profitable. Its extent is chiefly limited by the scarcity of markets and the fishermen, not having sufficient practice, are not bold seamen.

The seasons for catching the different kinds of fish are as follows: cod from October to March, haddock from October to March, salmon from April to September, white trout in abundance from May to July, sole in abundance from April to November, ling from October to March, flounders, breams and plaice from April to November, skate all the year round.

Seals are seldom taken but they usually come about August or September (as formerly herring about the same period but not in such shoals). Porpoise are seen at all seasons but not taken. Grampuses are sometimes seen in the herring season but are not taken; no oysters; crabs and lobsters abound from August to November.

Periwinkles and limpets are taken at all times. They are either sold on the spot to the peasants or carried to market according to the quantity to be taken.

The salted herring sell for 30s a barrel and the owners of the 8 boats from Urris to Dunaff may probably sell about 50 barrels a year. Salted ling or cod are sold in Buncrana for 6d apiece.

Seals

Seals are sometimes shot at Glassheady. They are seen from a few to 20 or 30 at a time. They frequent a bank in Strabraga bay opposite Malin but are described to be timid and wary. When obtained they produce, in oil and skin, (the latter is dressed at Derry and used for caps) about 2 pounds apiece. Sometimes 3 or 4 are procured at a time, but the difficulty of getting them or the ignorance of the people prevents this otherwise lucrative employment from being much followed.

The people at Malin live very much by fishing. Those of Clonmany hold land and fish occasionally. There is no encouragement given by the proprietors, no curing houses or depositories of salt.

River Fishing

Salmon and white trout also frequent the rivers. They are taken on the shore by stake-nets from Binnion to Desertegney.

The right of fishing belongs to the Revd W.H. Harvey and he has let it for 5 years to Mr Halliday <Hallyday> of Derry, from Binnion to Ned's Battery in Lough Swilly, for 30 pounds a year. The right of fishing or other parts of the coast belongs to the proprietors.

General Remarks on Economy

The general height to which cultivation has been carried is about 500 feet above the sea. There is not much water in the parish but the streams are well adapted for irrigation where required. It is much exposed to northerly winds and the climate is moist. The prevailing good soil is reclaimed bog manured with seaweed and sand. There is no lime in the parish.

No lands could be better adapted for tillage than part of Lennan, Urrismanagh, Tullnabratley and Ballyliffin. There are no tracks well adapted for sheep-walks, although there are a good many kept, and few lands for grazing except in the townlands of Clontagh and Mindoran.

There is not an abundance of fuel or water and no convenient ports for shipping. The products of the coasts and seas are neglected. The roads are well adapted to the country.

DIVISIONS

Isle of Doagh

The only divisions otherwise than townlands is the peninsula called the Isle of Doagh, derived from Illan-na-doo'cagh or "isle of sand fields," an appropriate name where 2 entire townlands and parts of others have been totally buried by the drifting of the beach and the breaking up of banks of indurated sand driven by westerly winds over fields and villages now deserted.

Townlands

List of townlands in Clonmany: Addervill lies between Rusky and Straid, on the north fall of Bulbin; Altahalla, west of Mindoran and Cloon-tagh, mingling with Mintiaghs; Annigh, the highest part of the promontory called Binnion, on the sea-coast; Ardugh, on the sea-coast, east of Binnion station.

Ballymacmurty, on the sea-shore south of Carrickabrackey; Ballyliffin, to the west of Tullnabratley and south of Ardugh; Binnion, the promontory east of the mouth of Clonmany river.

Carrareagh, in Isle of Doagh, on Strabraga bay; Carrickabrackey, the northern townland at entrance of Strabraga bay; Cleagh, north of Clonmany river, in the vicinity of the chapel; Cloontagh, the most south eastern corner and marches with Donagh; Crossconnell lies on the left bank of Clonmany river, on the coast.

Dunaff, the north west promontory of the parish; Fugart, on the east of Doagh opposite Malin; Gaddyduff, east of the parish church near the centre of parish; Keenaght, to the west of Tullagh, on the coast.

Leenan, the south west townland of the parish, on Lough Swilly; Legacurry, on the shore of Strabraga bay opposite Malin; Letter, on the western fall of Slievekerogue mountain.

Magheranal, the south eastern town of the Isle of Doagh, on Strabrega bay; Mindoran marches with Mintiaghs, right of Carn road; Rashany lies on the south side of Strabrega bay, west of Straas; Ruskey mears with Mintiaghs and Desertegney, east of Addervill.

Straas marches with Donagh on the south side of Strabrega bay; Straid, east of the Slievekeroge range, on mearing of Desertegney; Tullagh, a headland between Binnion and Dunaff; Tullnabratley marches with Ballymacmurty on the north, and lies to the west of the bay; Urrismanagh, to the east of Mamore, on the Slievekeroge range and mearing down to Lough Swilly.

Buncrana

The market town of Buncrana is about [blank] miles [insert marginal query: 6] from the Gap of Mamore and [blank] miles from Mindoran; that of Carn is [blank] miles from Straas. [Insert footnote: Queries cannot be properly done without the adjacent plan]. [Signed] W. Lancey, Lieutenant Royal Engineers, 14th May 1834.

Parish of Culdaff, County Donegal

Statistical Enquiries on the Coast Fisheries

NATURAL FEATURES AND PRODUCTIVE ECONOMY

Queries and Answers No.1

9. Is fishing a favourite pursuit of the people or is it uncongenial to their habits and feelings? [Answer] It appears to be a favourite pursuit with the people. At the same time, it must be stated that the land is so highly let that they are obliged to fish, to make up those rents which the land itself could never produce.

10. Does the fish taken form a large portion of the food of the inhabitants of the coast; is a considerable portion of it sent to inland parts of the country or to any principal market? [Answer] It does form a considerable part of the food of the inhabitants. A very considerable portion is sent to Londonderry and to the inland parts of the neighbouring counties and, since the steam-boats have been established, to Liverpool and Glasgow. The greatest part of the best fish is sent out of the country by them.

11. Can you enumerate the edible fish which most abound at all times in the deep water or on the banks, and those which visit periodically the shores of the parish? [Answer] Cod, haddock, ling, turbot, gurnets, skate and sometimes mackerel. Lobsters and crabs are also found among the rocks. The shore is periodically visited by herrings and salmon.

Queries and Answers No.2

2. Are they constant or periodical fishermen? [Answer] They are periodical fishermen.

3. Are the boats and tackle employed the absolute property of the fishermen or hired as occasion may require? [Answer] The boats and tackle are the absolute property of the fishermen. The boats are Norway yawls and square-sterned boats about 26 feet long and 6 feet beam. The Norway yawl costs 8 pounds, the square-sterned boats from 11 pounds to 12 pounds, including oars, sails, cables and anchors, and they are built on the coast.

4. Are there any banks adjacent to the coast well stocked with fish? [Answer] There is a shoal called Hempton's bank about 20 miles north of the parish. It is well stocked with fish but the boats are not sufficiently well found to venture to it, except in very fine weather. The best fish are to be found in its vicinity.

5. Are the deep waters near the shore generally well supplied with fish? [Answer] Yes.

6. Are the shores rocky and precipitous, or do they afford good landing places for nets and convenient spots for drying fish, either in bays or along sandy beaches? [Answer] The shores are very rocky and precipitous. There are, however, small bays and sandy beaches convenient for the purpose.

7. Is the fishing limited by insufficiency in the number of boats? [Answer] No.

8. Is the fishery limited by want of salt or other means of curing the superfluous fish? [Answer] There is not any fish cured except a few herrings for home consumption, the quantity taken being nearly equal to the daily demand.

Queries and Answers No.3

1. Do many of the inhabitants of the maritime coast of the parish of Culdaff apply themselves to fishing? [Answer] Yes, about 200.

2. Are they constant or periodical fishermen? [Answer] Periodical.

3. Are the boats and tackle employed the absolute property of the fishermen or hired as occasion may require? [Answer] They are the absolute property of the fishermen.

4. Are there any banks adjacent to the coast well stocked with fish? [Answer] Yes, one bank called Hempton's bank about 20 miles distant from Culdaff bay.

5. Are the deep waters near the shore generally well supplied with fish? [Answer] Not generally well supplied.

6. Are the shores rocky and precipitous, or do they afford good landing places for nets and convenient spots for drying fish, either in bays or along sandy beaches? [Answer] The shores afford very good landing places and convenient for drying fish.

7. Is the fishing limited by insufficiency in the number of boats? [Answer] No.

8. Is the fishery limited by want of salt or other means of curing the superfluous fish? [Answer] No.

9. Is fishing a favourite pursuit of the people or is it uncongenial to their habits and feelings? [Answer] Yes.

10. Does the fish taken form a large portion of the food of the inhabitants of the coast? Is a con-

siderable portion of it sent to inland parts of the country or to any principal market? [Answer] The fishermen use some, but the principal part of the fish is sent inland and also to the market of Carndonagh.

11. Can you enumerate the edible fish which most abound at all times in the deep water or on the banks, and those which visit periodically the shores of the parish? [Answer] The deep water and banks abound with cod, ling, pollock, glasson, turbot, fluke, sole, skate, dogfish and garvin or sea bream, also haddock and shelog. Those that visit periodically are principally herrings.

12. Can you state the periods at which the great shoals of fish arrive and the ordinary length of their visit? [Answer] The herrings arrive in August and September, but the ordinary length of their visit is uncertain.

Queries and Answers No.4

[Insert note: Mr John Eivers will endeavour to procure the information required in this paper [signed] R. Fenwick, Lieutenant Royal Engineers].

1. Do many of the inhabitants of the maritime coast of the parish of Culdaff apply themselves to fishing? [Answer] The greatest part.

2. Are they very constant or periodical fishermen? [Answer] Constant.

3. Are the boats and tackle employed the absolute property of the fishermen or hired as occasion may require? [Answer] The property of the fishermen.

4. Are there any banks adjacent to the coast well stocked with fish? [Answer] There are.

5. Are the deep waters near the shore generally well supplied with fish? [Answer] Yes.

6. Are the shores rocky and precipitous, or do they afford good landing places for nets and convenient spots for drying fish, either in bays or along sandy beaches? [Answer] They are very rocky.

7. Is the fishing limited by insufficiency in the number of boats? [Answer] It is.

8. Is the fishery limited by the want of salt or other means of curing the superfluous fish? [Answer] No.

9. Is fishing a favourite pursuit of the people or is it uncongenial to their habits and feelings? [Answer] It is a favourite pursuit.

10. Does the fish taken form a large portion of the food of the inhabitants of the coast? Is a considerable portion of it sent to inland parts of the country or to any principal market? [Answer] It is their principal food; the remainder they send to the inland towns.

11. Can you enumerate the edible fish which most abound at all times in the deep water or on the banks, and those which visit periodically the shores of the parish? [Answer] The fish which are constantly taken are holbert, cod, haddock, ling, greylord <load>, fluke and skate. Periodical: creggig, salmon, glassin, garvin, sheelog, whiting and hake <haick> and herring.

Analysis of Fishermen

Table shewing the number of fishermen of each class in the parish of Culdaff, county of Donegal.

Periodical fishermen: 120 men, 60 lads, 20 boys; 50 boats, amount of tonnage 75, value 300 pounds [insert alternative: 450 pounds], value of nets 100 pounds.

[Key]: lads 12 years to 17, boys under 12 years, girls above 12, children including boys unemployed, wives including all women who have been married.

Answers are requested to be addressed to Lieutenant-Colonel Colby, Royal Engineers, Ordnance Survey Office, Dublin.

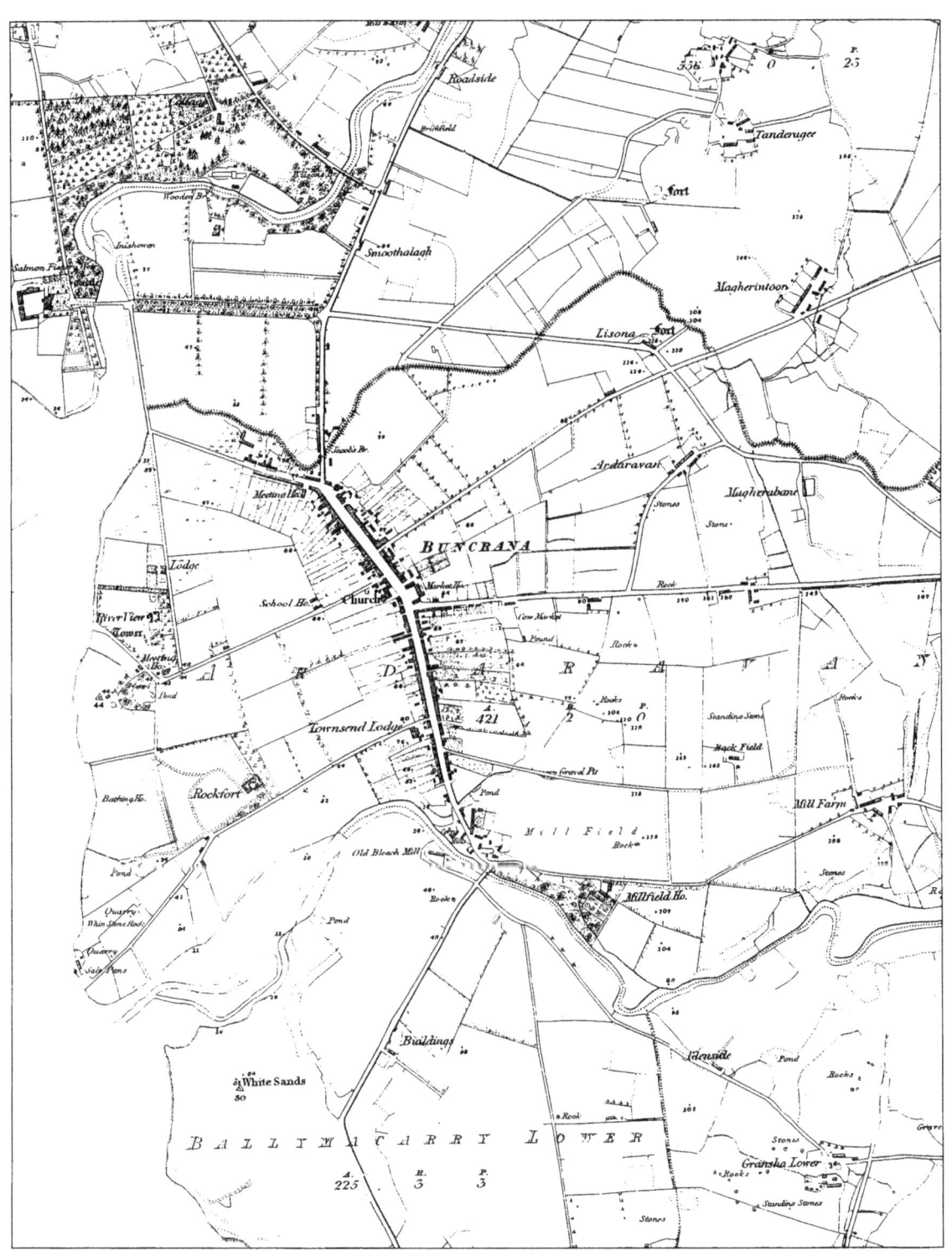

Map of Buncrana from the first 6″ O.S. maps, 1830s

Parish of Desertegney, County Donegal

Statistical Report by Lieutenant W. Lancey, May 1834

NATURAL STATE

Name and Locality

The name of this parish is pronounced Desertagney and is derived from "desert" and "agnus," a saint, "the Easter of St Agnus." [Insert marginal query: *disart* "a hermitage" and *Eighney*, a name].

And is situated in the county of Donegal, on the west side of the barony of Inishowen, on the right bank of Lough Swilly to the north of Buncrana. The Urris mountains separate it from Clonmany on the north and east, and it is enclosed by Mintiaghs and Lower Fahan on the south and south east.

The extreme length is 4 and three-quarter miles and breadth 4 and four-fifths, and contains 7,532 acres, of which a third are cultivated, the rest being waste and bog. The valuation to the county cess amounts to [insert note: could not be obtained].

NATURAL FEATURES

Hills

The principal range of hills is that of Urris, which rises in fine precipices from Lough Swilly and bounds the north of the parish. It attains the height of 1,375 feet and runs east for 1 and a quarter miles towards the south east corner. The hill of Aughaweal rises in gradual slopes from the lough to the height of 1,106 feet and is the commencement of a second range running into Mintiaghs and Clonmany. These 2 ranges are divided by a small rapid river flowing at the foot of Urris.

Lakes and Rivers

There are no lakes in Desertegney and the only river of consequence is that just mentioned. It rises in the townland of Ballyannon within the parish, about 5 miles from Lough Swilly, and runs north for 2 miles, then turns west and is joined by a stream which rises in Straid and Urrismana in Clonmany, about 4 and a half miles from the lough. The stream flows to the west for 2 and a quarter miles over quartz and talc-slate rocks to a small bay called Port Bawn in Lough Swilly. Its breadth is 40 feet and depth about 4 inches. It is well situated for water power and does not overflow as it lies in a deep rocky bed in a confined glen.

There are several small brooks in the parish, well adapted for draining the adjacent lands but not sufficient to ensure a constant supply of water for mills.

Bogs

The bogs are not very extensive. Those in Ballyannon, Aughaweal and Culhame are considered the best and are about 550 feet above the sea. Bog fir and oak occur but they are not very abundant. The turf is from 3 to 8 feet in depth.

Woods

There are no remains of any woods. A scrog existed in the memory of man at the foot of Lederig.

Coast

The general direction of the coast of Lough Swilly in this parish is to the north for 3 and three-eighth miles, to the headlands of Dunree on which a strong battery is built. It then runs north east for about 2 miles by Urris and Dunree, where there are fine precipices of quartz rock, but towards the south, although bold and generally inaccessible for boats, the coast seldom exceeds 50 feet in height.

Port Bawn, lying between Dunree and Urris, is the only bay. It is about 1,450 feet wide at the entrance and has a fine level strand. There are also landing places for boats at Mount Paul, the Curragh Hole, Mr Harvey's at Linsfort and at the foot of Dunree.

There are a few small caves but none of any consequence. Pigeon Cave is the principal one.

Climate

The harvest commences on the shore at Lammas and in the high grounds about 14 days afterwards. There is usually plenty of rain and wind, and in the memory of man the winter of 1833 and 1834 has never been exceeded.

NATURAL HISTORY

Botany

"One-pointed grass" springs up in the meadows and rye grass is planted by only 4 farmers in the parish.

Parish of Desertegney

Zoology

Foxes with white rings half round their necks abound. They live on the sea-shore among the rocks. There are hares and a few rabbits at Mr Harvey's; plenty of partridges, some grouse, snipes and a few woodcocks; occasionally eagles; plenty of crows, wild pigeons and the usual common birds.

Cod, haddock, mullet, sole, ling, flounders, salmon, skait, crabs, lobsters, periwinkles <perrywincles>, limpets, shrimps, razor-fish but no oysters and sometimes seals.

Geology

Desertegney lies on a primitive formation of quartz rock and talc slate, the former being principally confined to Urris and Dunree. A basaltic porphyritic dyke is found above Mr Harvey's house.

MODERN TOPOGRAPHY

Towns

There is no town in Desertegney but some large villages: the principal are Toneduff and Magherabane. The former is the largest agricultural village I have yet seen, but it differs from others only in its number of houses. They consist, as usual, of 1, 2 or 3 rooms with low roofs, thatched and bound down with straw ropes. They are not whitewashed, are unclean in the interior and present an appearance of meanness and poverty.

Public Buildings: Church

Linsfort church was built by the late General Hart's father, who was rector of the parish about 60 years ago. The Bishop, Lord Donegall and the parish paid for it [insert marginal note: cost could not be obtained]. It can contain 100 persons in pews but has no gallery. The body of Lieutenant Salter of the Royal Marines, lost in the *Saldanha* frigate, is buried in the church.

Catholic Chapel

The Roman Catholic chapel in Gortlack was erected on the site and with the stones of the old church about 20 years ago. It was lengthened 20 feet in 1826 and a gallery is now being added. These expenses are paid by subscription. About [insert marginal note: perhaps 600 or 700] persons usually attend mass.

Dunree Fort

Dunree Fort is strikingly situated on the coast of Lough Swilly immediately opposite to Knockalla battery. It stands on a little rocky peninsula whose isthmus is a mass of rocks having a natural arch below, through which the sea flows, and a chasm above 25 feet deep by 9 feet wide.

The fort occupies the whole of this peninsula and is inaccessible except by a drawbridge thrown over the chasm. It is an irregular 4-sided figure measuring about 650 feet round the inside of the walls and parapets, and presents a fire of 9 24-pounders on traversing carriages, and 3 others can be mounted in embrasures if required.

A ship on entering the lough would have to contend with the direct fire of 4 guns. In passing by the fort she would also receive the direct fire of 4 others and, after passing it, the same number. The principal battery consists of 6 24-pounders, 4 of which cross the fire of Knockalla, 1 fires up, the other down the lough. Towards the entrance of Lough Swilly, and above the main battery, is a single gun, and immediately above it, on the most commanding part of the rock, 2 are mounted on a Martello tower which fire over the fort. The terreplein of the main battery is about 90 feet above the sea and that of the tower 35 feet above the battery.

Dunree is commanded by musketry from an adjacent hill but the 6-gun battery is protected by the buildings and the single gun battery by the tower, the wall of which is raised towards the country to protect the gunners.

A company of men and officers can be accommodated in the barracks with all the usual requisites for infantry soldiers, and the fort possesses a fine spring which issues out of the rock.

Dunree Fort was built in the years 1812-14 under the superintendence of Captain Spicer, Royal Engineers, at an expense of [blank] pounds. Its present garrison is a master gunner and 7 artillerymen detached from Buncrana. Mr Edgar of Buncrana contracted for the building of Dunree and the other 5 forts in Lough Swilly.

Gentlemen's Seats

The Revd W.H. Harvey's house in Linsfort is the only gentleman's seat. It was built 3 years ago and cost about 3,000 pounds. It is pleasantly situated on the bank of Lough Swilly and it is a neat, whitewashed, slated building of moderate dimensions built on an English model, with farm offices, barns, stables etc. of a superior description. There is no demesne but a garden, lawn and a little ornamental ground about it.

The Glebe House is a plain building apparently without design. It was built in 1827 by Dean Blakely and has 7 rooms. It cost 800 pounds, about 4 times [insert marginal note: say 3] its value at the most extravagant computation.

Mr Baldrick's house in the townland of Linsfort was rebuilt by Captain A. Belsom in 1720. Mr Baldrick, a very respectable yeoman, purchased it with 60 acres of land having 13 years to run, from the Revd Oliver McCausland, the present rector of Finlagan, for 200 pounds, who purchased it from the Revd Mr Hart before mentioned.

Mills

There are 2 undershot corn mills in Desertegney: one in Toneduff, on the river at the foot of Urris, with a slate roof, has a wheel 14 feet in diameter and 2 in breadth with plenty of water and a drying kiln, and receives the 30th grain; the old price was the 16th. The other mill is in Linsfort with a wheel 12 feet in diameter and 2 feet in breadth, has a kiln and fans and consequently does the most work at the same price, but has not sufficient water.

The erection of mills in Desertegney is not prevented by any legal disputes but there is only 1 river which is well calculated for them.

Communications

The principal roads are those from Buncrana to Dunree Fort and the Gap of Mamore, which are connected at the foot of Urris by a crossroad leading from the fort to Clonmany church. These roads are scarcely passable for spring cars but they answer the purposes of the country people, who convey most of their goods and produce to market on the backs of horses. They are about 25 feet in width and their extent from the south mearing to the Gap is about 4 and a half miles. The expense of repairing is paid by the grand jury. They are tolerably well laid out.

Bridges

The only bridge of consequence is near the foot of the Gap of Mamore. It was built in 1806, has 3 arches and cost [insert note: no cost], at the expense of the county.

There is a smaller one on the Dunree road, built in 1814 at a cost of 445 pounds by the county.

General Appearance and Scenery

In ascending the Gap, the road is good until near its summit, when it becomes extremely rough and absolutely dangerous to ride on. The scenery is strikingly wild and bold, and the view either towards Clonmany or Desertegney is remarkably fine. In descending the Gap, the landscape increases in beauty and the fine cultivated lands of Leanan <Lennan>, with the headlands on the coast and the extensive view of the ocean, constitute no ordinary landscape.

[Insert marginal note by Lancey: Belongs to Clonmany, not to Desertegney].

ANCIENT TOPOGRAPHY

Pagan Remains

There are no ecclesiastical or military remains in this parish except a fort in Linsfort, 1 in Sharagone, Toneduff and Munniaghs.

Under the head Pagan may be noticed the standing stones in Munniaghs, Ballyannon, Leafin and the Glebe, and the cloghogle stones on the mearing of Sharagone and Toneduff. [Insert marginal note: The cloghogle stones consist of 9 slabs, 7 upright and 2 horizontal thus: [diagram with annotation]. Those to the east, marked X, are covered with 2 horizontal slabs and are 22 inches from the surface; the 3 to the west are uncovered. 2 are 8 links and that on the extreme west 22 inches high [drawing]. The upright stone in Munniaghs is west of the above and is about 6 feet high.

The peasants dug around some of these upright monuments in hopes of finding treasure. No persons know anything about them: complete ignorance prevails on this subject and on most of the antiquities met with in the north of Ireland.

Old Church

The ruin of the old church was built up in the new Roman Catholic chapel as before stated and I obtained no account of its former state.

MODERN TOPOGRAPHY

General Appearance and Scenery

On entering Desertegney by the Buncrana road, the lofty, barren and rugged ridge of Urris, rising from Lough Swilly to the height of 1,376 feet on a short base, presents the most striking feature. To the right is the Gap of Mamore, to the left the scenery of the lough with the opposite bold coast. The hill of Aughaweal stands in the foreground

Parish of Desertegney

to the right and, falling in gentle and regular slopes to the west, presents the different gradations of rock and bog, waste and cultivated land to the coast, where it terminates in steep rocks varying from a few feet to about 50.

The road to Dunree Fort passes to the right of the best land in the parish and the unvaried monotony of stone walls and the almost total absence of trees [crossed out: plantations] is relieved by Mr Harvey's neat house and small plantations on the coast.

The general appearance of the parish is as wild, poor and mean as any I have yet seen.

SOCIAL ECONOMY

Early Improvements

The sea-coast appears to be the chief attraction, next to the common interests of tillage, that has located the people in Desertegney.

Obstructions to Improvement

The disturbed state of the country tends to prevent improvements. No plantations can be expected to thrive where the people cut the young trees as soon as they are fit for their purposes. Even peas and beans can scarcely be grown for depredations constantly committed on gardens, and the few persons who are willing to improve are overawed by the peasants.

Local Government

There is no magistrate in the parish. All magisterial business is settled in Buncrana or Carn.

Dispensaries: the poor requiring medical relief apply to the Buncrana dispensary.

Schools

Linsfort school consists of 32 scholars and is the only regular establishment in the parish. Males 14, females 18, Protestant males 10, Protestant females 9, Roman Catholic males and females 13. Patron and supporter the Revd Mr W. Harvey. The master resides and is the parish clerk. The scholars pay 2s 6d a quarter.

There is also a hedge school in Leafin which educates 35 Catholic children. The male and female children in both schools sit together and they pay in Leafin the same price as at Linsfort.

Poor

There are a great many poor, who are principally Roman Catholics. There are no almshouses or endowments of a charitable nature for their relief.

Religion

The majority of the people are Roman Catholics. There are only 30 families of Protestants of all denominations. The rector receives 140 pounds under the Composition Act and a glebe of 60 pounds. The Roman Catholic priest is a curate of the Roman Catholic rector of Buncrana and he receives one-quarter of the dues etc.

Habits of the People

They live in low stone cabins with glass windows and thatched roofs bound down with straw ropes. Very few are whitewashed as there is no lime nearer than Carn. The cabins consist of 1, 2 or 3 rooms. Those of 2 rooms prevail. They are not clean or comfortable. The English language is increasing. The food of the people is potatoes, water, milk and some meal. Most people keep a cow and all burn turf and a little bog wood.

They live from 60 to 80 and are about 6 in a family. They marry very early, frequently at 16, and in one instance in the memory of man the united ages of one couple did not exceed 28.

Amusements and Traditions

They keep St John's Eve and jump over bonfires in which they burn bones. There are no patrons' or other saints' days peculiar to the parish. Malin is the chief resort for the people of Inishowen to celebrate these superstitions, but women frequent a place in Gortlack to obtain clay to cure their complaints.

Emigration

They are beginning to emigrate to America. About 20 have gone this year. Many go to England and Scotland for harvest and some to the Scotch spinning and carding factories. Only a part of the household leaves home and the others plant the family potatoes for the winter's support.

Remarkable events: none.

PRODUCTIVE ECONOMY

Manufacturing

There are a good many looms but they are principally idle at present for want of encouragement. Spinning is general in the cabins. One lb. of flax will produce from 4 to 6 hanks of yarn and a woman can spin 8 cuts in a day. Shirting will sell for 6d to 8d a yard and a weaver will make 6 to 8 yards a day. If employed as a journeyman, he will charge 3d a yard for 8d cloth and 2d for woollens. Grey woollen cloths are also made and sold for 12d to 18d a yard; when dressed at the tuck mill in Buncrana are sold for 2s 6d to 3s a yard.

Blankets and flannels are made for home use. The latter brings 10d a yard if sold. The quantity made depends on the demand and the looms, as stated above, are nearly idle for want of employment.

Fairs and Markets

There are none in the parish. Buncrana, Carn and Derry are the markets to which the produce of Desertegney is carried.

Proprietors

The lands of Desertegney are held by 2 landlords, the Revd W.H. Harvey and the Revd W. Knox of Lifford. Mr Harvey resides, and the revenue of the parish at the king's death will be worth about 1,500 pounds a year, 700 pounds of which belongs to Mr Knox and 800 pounds will be the revenue of Mr Harvey. Ballyannon, Gortlack, Tonduff and Sharagone belong to the former and the rest of the parish to the latter, with the exception of the glebe. [Insert marginal note: Mr Micky Dogherty of Clonmany receives Mr Knox's rents and Mr Joytown of Belfast those of Mr Harvey. Each receives 5%].

Holdings and Leases

The usual size of the holdings is about 4 acres arable and 6 pasture. There are only 3 above 20 acres arable, one of which has 30 acres in total extent; about 8 farms are above 10 acres each. Mr Harvey's lands are held by leases, many of which will terminate at the present king's death; other leases by Lord Donegall (the former proprietor) run for 40 years and 3 lives or 61 years without lives.

Mr Knox's lands are let in the usual manner of churchlands for 21 years. The lands are generally held by middlemen. The rents vary from 30s to 40s an acre with sufficient grazing. Those who have bad land have more mountain. Those who have the best arable have less for their money.

There are 4 very respectable Protestant yeomen in Desertegney. The rest farm for subsistence. The fields are small, enclosed in stone walls and little attention is paid to their shape.

The local taxes are tithe and county cess.

The farm buildings are very indifferent and are built and kept in repair by the tenants.

Manures

There is some good land about the sea-shore manured with seaweed, sand and farm composts. Lime is not used for manure as it costs at Carn 12d a barrel and is 10 miles from the middle of the parish. The seaweed is an excellent manure for potatoes and the cheapest that can be obtained. Burning land except for reclaiming wastes is not practised.

Implements of Husbandry

There are 2 winnowing machines, 3 iron ploughs and a few cars. The nature of the country is well adapted for carts, but the roads are not in good order and the general poverty of the people and the smallness of the farms prevent them being generally used. Horses are the chief means of conveyance.

Rotation of Crops

The usual rotation of crops by the best farmers is on a lea field: first oats, a second crop of oats, flax, oats, potatoes, barley and grass and then lea. The inferior lands are cropped with potatoes, 2 crops of oats and then allowed to run lea.

Seed and Produce

The seed for an acre of oats is 20 to 24 stone, the seed for an acre of barley 15 to 16 stone, flax 32 gallons of New York seed, flax 36 gallons of Riga, potatoes take 8 barrels of 16 stone, clover 10 to 12 lbs to an acre with rye grass seed.

The produce of oats sells on the ground for 5 pounds, barley 6 to 10 pounds, flax 6 to 10 pounds, potatoes 10 to 12 pounds. The expense of sending to market is about 2s 6d a day for cart hire, but this is never incurred as they take it on their own carts or horses.

The price of oats in Buncrana market is 7d ha'penny per stone, barley about 8d, flax undressed 5d, dressed 11d [per] lb., potatoes about 5s a sack of 24 stone, forced-grass hay 40s a ton, meadow hay 25s and there are about 26 acres in the parish.

Grazing

There are no farms exclusively laid out for grazing. Each tenant has a portion of the mountain or wastelands. If any cattle should be taken in, they charge 4s to 5s a head for the season. The culture of artificial grass is conducted by 4 persons, and that only for their working and common stock. The

Parish of Desertegney

meadows are irrigated and sufficiently drained. Common "one pointed grass" springs up in them.

Wages

Wages of male servants vary from 56s to 60s and women receive 20s to 21s each the half-year, with board and lodging.

Livestock

Inishowen ponies worth 8 pounds to 10 pounds, common Irish cattle worth 3 pounds to 6 pounds; pigs bring 14s a hundred [cwt?] and sometimes run 2 and a half cwt, the usual size being 1 cwt.

Common poultry of all kinds is usual. Every family that has lands keeps at least 1 horse. There are no improved breeds or stall-fed cattle, no cattle jobbers or horse dealers in Desertegney.

Uses made of the Bogs

They are grazed and used for fuel. There are 4 blacksmiths in the parish whose forges are supplied from the bogs. The timber usually is not sufficiently good for building. A day's cutting for 1 man and 3 helpers is about 5s. They are allowed to use only 1 spade in the bog and 1 to pare the upper surface, 1 man to pack the barrow and 1 to wheel it. The party works from daylight till dark [insert addition: and can cut on an average 30 cages [gauges?], each cage being 16 bushels and worth 11d a cage when dragged out of the bog. A car and horse is hired for 2s 6d a day and will travel about 20 miles a day to and from the bog].

Drainage

The bogs are well situated for draining and it is carried on where required by simple trenches cut through them and conveying the water into the nearest stream.

Planting

Mr Harvey has ornamented his house at Linsfort with a few young trees and there are a few round some of the farmhouses, but generally the parish is destitute of timber.

Seaweed

Kelp is not made at present as the bleach green at Buncrana has long since ceased to be used, and the people make more of the seaweed by the potato crop than by burning it.

Fishing

The salmon fishing on the whole coast of Desertegney, belonging to Mr Harvey, and his interest in Clonmany as far east as Binnion are let to Mr Halliday, a Scotchman residing in Derry, for the sum of 30 pounds annually for the next 5 years as a trial. Mr Halliday has erected 2 stake-nets in Port Bawn and 1 at Linsfort. To each net are attached 2 men who are provided with a boat by Mr Halliday, who has an agent in Buncrana who receives the fish and forwards it to Derry, none being sold on the spot. The chief boatman receives 7s 6d, the other 6s a week.

There are about 75 men employed occasionally in fishing in the lough and on the banks, having 15 boats, each boat a set of herring nets, 5 or 6, of 17 fathoms long and 120 meshes deep. The boats are their own property and the seas abound with fish, but the herring shoals do not frequent the coast so much as they used, for which I have heard no good reason. [Insert note: The people say that the quantity of seaweed taken for manure has driven the fish from the coast].

Cod, haddock, sole, ling, flounders, skate, herrings, crabs, lobsters, periwinkles are the usual kind of fish. The deep-sea fishing is now the most profitable and is quite capable of extension, and would doubtless succeed better if good decked smacks were employed which could stand the open sea, but the crazy boats in use are unfitted for any wind and consequently the people are not bold seamen.

General Remarks on Economy

The highest point to which cultivation has been carried is in the townland of Lederig, 650 feet above the sea. The lands are generally well situated for irrigation and drainage. The former might possibly be useful, the latter is almost unnecessary. It is much exposed to the prevailing westerly winds and not at all protected by artificial means. The soil, lying on talc slate, is generally bad, but towards the coast the land is very tolerable and, having the constant advantage of sea manure, produces good crops.

The poverty of the people and the distance from any lime quarry prevents that useful mineral being used in agriculture, but its absence is less felt in consequence of the abundance of seaweed. The parish is not adapted for sheep-walks or grazing, but much waste and useless land might, with little expense, be advantageously planted, especially in Lederig, where rocks occupy so much space that oaks might flourish where grass and heath will scarcely grow.

Facilities for water power exist with advantage only at the foot of Urris, and fuel is too scarce to be burned in machinery. The people find it more to their advantage to turn this seaweed into manure than kelp and, from the want of market and money, fishing is comparatively neglected.

The roads are well laid out.

Mr Harvey this spring reduced his rents 25%, which has given great satisfaction to his tenants.

DIVISIONS

Townlands

There are no other division besides townlands known in Desertegney. Townlands are not entered: they will be found in the name book. [Signed] William Lancey, Lieutenant Royal Engineers, 20th May 1834.

Parish of Donagh, County Donegal

School Statistics by Lieutenant W.E. Delves Broughton, April 1834

SOCIAL ECONOMY

Table of Schools

[Table contains the following headings: name of townland, number of pupils subdivided by religion and sex, remarks as to how supported].

Churchlands, 22 Protestants, 12 males, 10 females; the salary received by the teacher yearly is 12 pounds, arising by voluntary contributions.

Glentogher, 20 Protestants, 36 Catholics, 40 males, 16 females; national school, teacher's salary from society 8 pounds per annum, from pupils learning arithmetic 2s 2d per quarter, writing 1s 6d, reading 1s 1d per quarter.

Town of Carn, 10 Protestants, 91 Catholics, 50 males, 51 females; St Patrick's national school, teacher's salary 10 pounds per annum, 1s per week from pupils. There is a private school besides, average about 40, of all denominations.

[Signed] W.E. Delves Broughton, Lieutenant Royal Engineers, 2nd April 1834.

Replies by Revd P. Rogers to Queries of North West Farming Society, [1820s]

DIVISIONS

Townlands

Section 1st. Townlands are Carrickfodin, Sulnaree, Magheradrimin, Glentaugher, Balkyloskey, Cashel, Carrabligh, Carramore, Glenmakeen, Carndonagh <Carndoagh>, Altashane, Cragnaherna, Kinnaglug, Moneyshanderry, Carrick.

PRODUCTIVE ECONOMY AND NATURAL FEATURES

Soil

(2) Soil of this [parish]: there is a great variety. Crofting constitutes a principal part of the arable. It is of excellent quality and capable of producing all the necessary crops raised here, viz. potatoes, barley, corn and flax, but in many places much injured by large quantities of small stones lying on the surface. There is also a great proportion of it thin and light, and being unenclosed and without drains that it scarcely pays for labour.

That which is reclaimed from bog differs in proportion to its quality. Where it lies at the bottom of hills, it is always best, being of a rich and loamy nature and lying on a rich loamy earth. That on low flat ground is very bad in general, as its bottom is of a red or white gravel and produces no crop with labour except potatoes.

Mountains and Rivers

Mountains are Slieve Snaght, i.e. "snow mountain," the highest in the barony of Inishowen, and part of Crock Rusky.

Rivers are those of Glinlougher and Glennagannon. They rise in the mountains to the south east of the parish and take a north west course in a direction nearly parallel to each other, and empty themselves in a saltwater lake called Strabraggy, the northern boundary of the parish. They abound with trout and salmon in their seasons and would become very valuable if proper care were taken to prevent the salmon from being killed at spawning time.

Lakes

The only one is Strabraggy, i.e. "the lying strand," coming from the Atlantic Ocean, forming at its entrance a dangerous bar which is seldom navigable, although sloops of 70 tons burthen have sometimes crossed it in safety.

Plantations

None except one in Glentaugher lately planted by the late Henry Alexander Esquire. Part of it is in a thriving state, the other, being planted among heath, is declining for want of care.

NATURAL HISTORY

Mines

A silver one was worked about 50 years ago in Glentaugher nearly at the southern extremity of the parish. It is supposed that it produced very good ore but no reason can be assigned why it was relinquished.

Quarries

Some of excellent bluestone can be had in many parts of the parish and 2 slate ones of a very middling quality, probably owing to their not being sufficiently sunk. The kind of stone, besides limestone and slate, is a sort of very hard granite commonly called whinstone by the inhabitants.

Modern Topography

Modern Buildings

(3rd) Scarcely any worthy of note. A great many slated houses of 2-storeys high have been lately built in the town of Carndonagh.

Towns

The principal one is Carndonagh, the only fair or market one in the parish; the other towns are scattered cottages.

Gentlemen's Seats

Robert Cary Esquire has a very handsome [house] within about a mile of Carn to the west. His house has been built within these 12 years. It is very commodious and well furnished.

About another mile farther to the west are the seats of the Revd George Marshall, rector of Donagh, and Fairview, the seat of James McGill Esquire. From these 2 last-mentioned places there is a beautiful prospect of Strabraggy lake and of the seat of John Harvey Junior of Malin Hall.

Scenery

There is nothing particularly striking in any part of the parish, but from the remains of an ancient oakwood in the neighbourhood of Carn, which forms a part of Mr Cary's demesne <domain>, there is good reason to believe [it was] there about a century ago, and by enclosing and attention might be renewed to great advantage.

Inns and Roads

Inns: none in the parish excepting in the town of Carn already mentioned.

As Carndonagh is nearly in the centre of the parish, there are 4 principal roads leading from it, viz. one going in a southerly direction to Derry, one going towards the north to Malin, one going westerly to Ballyliffin and Clonmany, and another going towards the east to Bonafoble and Greencastle. Besides these, there are others branching off to other places such as Buncrana, Culdaff.

Ancient Topography

Ancient Buildings

There are none, neither are there any castles. There is 1 church in the parish called Donagh church, a quarter of a mile to the west of Carn.

Social Economy

Food

The principal food of the common people is potatoes, fish and milk; sometimes they use oaten bread and stirabout made of oatmeal.

Fuel

That made use of in this parish and in the barony in general is peat moss or turf, of which there is a great abundance in the parish.

Diseases

The smallpox greatly diminished by the cowpock inoculation, whooping cough, measles. The pleurisy and different kinds of fever sometimes attack grown persons, but there is no particular disease prevalent here, no more than in any other part of the country.

Longevity

Widow Casey of Glentaugher, 102; Widow Campbell, of the same part, lately died, 92.

Character of the People

Genius: the inhabitants are endowed with a lively and fanciful turn, but although they are for the most part confined to different occupations, they seldom attempt anything worthy of note.

The people in general are of a hospitable peaceable disposition, but being once roused they are rather violent in their passions and sometimes they are actuated by a spirit of revenge which may be principally attributed to the want of an early education.

Language

English is principally spoken here and made use of in public, but they can also speak a dialect of the Irish language which they often make use of as occasion may require.

Manners

They are sufficiently polite, as much so as can be expected from their opportunities and in proportion to their intercourse with people of a superior cast. Their desire and degree of improvement may be easily traced.

Customs

Particular customs are few in number. Striking a small wooden ball with a crooked stick called a common *caman* is customary among the boys at Christmas times, who make matches for such sport. Another is to make bonfires on the eve of every 24th of June.

Christenings and Marriages

When a child is born to one who is able to entertain his friends, he assembles them and gives them plenty of fish, flesh and bruised potatoes to eat, and to crown the whole, plenty of Inishowen whiskey to drink.

The nuptials are celebrated by giving a dinner to the friends of the bride and bridegroom; but among the lower orders on the Sunday following the marriage, all the males who are invited treat the newly married couple to a hearty drink of whiskey.

Wakes

Wakes are usually visited by youths of both sexes. Among the lower orders, if the person who dies be very young or very old, a great deal of merriment is expected to take place; consequently they amuse themselves with a variety of sports. But if the person who dies be respectable, then much gravity and all decorum is observed.

Sometimes matrons who are adapt in the art of crying over their Catholic friends exert their ingenuity in reducing their wild plaintive notes into a kind of musical humming over the corpse of the deceased, and are so tenacious of them that their friends must drag them from the mournful scene.

The corpse is conducted to the burying place by a number proportionable to his respectability when alive; and if he be a Roman Catholic, sometimes attended by a few of the crying women.

The parish priest attends and celebrates mass. After that he receives a collection, called offerings, originally intended to be distributed for charitable purposes or secure an interest in the priest's prayer to obtain a final repose for the deceased person's soul.

There are no traditions.

Education

Children are sent to school at about the age of 5 years. As they are not constantly kept there, it is a long time before they can read and often lose what they have obtained, on account of the parents being poor and obliged to hire them, and many of them keep them at home very uselessly employed.

There are 3 schools in the parish, 1 at the meeting house a mile from Carn, where the English language is grammatically taught, arithmetic, geography and many branches of the mathematics; 1 in Carn, the other convenient to Donagh church, but these 2 last deserve no notice.

There is also a Sunday school well attended and conducted at the meeting house.

Libraries and Manuscripts

There is no public collection of books and very few manuscripts. A Mr Dougherty in Carn has a manuscript in the Irish language which he says was written by an Irish monk while he was studying in Spain. It contains a system of astronomy. The figures appear to be drawn by the hand and the calculations in it respecting the moon are founded on the Metonic cycle of 90 years, which makes of it little consequence when compared to the advanced state of the science at present.

Religion

The religious establishments are the Protestant, Presbyterian and Roman Catholic. The people attend their respective congregations with great regularity and devotion. The Protestant clergyman's glebe and tithe at present amount to 466 pounds, the Presbyterian arising from his congregation about 30 pounds and the Roman Catholic 150 pounds.

Oats, barley, flax, potatoes and meadow are received here for the purpose of valuing for tithe.

The houses of worship are Donagh church near Carn, a Roman Catholic chapel at one end of it and a Presbyterian meeting house at a place called the Mill-head, at about 1 mile west from Carn.

PRODUCTIVE ECONOMY

Modes of Agriculture

The old system of kibbing is principally pursued except when mossy ground is to be reclaimed. Then it is trenched into ridges, the sods cut into a triangular shape and placed on one side. When dried, they are put into a heap and burned. The ashes when a little cooled are thinly scattered over the ridges, the seed laid and sods cut from the edge of the ridge which cover them.

The drill mode is advancing slowly: there are 2 only adopted it, one lately, the other many years. As his mode, I think, is better for producing a longer succession of aftercrops than any other I have heard of, I shall describe it, viz. a quantity of bog in summer is collected, drawn out and scattered on the land in January; 50 barrels of lime to the acre spread over it, 2 furrows ploughed together and cast over all with a shovel, all ploughed down in the month of March. Then the cross ploughings till the drills are found, which are filled with good compost or strong dung.

Green crops are raised only by a few farmers, owing to the great quantity of sheep roaming through the country without control and no enclosures to stop them. Notwithstanding these advantages, I have persevered in them to greater advantages than could be imagined.

Meadows are generally small and unenclosed except in Glentaugher, where there is, I suppose, about 30 or 40 acres laid down for that purpose and judiciously irrigated; but the water not being properly attended to, I suppose, they don't produce more than half-crop.

Rotation of Crops

Rotation of crops is badly attended to here. After they raise their crops of barley, they sow corn after corn until their land is exhausted, before they begin to potato it. As I sow clover, I am enabled to adopt a better mode, viz. I lay down my barley with clover and grass seed, a second year I cut them for soil, third I graze it, fourth I take a crop of corn, fifth a crop of flax, sixth a crop of oats and then lay it down with grass seed for pasture or prepare it for potatoes.

Livestock

Our stock of horses is various: we have the high-mettled racer, the carthorse, the hardy Inishowen nag and the humblest of the class.

Cows, sheep and pigs are all of the Irish breed, with a few exceptions.

Fairs and Markets

Carndonagh being the only fair and market town in the parish, the fairs in it are held on the 21st of the following months, viz. February, May, August and November. Weekly markets are held on every Monday.

Wages and Trades

Servant boys get from 50s to 3 guineas the half-year, labourers from 6d to 10d with food per diem.

The trades in common use are the blacksmith, the carpenter, weaver, tailor, shoemaker, cooper, fuller, flaxdresser, saddler, slater and stone mason.

General Economy

No manufactures.

Commerce is carried on by selling and buying barley, corn, potatoes, flax and codfish. No navigation of consequence.

Suggestions for Improvement

This parish is advanced but little above the others in improvement as all, with a few exceptions, are in a state of nature with respect to enclosures. It is divided between 14 landlords; few of them are seen amongst us, though the farthest off is not more than 20 miles. They hold out no encouragement to their tenants to improve and the most of their tenants have neither the means nor the taste to attempt it otherwise.

All the landlords, except Andrew Ferguson Esquire, have their lands divided into very small farms, so small that the tenants must sell all the produce except the potatoes and seed oats for the rent, and many of them have to buy their summer's food on trust at a very high price.

This, I can see, is a principal reason why our country has such a naked and, were it not for the cabins dispersed through, a deserted look. But would the landlords divide their lands into respectable farms of 20 or 30 acres each, give long leases, give encouragement to enclose, reclaim, drain and plant, would they visit their lands once or twice a year, show their tenants that they have an interest in their prosperity, labour would take a new direction, the morals of the people improved, indolent and illegal habits banished, and change the preconceived tyranny of their landlords into the full conviction of his being their friend and benefactor.

Poor

With respect to the means of ameliorating the condition of the poor, the above observations are what I conceive to be most necessary as the cottiers, of whom there are a great number at present, live more at ease than their landlords. There is another means of the highest importance that I would lastly suggest.

As education is so highly conducive to the prosperity of civil and religious society, the landlords would bestow a great blessing upon their tenants if they would raise a subscription among themselves and co-operate with the Kildare Street Society in establishing schools for the use of their children.

There are 6 landlords' tenants' children, tenants who for the most part attend or could attend at the Hillhead school. A trifling subscription from each of these, according to the above plan, could establish one of these of greater consequence than probably any other in the country.

[Signed] R. Rogers, Presbyterian minister of Donagh.

Parish of Killygarvan, County Donegal

Statistical Report by Lieutenant W. Lancey, November 1834

MEMOIR WRITING

Letters between Lieutenants T.A. Larcom and W. Lancey

My Dear Lancey,

You say much bog timber was procured when Tamney lough was drained. Was there anything peculiar in its position: did it lie on the bottom as if floated there, for instance? Was the lake area large or could it be in any way connected with the destruction of the forest? The destruction of so much wood all over the county is very curious and well worth investigation.

Your account of Dunree Fort in Desertegney struck me as very engineer-like and good. You do not say anything of the form of Knockalla in Clondavaddog <Clondavaddoc>. I wish everybody took as much pains as you do with Memoirs. Yours faithfully, T.A. Larcom, 30th April 1835.

My Dear Larcom,

Many loughs in the barony of Kilmacrenan have timber in them and this is not a singular instance of the people raising it for common purposes. In one lough in Killygarvan, near McAmish Fort, I should think the timber grew first and the lough was formed afterwards, as some stumps appear in the water favouring this supposition. Knockalla battery being drawn on a large scale, I considered did not require so much description. All the guns are on traversing carriages en barbette.

The reason I have not been so explicit whether the guns are in casemates, and in many things in the 2 last Memoirs, is my want of taste and time for such things, and feel my inefficiency to do common justice to the various subjects embraced in a Memoir. All I consider I am doing is to point out the things worthy of notice for better hands to examine more fully. I have 2 parishes amounting to 43,000 [acres?] this quarter and 2 amounting to 52,000 September quarter to finish, being 6 weeks for each. This keeps me busy and leaves little time for Memoirs or geology. Yours faithfully W. Lancey, 2nd May 1835.

Memoir Writing

This Memoir was written prior to the order respecting the 1st and 3rd pages [signed] W. Lancey, Lieutenant Royal Engineers, 17th November 1834.

NATURAL STATE

Name

Killygarvan is pronounced by the inhabitants as it is written and is said by some to mean the "woods of St Garvan," by others the burial place of the Garvans. The former I conceive is the probable derivation, as there are remains of extensive woodlands in this parish and an old religious house, now called McSwine's Castle but once occupied by 400 Carmelite friars. It is also said to be called Fahan-art in the old title deeds, which means "at the valley."

Locality

This parish is in the county of Donegal, on the east side of the barony of Kilmacrenan and lies on the west margin of Lough Swilly. It is bounded on the north by Clondavaddog, on the south by Tullyaughnish and on the west by portions of these parishes. Its extreme length north and south on the shore of Lough Swilly is 8 miles; contains 9,132 English acres, 3,828 of which are cultivated, 4,902 acres bog and waste, 365 acres of wood and 37 of water in 11 loughs. Its valuation to the county cess amounts to 245 pounds 12s 9d.

NATURAL FEATURES

Hills

Killygarvan is divided into 2 cultivated districts by a range of quartz rock hills rising at the Long lough near the Salt Pans on the coast and running towards the south west. This range includes Upper Killygarvan, 559 feet above the sea, Glencross, 534 feet and Crohan, 1,007 feet. The summit of the range then turns north west to Glenalla, 1,132 feet and proceeds to Neskinmore and thence sweeps round to Knockalla, both of which are in the parish of Clondavaddog.

The northern part of Killygarvan lies encircled in the hills described above and the southern part on the southern slopes of that range as far as Crohan. Two-thirds of the northern part of the parish are intersected by porphyritic greenstone dykes running south west in the same direction with Glencross ridge and the principal valleys. These dykes, meeting the Glenalla ridge at an oblique angle, have serrated its top to a considerable degree.

The principal valley runs from Drumhalla bridge to the chapel, the next from Killygarvan bridge to Monreagh, third is occupied by Gortlough, Gibbons and Fullarton's loughs, all of which, but especially the 2 first, are interesting and picturesque.

Lakes

There are 11 loughs situated thus: Long lough in Salt Pans contains 10 acres 1 rood 18 perches and is 64 feet above the sea; Carrick lough in Clondallon, 3 acres 34 perches, 73 feet above the sea; Short lough in Lower Killygarvan, 3 acres 34 perches, 74 feet above the sea; Gortlough in Upper Creavary and Gortlough, 3 acres 34 perches, 300 feet above the sea; Gibbons lough west of Gortlough, 3 acres 34 perches, 296 feet above the sea; Lough Fullarton west of Gibbons, 80 acres 28 perches, 328 feet above the sea; Lough Caan in Gortlough, 323 feet above the sea; half of Blind lough in Kinleatragh, 557 feet above the sea; part of Lough Rogan north of last, 563 feet above the sea; a lough in Oughterlin proper, 415 feet above the sea; and one on the mearing of Legland and Gortlough, 106 feet above the level of the sea.

Rivers

There are no rivers properly so called in the parish. The largest watercourses amount but to brooks. The March burn, dividing Killygarvan from Tullyaughnish, and that flowing from Crohan mountain to Drumhalla bridge are the principal. This last, rising in Crohan at about 774 feet above the sea, flows to the coast in 2 parallel branches to the north east for 3 and half miles when, uniting at the north east of Newtown Carradowan at half a mile, empties itself into Lough Swilly a little beyond Drumhalla bridge.

The March burn is the southern mearing of this parish and is smaller and more impetuous than that described. Both are well situated for mills. They flow over rocky and stony beds but their waters are not of great power. The scenery on the banks of that running through Keranstown and

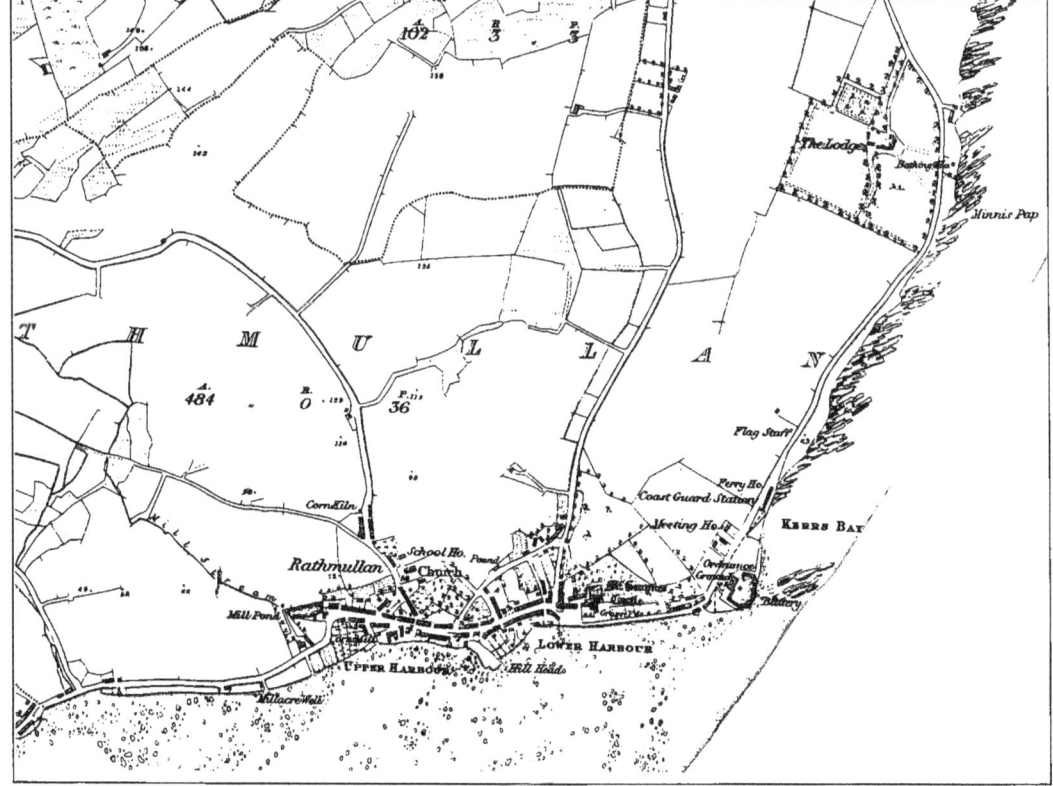

Map of Rathmullan from the first 6" O.S. maps, 1830s

Carrodowan, being enlivened with natural woodlands, is more than ordinarily pretty.

There are several smaller rills of water sufficient for the purposes of the district. That dividing Laherdan from Lower Drumhallagh turns a corn mill of small dimensions.

Bogs

The bogs are not extensive, the mountains being principally covered with rough pastures. Their general height is about 450 feet above the sea and the best are in Creeveoughter, Elagh and Upper Drumhalla, from 5 to 7 feet deep. Fir, oak and birch occurs continually. The former appears to have been broken off at the surface and, although found in every direction, the largest trees usually lie as if blown down by the westerly and north western cycles.

The boughs in the Salt Pans evince the remains of a thick fir wood. There are several roots of large trees to be seen in Long lough, and 1 stem of fir lately taken out of Lough Fullarton at the southern end of the parish measured 40 feet by 9 in girth.

Woods

Traces of considerable woodlands remain in Killygarvan. To the west of Rathmullan, on the shore of Lough Swilly, there are about 171 acres of oak, fir, birch, ash and alder, and on the northern fall of the Glencross and Killygarvan hills, in the townlands of Glencross, Gortfugh, Keranstown, Caradowan, Clondallon and Salt Pans, there are about 194 acres of wood, principally oaks.

No good timber exists at present. The largest oaks are not more than 18 inches in diameter and the greater portions considerably less; but in the memory of man very fine oaks were common in the parish.

The readiest plan to turn these woods into profit would be to cut them down and train them as natural copses to be cleared every 20 years for barking.

Coast

The general direction of the coast is north and south from Rathmullan to McAmish battery, then north west towards Knockalla, and from Rathmullan south west to the parish of Tullyaughnish.

Bays and Harbours

There are no bays except for fishing boats; these exist in many spots. The coast seldom exceeds 50 feet in height and landing places are continually met with, especially towards the southern end of the parish. Kerr's bay, to the north of and close to the Martello tower of Rathmullan, is the principal one. Opposite to it, at a quarter of a mile from the battery, is the best anchorage in the lough in 10 fathoms water.

Killygarvan bay is very shallow and left dry at low water. Its strand is composed of shells. The lower harbour opposite Rathmullan is also shallow and only fit for small boats.

Climate

The climate of Killygarvan is considerably more favourable to cultivation than that of the opposite shore, being protected from the western gales by ranges of hills already described. The usual times of harvest in the lowlands is about the 12th September, that of the hills a few days later. Fine weather does not continue for many days together, and it has been remarked that there is less rain in the latter quarters of the moon than the early ones, and in rainy weather the showers cease at the same period of the tides, generally at high water.

NATURAL HISTORY

Botany

There is a variety of wild flowers. The lotus grows in perfection in the Long lough. Sea pinks are in abundance.

Oak, alder, birch, sycamore, ash and fir are found in the woods and fiorin grass is common.

Zoology

Salmon, trout and salmon trout, turbot, soles <soals> and flounders, mullets, cod, ling, herring, mackerel <mackerell> with crabs, lobsters, oysters, scallops, razor-fish and cockles are all obtained in Lough Swilly.

Martins and otters are not scarce. Foxes abound in Crohan. The usual common birds are plentiful, with hawks and cormorants. The golden wren is a native. Game is scarce but woodcocks are plentiful in the woods in their season.

Insects

The death-head moth and another rare species, white with black spots, with the underwings of an orange colour, have been taken in this parish.

Geology

The whole parish consists of primitive rocks intersected with numerous porphyritic greenstone dykes, the general direction of which is north east and south west, in the same direction with, and evidently a continuation of, the dykes on the opposite coast of Clonmany, Desertegney and Mintiaghs. The rocks are of quartz and talc slate with a run of primitive dark blue limestone to the south of, and close to, the dyke running from the Drum House to Monreagh.

These strata rise at steep angles averaging from 60 to 80 degrees, dipping by the needle due south. They are not turned to any profit except those of the limestone, and this mineral is not used in cultivation in consequence of Lieutenant-Colonel Knox's prohibition arising from the scarcity of turf on his estate.

Lead ore has been found in rolled masses in the south of the parish, specimens of which were presented to me by Colonel Knox in 1826; and it was reported that a thin vein of ore was discovered near the narrow part of Millbrook in the stream. I endeavoured to find it but was unsuccessful.

A good deal of bog iron ore is found in the parish.

MODERN TOPOGRAPHY

Towns: Rathmullan

Objects of art, modern and ancient.

Rathmullan is the only village. Its ancient Irish name was Larchnamaalla. The present name signifies "the fort on the round hill," most probably derived from the situation of McSwine's Castle. It is about 3 furlongs in length and consists of a narrow, ill-built and dirty street of fishermen's houses and about half a dozen residences for persons of middling circumstances. Its situation was probably determined by the erection of McSwine's Castle. In 1622 it contained 100 British settlers.

Public Buildings

The public buildings in the town are the parish church, Presbyterian meeting house and the battery. The chapel and McAmish Fort are in the central parts of the parish.

Church in Killygarvan

The church was erected about 21 years ago at an expense of 900 pounds, 600 pounds of which were given by the Board of First Fruits and advanced by way of loan to the parish. It has a gallery at the west end, can contain 230 persons and is usually well attended. The style of architecture is modern Gothic and the building is neat and substantial, with a tower 45 feet in height.

There are 2 tablets of the Knox family within the church, the oldest of which (1774) is to the memory of Colonel Knox's father, who represented the county of Donegal for 27 years. At the head of this tablet is engraved "Mariana filia obiit November 1761;" the unfortunate young lady who was shot by her lover McNaghten, for which he was tried, condemned and suffered at Strabane the utmost penalty of the law.

The other tablet is to the memory of Lieutenant-Colonel Knox's second son, who died 9th December 1831.

The church stands at the west end of the village in a spacious burial ground.

Meeting House

The Presbyterian meeting house belongs to the Synod of Ulster and is at the east end of Rathmullan. It was built by subscription about 5 years ago, cost 115 pounds in money, besides much free labour; can contain 180 hearers and is well attended.

Battery

The fortified Martello tower at Rathmullan mounts two 5 and a half inch howitzers on traversing platforms 24 feet above the level of the sea battery, which mounts 5 24-pounders on traversing platforms 19 feet above the lough at high water. It stands immediately opposite the battery on the island of Inch and their crossfire presents at least 12 guns to the channel, which is about 1 mile and a half wide. A powder magazine and stove for hot shot, with barracks for 42 men, are in the body of the work, but an invalid in charge of the stores and 7 gunners comprise its present garrison.

Other Buildings

The town of Rathmullan is accommodated with a daily penny post.

The public buildings detached from the village are the chapel and McAmish Fort. The former is in Legland and was erected by subscription in 1792; cost 200 pounds, can contain 1,200 persons and is well attended. It is placed in a commanding and conspicuous, though remote, place, but well chosen for the general accommodation of the people.

McAmish Fort

McAmish Fort lies on the coast of Lough Swilly, on a narrow tongue of land (a basaltic dyke) about 320 yards long and 12 broad running into the lough. It is about 3 and a quarter miles north of Rathmullan and stands opposite to Ned's battery at Buncrana, the crossfire of which, with McAmish, defends the channel about [blank] miles in breadth.

McAmish consists of a Martello tower mounting 2 24-pounders on traversing platforms and a sea battery of 3 guns of equal calibre. The base of the tower stands on the terreplain of the battery and is 25 feet above high water mark. The fort is secured from the mainland by a gulf <gulph> over which is thrown a drawbridge. Barracks for 30 men with magazines and stoves for hot shot are within the walls, and the present garrison is the same in number as that of Rathmullan. These gunners are detached from Buncrana, the headquarters of a captain and company of artillery.

The 6 forts in Lough Swilly were erected by the engineer department in 1812.

Gentlemen's Seats

The principal residence is Fort Royal, the seat of Charles Rae Esquire. It is well situated, only a few yards from this shore and three-quarters of a mile north of Rathmullan. Its ornamental ground is about 5 acres, kept in the neatest order with gardens and 3 small glasshouses for grapes, exotics etc. Mr Rae erected this house in 1807 and is enlarging it at present.

The second house is the Lodge, the summer seat of Lieutenant-Colonel Knox, the most extensive proprietor in the parish. It is a modern erection of about 1820 and is well secluded, a few yards from the shore and half a mile north of Rathmullan. It has 4 rooms on the ground floor and 5 above, with convenient kitchens, cellars, stables, coach house and garden, and stands in about 4 acres of land encircled with young trees.

The Drum or Drumhalla House at the north end of Killygarvan bay is well situated on limestone and greenstone rocks, and commands a beautiful view of the adjacent lough. It was built in 1789 by Dr Knox of Lifford, grand-uncle of the present Colonel Knox, at an expense of about 500 pounds, which was then considered an overcharge.

Glebe House: it is at present the residence of Thomas Smith Esquire. The Glebe House stands about a furlong to the north east of Drum House and adjacent to the old parish church. The extent of its ground is a little more than 6 and a half acres. The Board of First Fruits gave 450 pounds and a loan of 50 pounds towards its erection, which was completed in the same year with the church (1813).

Carolina, belonging to the Presbyterian minister, and Hollymount, Captain McGee's, a little to the west of it, are the other houses in the parish that would attract attention. They are comfortable residences but do not require particular description.

Mills

There are 2 undershot corn mills, one situated in the south east corner of Laherdan, the other in the village of Rathmullan. The diameter of the wheel of the former is 10 feet, that of the latter 14 feet; each are about 24 inches in breadth.

There are no legal disputes about rights of water or fisheries to prevent the erection of mills for any purpose.

About 70 years ago there was a distillery in the village and a wood-cutting mill at the north of the parish, at the March burn.

Communications

There are leading roads but no good ones passing through Killygarvan. The road from Rathmelton to Rathmullan is good but from thence to Knockalla Fort, after it passes Killygarvan bay, it becomes almost impassable for spring cars.

The country roads which lead from the shore and meet in the vicinity of the chapel are still worse, and the leading line to Kerrykeel <Carrowkeele> by Meskinmore is in many places dangerous to ride upon. Their average breadth is 26 feet and are repaired at the expense of the county, the presentment for this half-year being 21d a perch. They are therefore of necessity in bad order, the labourers having continually to contend with rocky and steep ascents.

There are 10 bridges, the 2 most expensive of which cost 50 pounds each.

Ferry

A passenger and cattle ferry, the property of Colonel Knox, passes from Kerr's bay between the island of Inch and the point of Fahan at the shortest notice. The proprietor finds boats and receives half the ferry money. Its gross value per annum amounts to 80 pounds. A report is in circulation that Mr Norman, the proprietor of the opposite coast of Fahan, intends to dispute the sole right of Colonel Knox to the advantage of this ferry.

A single passenger pays 10d; if more than one, each pays 5d; 10d are charged for a horse or cow; 20d for a car and 30d for a carriage.

This ferry is better adapted for passengers and cattle than for carriages, which can be passed over in a more secure way at Fort Stewart in Tullyaughnish. The communications to Fahan is subsequently stopped for 2 or 3 days in rough weather.

ANCIENT TOPOGRAPHY

Antiquities: Giant's Beds

The most ancient remains in Killygarvan are the giant's beds or standing stones, the most perfect of which is in Upper Drumhallagh. It lies east and west and is in good preservation, with the exception of the horizontal covering stones (d,m) which are broken in pieces. The following sketches represent its ground plan and elevation viewed from the south. [Ground plan of grave with numbered stones, view of giant's grave with numbered stones].

Key: A equals 8 feet long, 16 inches thick, 4 feet high; B equals 4 feet 6 inches high, 3 feet 3 inches long and 9 inches thick; C equals 6 feet 2 inches high, 3 feet broad and 1 foot thick: composed of gneiss.

The second giant's grave is in Creeveoughter, in ruins and is being broken up for roads.

The third is in Upper Creavary <Crevery>, consisting of 2 upright slated and a cross one thus: [drawing]. On the mearing of Killygarvan and Clondallon there is also a large stone called Crawford's Table.

Ruined Church

The most ancient ruin is Killygarvan parish church, evidently built before the introduction of glass, having narrow loopholes for the admission of light. The style is very plain and rude: 4 walls and gables. It was used as a Protestant place of worship up to the period of the rebellion of 1641, when it was destroyed and the bodies of the Protestants disinterred, since which time they have ceased to be buried in its graveyard. Its founder's name is not known in the parish.

Castle

The castle of McSwine is situated in the village of Rathmullan and is an extensive ruin. It is said to have been originally an establishment for Carmelite friars, 400 of whom once belonged to it. It was dedicated to the Virgin. It came afterwards into the hands of the owner of the soil, McSwine, who fortified it.

McSwine's property was confiscated at the latter part of Elizabeth's reign and this castle, with a large tract of land, was given to Knox, late Bishop of the Western Isles, then located in the see of Raphoe, to whose descendants it still belongs. The bishop converted it into a residence about 1618, as is supposed from the following inscription over one of the doorways: "AN.KN.SC 1618." It is supposed the building suffered from fire in the rebellion of 1641.

The east transept was used as the Protestant place of worship until 1813 but is now unroofed and falling into total decay.

Mouldings of good workmanship are seen in various parts of the building cut in freestone and blue limestone, and the remains of a shrine and basin for holy water are in good repair. [Drawing of doorway 4 feet 5 inches wide, 5 feet high, with detail of archway; pattern of holy water stoup; 3 sections of decorative plaster mouldings].

A remarkable stone is built up in the enclosure wall near the entrance, bearing the armorial effigies of McSwine. Musket and larger balls have been taken out of the walls, most probably used against the castle in the time of the rebellion. An iron ball of very rough workmanship was discovered only a few weeks ago.

Holy Wells

There are no places of penance in Killygarvan. A holy well for the cure of sore eyes and a weekly station every Friday morning for bone complaints at the bridge at the March burn constitutes the only places of super[stition] I have heard of in this parish.

MODERN TOPOGRAPHY

General Appearance and Scenery

The scenery of Killygarvan combines a greater variety than is usually met with: deep valleys running from the coast into the interior, terminated by bold and rough mountains, high basaltic dykes and loughs combine to render this parish more picturesque than those usually met with.

On entering it by the Rathmullan road, the village on the banks of Lough Swilly, with its church ruin and battery, the road running on the margin of the lake, the hills clothed with thick wood, with Inch Island to the right and Inishowen, seen over the masts of a few vessels anchored in the bay, present an interesting landscape.

The view from the Kinagar towards Crohan at the setting sun is worthy of notice and the neighbourhood of the Salt Pans, McAmish Lower and the valley of Carrodowan, combining sea, lakes, rocks and woodlands, affords a rich variety.

PEOPLE OR PRESENT STATE

Early Improvements

The most probable reason for the occupation of this parish was its sea-coast and sheltered situation. In the settlement of Ulster it appears that 100 persons were located in Rathmullan. It is well known to have formerly been the territory of McSwine, but few of his family name are now to be found in the parish.

Obstructions to Improvement

I have not heard of any legal disputes to retard improvements. Gavelkind does not exist and run and dale is almost discontinued.

Local Government

The magistrates are Charles Rae Esquire of Fort Royal and Thomas Smith Esquire of Rathmullan. The people are remarkably quiet. The constabulary amounts to 1 sergeant and 1 private, and the laws are respected.

There are 16 gunners in the 2 batteries and the coastguard amount to 1 lieutenant and 7 men in charge of 3 boats.

Petty sessions are held every 14 days in the village in a private house; the crimes are of a common nature.

There are no houses insured except Fort Royal.

Illicit Distillation

The habit of private distillation has not been given up but the practice is not so systematically carried on as formerly. The shebeen <shibbeen> or unlicensed public houses are numerous and mischievous.

Dispensaries

The dispensary is combined with that of Clondavaddog, the medical attendance in Rathmullan being twice a week. It was established on the 23rd May 1833.

Schools

There are 2 schools in Killygarvan. The parish school near the church is supported by Colonel Robertson's charity. Colonel Robertson made a large fortune in the East Indies and at his death bequeathed sufficient funds to allow 12 pounds for a schoolmaster and 3 pounds for books annually in each parish in the dioceses of Armagh and Raphoe. In Rathmullan school the master teaches 60 scholars, 40 boys, 20 girls, one-half of whom are Roman Catholics, varying from 5 to 16 years of age. 8 scholars are free, the rest pay 1s 6d a quarter. There is no accommodation for the master's residence.

Mr Rae's school near Aughavannan was established in 1819 and was under the Kildare Street Society until the government grant was stopped. It is now supported by Mr Rae, who gives the master and mistress 6 guineas a year, potato ground and all school requisites. The children amount to 124, 55 male and 29 female Protestants, 26 male and 14 female Roman Catholics. The average age is about 8 years. The master does not reside. The children pay 1s 6d a quarter and females for instruction in needlework 6d extra.

Poor

No established relief exists for the poor. Here, as elsewhere, they beg periodically during the week from door to door.

Religion

By the last census, the inhabitants amounted to 3,400, 2,605 of whom are Roman Catholics, 320 Church men, 50 Covenanters and 425 Presbyterians.

The ministers are paid as usual. The income of the perpetual curate is 75 pounds Irish and a glebe of 6 and a half acres, with 25 pounds added by the Board of First Fruits. The Presbyterian minister receives 20 pounds stipend and 50 pounds regium donum. The priest is paid in the usual manner by offerings etc.

Habits of the People

The people dwell in stone cottages of 1-storey high, occasionally whitewashed, with thatched roofs and glass windows without comfort or cleanliness. There are, however, some exceptions to this general rule which are chiefly found amongst the Protestant people.

Potatoes, water and occasionally meal or fish

Parish of Killygarvan

comprise their diet. Bog and fir are used for fuel. Their dress is usually very indifferent. They live to advanced life: in the Protestant congregation there are 8 individuals whose ages average 88.6 years.

The usual numbers in a family are about 6. The Church people marry late: the Presbyterians from 18 to 25, the Roman Catholics earlier.

Amusements

The peasantry have no peculiar amusements or recreations. The gentry of Lough Swilly established an annual regatta at Rathmullan in 1833, which brings a great number of boats, booths and beggars together, attended by no inconsiderable degree of fighting and unnecessary idleness. I have not heard of any advantages arising from this regatta.

Emigration

About 50 persons annually emigrate to America. The families are Protestant, the individuals Roman Catholics.

Remarkable Events

I have not heard of any remarkable circumstances connected with Killygarvan in addition to those described under the head Ancient.

PRODUCTIVE ECONOMY

Spinning and Weaving

The people on the coast hold lands and catch fish when opportunities present themselves.

Spinning and weaving are usual both in linens and druggets. Common druggets sell for 10d a yard, women's druggets 2s a yard, striped blue, red, green, white etc. Linen cloth from 7 to 13 hundreds: the common kinds vary from 6d to 18d a yard. Flannels and blankets are also made: the former run from 13d to 14d a yard and a pair of good blankets will sell for 18s. Worsted stockings cost from 18d to 20d and socks 1s a pair. A weaver at work at 6 penny cloth can earn 2d a yard, at a better kind 2d ha'penny. The best drugget he will weave for 4d but can seldom at any work at the loom make more than 12d a day. The druggets are not taken to market but made to order.

Fairs and Markets

There are 2 annual fairs held at Rathmullan, one in August and the other in November. Nothing is sold of any consequence; they are more for pleasure than for business. The linens are taken to the markets of Derry and Rathmelton, at which latter place there is a bleach green. The general farm produce is usually taken to Rathmelton market.

The British standard weights are those by which they desire to purchase their commodities, but the Irish weights and measures are still frequently used. Rathmullan possesses a patent for a weekly Saturdays market which is not put in force.

Proprietors

The principal landed proprietor is Lieutenant-Colonel Knox of Prehen in the county of Londonderry; Mr Mortimer and Mr Cochran possess the rest of the parish. The chief part of Colonel Knox's lands are held for 31 years and His Majesty's life, the years being expired. The other lands are generally held at will. The landlords are all absentees from the parish, Mr Smith of Rathmullan being the principal agent.

Rents

The agents receive 5 pounds per cent on the monies stated in the rent rolls which the tenant has to pay, as also 2d a pound to the bailiffs on the sums collected. The average rent varies from 35s, 25s and 15s the Cunningham acre, and the size of the farms runs from 5 to 10 acres arable, and 16 and 20 acres including mountain.

The poor cottier pays his rent by the sweat of his brow. He receives from the farmer a cabin and about the 10th part of an acre for potato ground with a day's cutting of turf, for which an average of 3 days' work per week is required. The cottier does not keep a cow. He has no means to buy one and if he had, he could not feed her. The conacre system is pursued in the neighbourhood of the village, at the rate of 6 pounds per acre.

Agriculture

The fences are nearly all stone and the fields very irregularly laid out. The farmhouses are built at the tenants' expense and are bad. Charles Rae Esquire keeps his house, grounds and farm in the neatest possible order, but the adjacent peasantry derive little, if any, advantage from his example, not having sufficient funds to follow it.

The nature of the soil is light loam and stiff clay with bog. The chief manure is seaweed; its value is about 1s a load and can easily be obtained. Sea-sand costs about 3d, shells about 6d to those who have to purchase them.

Strange to say, although limestone abounds, the proprietor, afraid of destroying his turf, will not suffer it to be burnt when many tenants are already obliged to purchase turf from adjacent towns; they would not hesitate to purchase for burning [in] their kilns. The land is not destroyed by fire unless to obtain ashes in reclaiming bogs.

Implements of Husbandry

Improved instruments of husbandry are unknown except one winnowing machine and a few iron ploughs. Carts are used in the neighbourhood of Rathmullan, but the state of the roads is not generally suited for them. The produce and manure are usually transported on the backs of horses or in boats. Oxen are not fed or used in the parish.

Rotation of Crops

The rotation of crops is usually oats on fallow, then flax followed by potatoes and wheat, oats or barley.

Oats require 17 stone of seed on a Cunningham acre and produce from 4 to 5 guineas "on the foot," at 6d a stone. [Insert note: "On the foot" is a country term for uncut grain].

Flax requires 28 to 32 gallons and the produce is 4 and a half cwt, and is worth 9 pounds.

Potatoes take 14 measures of 8 stone in drills and 18 in lazy beds, and are worth 10 pounds at 2d a stone.

Wheat requires 14 stone and yields 10 barrels of 20 stone, now selling for 22s or 23s a barrel, equal to 11 pounds.

Barley takes 10 stone and produces 8 barrels of 20 stone, worth 16s a barrel, equal to 6 guineas.

The usual method is to take the produce to Rathmelton market, nor would the farmer sell it at a cheaper rate if bought on his own farm.

Payment of Rent

The old method of paying the rents by the produce on a farm of 6 acres was thus: the potatoes and oats fed the family, the oat straw the cow, the barley paid the November rent, its straw thatched the cabin. The flax turned into cloth kept the family engaged in the winter and paid the May rent.

Grazing

No farms are devoted to grazing. Drainage is extremely easy but little attended to. The north western district of the parish is well adapted for cattle and sheep in summer, but there are no permanent pastures for their support and protection during the winter months.

This parish might be rich in flocks and herds, and thousands might be fed and much wealth reaped from that which now goes comparatively to loss, by which the farmers, the public and the landlords might be much benefitted.

Wages

Farm servants receive 6 pounds per annum, women 2 pounds 8s with board and lodgings.

Cattle

The common mixed country breed of cattle prevails. Small, hardy, sure-footed ponies worth about 10 guineas, with common pigs and poultry, are plentiful. Mr Rae has introduced a good breed of pigs. About 2 or 3 persons live by jobbing cattle in a small way at the adjacent markets. A milch cow can be purchased for 5 guineas.

Uses made of Bogs

The bogs are grazed and those in Creeveoughter, Elagh and Upper Drumhalla are well adapted to this purpose. The people usually have turf, but in Colonel Knox's property, where it is getting scarce, if they purchase from their neighbours they pay 8s a dark: a day's cutting for 1 spade and 4 men.

Drainage: no efforts on a large scale are made to drain the bogs. French drains are common.

Planting

Planting has scarcely been tried in Killygarvan. Nature has done much in this way, art little or nothing. The natural woodlands lie on the south slope of one range of hills and the north slope of another. The first consist of oaks, birch, holly, ash and alder, with a few planted larches and firs. The latter is principally oak of about 30 years' growth. The former woodland is close to the sea and appears to be in a more flourishing state than the latter.

There is no good timber in the parish, but this arises more from its having been cut down and sold than any natural impediment to its growth. Many persons remember when fine oak trees were common in the woods of Killygarvan. The present woods, however, with the exception of deals, are sufficient for the consumption of the parish.

Parish of Killygarvan

Sea-Coast

The produce of the coast, shells and seaweed are used for manure. The latter is not burnt for kelp but it is occasionally used for feeding cows.

Fishing

By referring to the schedule, it will be seen that Killygarvan possesses 109 undecked boats of about 2 tons burden, carrying 5 men each, 47 of which belong to the townland of Rathmullan. Sometimes 200 men in 40 boats go to Fanad lighthouse or between Inch and Buncrana, with 5 or 6 nets to each boat, for the purpose of taking herring. These nets are 200 meshed or 3 fathoms deep, made in 2 sheets of 100 meshes each and fastened together. They are 16 to 18 fathoms long.

The fish are taken in 8 to 18 fathoms' water and the men divide the produce of the night's work, each sharing for his net; and if he possess the boat, he receives half a share extra.

The herring fishing is of course periodical. The shoals generally arrive about the 20th July. There are several boats constantly engaged off Rathmullan taking inferior fish, small codlings and flounders, 1 trawl boat fishing for soles and turbot and 2 or 3 in taking trout and salmon-trout during their seasons. These are all sold on the spot or brought to the village, except the sole and turbots which are usually taken to Buncrana or even to Derry.

Cod, mullets etc. are also taken. A codfish can be purchased for 6d, a mullet for 4d a lb., a string of flounders about 10 lbs for 6d, large crabs for 3 to 4 ha'penny apiece and a lobster of 5 lbs for 1s. Fine shrimps abound on the coast but are not taken. Oysters are obtained from Inch Island for 3d a hundred.

Razor-fish abound on the sands at low water at the great springs. The fishermen run backwards with an iron arrow in his hands, the weight of his foot discovers the fish, which throws up water and, in an instant, he drives the arrow through the length of the shell, turns the barb and draws the fish out of the sand in which it lay concealed. On a moonlight night they come to the surface of the sand for 2 or 3 inches and are easily taken by the hand. By some they are esteemed and can be purchased for 1d a dozen.

The herring fishery has much decreased in Lough Swilly compared with what it was 40 years ago. No sufficient reason can be given for the caprice of these fish. Some say the trawling boats destroy their spawn, others that too much seaweed is taken for manure. Lough Swilly herrings were once an article of great traffic and the fish much esteemed. At present the shoals do not afford a regular or sufficient supply for the inhabitants of the adjacent shores.

Deep-Sea Fishing

Deep-sea fishing is quite neglected and the craft of the parish are totally unfitted for it. They are principally intended for transporting the people and produce about the lough, and are only occasionally used in fishing. If a company were to establish good boats similar to those of Scotland or the Isle of Man, they would doubtless be repaid for their trouble on the banks outside the Swilly. The fishermen are considered superior to those at the mouth of the lough. For the seasons in which the fish frequent these shores, see the Memoir on Desertegney parish.

Salmon Fishing

Mr Halliday, the agent of the salmon fishing at Derry, has erected a stake-net at the village of Rathmullan. The right belongs to Colonel Knox, who receives one-tenth of the produce for permission. All the fish caught belong to Mr Halliday, who keeps the salmon and trout and gives the rest to the fishermen employed. The establishment consists of a small boat with 2 men, who receive 9s and 7s a week, and the produce is about 48 lbs of salmon daily. If not sold on the spot for 5d a lb., it is sent to Derry for exportation to Liverpool.

This is the second year the net has been erected and it is considered to be a profitable one. Since the fishing laws have expired and the bounty ceased, much fewer fish have been taken in Lough Swilly.

General Remarks on Economy

The parish is capable of great improvements and is considered by those who are sufficient judges to be easily rendered a flourishing agricultural district. If farmers of capital and intelligence were introduced and the farms consolidated and let on encouraging leases, the happiest results might follow. The lands, with good management, might be made highly productive and the waste uplands now lying idle and unstocked might sustain an immense number of sheep, cattle and horses for exportation. The seasons being early, the drainage easy and its slopes protected from injurious winds render Killygarvan as susceptible of improvement as any part of the country. Mr Rae's farms are excellent specimens of what can be effected.

The highest point to which cultivation has been carried is 500 feet, in the lowlands of Creveoughtar, Elagh and Monreagh, the general height being about 60 to 180 feet. Much of the district might be advantageously planted, and many patches, if enclosed, would in a few years be covered with copses from the remains of brushwood still existing in wattles.

The scarcity of fuel, except in certain localities, prevents any hope of its becoming a manufacturing district.

Although the port for vessels is of the best description, the communications are but indifferently laid out but could easily be changed or repaired to make them fully answer all demands of the district.

I have already stated the products of the seas to be considerably neglected and, unless the proprietors or a company improve the fishing craft, this state of things must continue as the fishermen have not sufficient means to do it.

It is supposed that veins of cyalena exist in the parish, but not in sufficient quantity to raise a hope they may ever be profitably worked.

The woods, if cut down and turned into oak copses, would be rendered profitable.

There are several excellent sites for bathing cottages, and if the proprietor would build them with a range of hot and cold baths and improve the ferry and village, Rathmullan would possess far greater advantages than any other bathing place in the north of Ireland, Portstewart excepted.

In the bay at Drumhalla, at the low water, the remains of wood are visible and under the shingle there is a layer of good bog. Mr Rae dug up 15 roots of black oak in the low grounds of Kinteal.

ANCIENT TOPOGRAPHY

Drawings

Ancient stone in wall, Rathmullan, 2 feet by 18 inches.

The arms of McSwine's family (in blue limestone); doorway built by Bishop Knox, 1618, in building.

Sea view of Rathmullan ruins drawn to scale (each chain on the 6-inch scale equal to 1 foot); east view of part (b), west and ground entrance.

Killygarvan old church [ground plan with orientation, 54 feet 7 and a half inches by 23 feet 4 inches; west end, east end with dimensions; south wall with dimensions of door and window openings, north and back wall with dimensions].

Killygarvan old church by A. Calder, Royal Sappers and Miners.

Arms of McSwine built up in wall, left, entrance to the burial ground [2 feet long, 18 inches wide]; original sketch, and is preferred to the copy. [Signed] William Lancey, Lieutenant Royal Engineers, 19th November.

DIVISIONS

Townlands

No other divisions but those of townlands are known in Killygarvan and the names of their proprietors, content in acres, quantity cultivated, waste, tenure and rent valuation to county cess etc. are described in the Name Book.

The county cess for the whole parish amounted in 1829 to 128 pounds 9s 6d, in 1830 322 pounds 9s 2d, in 1831 248 pounds 2s 11d, in 1832 321 pounds 3s 7d, in 1833 297 pounds 11s 9d, in 1834 308 pounds 8s 4d.

Table of Townlands

[Table contains the following headings: name, English translation, rent per acre of arable land, name of proprietor and agent, quality of land, tenure, size of farms, number of boats with fishing tackle, number and cost of bridges, freshwater loughs, remarks].

Aughavennan "kids' place:" proprietor Lieutenant-Colonel Knox, agent Mr Smith, Rathmullan [insert superscript: Rathmelton]; soil light loam and bog, leases for years and lives, farms from 16 to 32 acres.

Anny "the place of massacre:" rent 20s to 21s for arable, proprietor Henry Irwine Esquire, agent Captain Hazlett, Rathmelton [insert superscript: Rathmullan]; soil stiff clay and cut-away bog, held at will, farms from 12 to 24 acres, 12 boats and fishing tackle; 1 bridge, cost 20 pounds.

Ballybo "the town of the cow:" rent 20s to 30s for arable, proprietor Lieutenant-Colonel Knox, agent Mr Thomas Smith, Rathmullan; soil light loam and bog, leases for years and lives, farms from 12 to 5 acres; 4 boats with fishing tackle.

Binn "rock or cliff:" rent 15s to 20s for arable, proprietor Lieutenant-Colonel Knox, agent Mr

Thomas Smith, Rathmullan; soil red till, leases for years and lives, farms from 10 to 30 acres.

Creavary "clay straight:" proprietor Lieutenant-Colonel Knox, agent Mr Thomas Smith, Rathmullan; soil light loam and bog, leases for years and lives, farms from 2 to 10 acres; 3 boats with fishing tackle.

Craigmadden "the fox's rock:" proprietor Lieutenant-Colonel Knox, agent Mr Thomas Smith, Rathmullan; soil loam and bog, leases for years and lives, farms from 2 to 10 acres; 3 boats with fishing tackle.

Coryfeagh "elk's garden:" proprietor Lieutenant-Colonel Knox, agent Mr Thomas Smith, Rathmullan; soil light loam and bog, leases for years and lives, farms from 5 to 20 acres.

Clondallon "blind or dark glen:" rent from 15s to 20s for arable, proprietor Lieutenant-Colonel Knox, agent Mr Thomas Smith, Rathmullan; soil light loam and bog, leases for years and lives, farms from 8 to 12 acres; 1 bridge, 9 feet long, 5 feet high, 18 feet broad, cost 20 pounds; eels in freshwater lough.

Caradoan "the hooks dent:" rent 15s to 20s for arable, proprietor Lieutenant-Colonel Knox, agent Mr Thomas Smith, Rathmullan; soil light loam and bog, leases for years and lives, farms from 3 to 9 acres; 1 bridge, 14 feet long, 7 feet high, 18 feet broad, cost 40 pounds.

Creeveoughter "a chasm:" rent 20s to 21s for arable, proprietor Mr Henry Irwine Esquire, agent Captain Hazlett, Rathmelton; soil stiff clay and cut-away bog, held at will, farms from 8 to 16 acres; 1 bridge, 13 feet long, 6 feet high, 15 feet broad, cost 20 pounds; freshwater lough 60 feet deep [insert note: supposed depth], 1 and a half acres wide, containing trout.

Drumhallagh "honey back or elevation:" rent 15s to 20s for arable, proprietor John Cochran Esquire, Edinmore, his own agent; soil light loam and cut-away bog, held at will, farms from 1 to 20 acres; 8 boats with fishing tackle; 1 bridge, 20 feet long, 16 feet high, 18 feet broad, cost 50 pounds.

Gortlough "park lough:" proprietor Lieutenant-Colonel Knox, agent Mr Thomas Smith, Rathmullan; soil red till, leases for years and lives, farms from 5 to 20 acres.

Gortcross "park cross:" rent 20s to 30s for arable, proprietor Lieutenant-Colonel Knox, agent Mr Thomas Smith, Rathmullan; soil red till, leases for years and lives, farms from 5 to 30 acres.

Gortflugh "west park:" rent 15s to 20s for arable, proprietor Lieutenant-Colonel Knox, agent Mr Thomas Smith, Rathmullan; soil red till, leases for years and lives, farms from 12 to 36 acres.

Glencross "glen of the cross:" rent 20s to 25s for arable, proprietor Lieutenant-Colonel Knox, agent Mr Thomas Smith, Rathmullan; soil red till, leases for years and lives, farms from 2 to 16 acres.

Inniskil "old kiln:" rent 20s to 21s for arable, proprietor Henry Irwine Esquire, agent Captain Hazlett, Rathmelton; soil stiff clay and cut-away bog, held at will, farms from 6 to 20 acres.

Kinteal "the head of salt water:" rent 20s to 30s for arable, proprietor Lieutenant-Colonel Knox, agent Mr Thomas Smith, Rathmullan; soil strong clay and sandy, leases for years and lives, farms from 1 to 47 acres; 4 boats with fishing tackle; 1 bridge, 29 feet long, 12 feet high, 36 feet broad, cost 50 pounds.

Killygarvan "wood of Garvan:" rent 20s to 25s for arable, proprietor Lieutenant-Colonel Knox, agent Mr Thomas Smith, Rathmullan; soil red till, held at will, farms from 12 to 40 acres; 2 boats with fishing tackle; freshwater lough with eels.

Kilcolman "Saint Colhom:" rent 20s to 21s for arable, proprietor Henry Irwine Esquire, agent Captain Hazlett, Rathmelton; soil stiff clay and cut-away bog, held at will, farms from 1 to 12 acres.

Lougher "wettish:" rent 15s to 20s for arable, proprietor Colonel Knox, agent Mr Thomas Smith, Rathmullan; soil cut-away bog and stiff clay, held at will, farms from 2 to 8 acres.

Millbrook "mill brook:" rent 15s to 20s for arable, proprietor Lieutenant-Colonel Knox, agent Mr Thomas Smith, Rathmullan; soil red till, leases for years and lives, farms from 30 acres.

Rathmullan "rath Mullan:" rent 20s to 40s for arable, proprietor Lieutenant-Colonel Knox, agent Mr Thomas Smith, Rathmullan; soil light loam and bog, leases for years and lives, farms from 1 to 20 acres; 47 boats with fishing tackle; 1 bridge, 9 feet long, 4 and a half feet high, 21 feet wide, cost 20 pounds.

Salt Pans "salt pans:" rent 15s to 20s for arable, proprietor Lieutenant-Colonel Knox, agent Mr Thomas Smith, Rathmullan; soil light loam and bog, leases for years and lives, farms from 30 to [?] 38 acres; 11 boats with fishing tackle; freshwater lough with eels.

[Total] 102 boats with fishing tackle, 6 bridges.

SOCIAL ECONOMY

Table of Schools

[Table contains the following headings: name of

townland, number of pupils subdivided by religion and sex, how supported, when established].

The parish school, 30 Protestants, 30 Catholics, 40 males, 20 females, total 60; supported by Colonel Robert0son's charity, 12 pounds a year for master and 3 pounds for books.

Mr Rae's school, 84 Protestants, 40 Catholics, 81 males, 43 females, total 124; supported by Mr Rae, 6 guineas a year etc., established 1819.

Trades and Occupations

Grocers 4, cloth merchants nil, smiths 4, coopers 2, butchers 2, boat builders 4, netmakers 4, carpenters 6, shoemakers 8, tailors 5, masons 2, wheelwrights 2, nailers 1, linen weavers 6.

Signed William Lancey, Lieutenant Royal Engineers, 13th November 1834.

Printed Notice for Lough Swilly Regatta

Regatta

Lough Swilly regatta will commence at Rathmullan on Tuesday the 1st July 1834 and continue for 4 days.

First day, Tuesday 1st July: a salver, value 20 guineas, given by John V. Stewart Esquire, to be sailed for by yachts not exceeding 10 tons, the property of any gentlemen residing in the county of Donegal. The owner of each yacht, or a gentleman for him, to be on board during the race. Won the first time last year by the *Hussar*, Francis Forster Esquire; entrance 1 guinea.

Same day: a prize of 4 pounds for rowing boats belonging to fishermen in Lough Swilly, not exceeding 24 feet keel; entrance 2s 6d.

A prize of 3 pounds for rowing boats belonging to fishermen in Lough Swilly, not exceeding 18 feet keel; entrance 2s. NB Norway skiffs or gigs not allowed to enter.

Second day, 2nd July: the *Lough Swilly Challenge Cup*, value 20 guineas, will be sailed for by yachts not exceeding 50 tons register, the property of gentlemen residing in the county of Donegal. The owner, or a gentlemen for him, to be on board each yacht during the race. Won the first time last year by the *Hussar*, Francis Forster Esquire; entrance 1 guinea.

Same day: 6 pounds for sailing boats of the first class, the property of fishermen residing on Lough Swilly; entrance 5s.

4 pounds for Norway skiffs or gigs belonging to fishermen in Lough Swilly, not to pull more than 4 oars; entrance 2s 6d.

4 pounds for sailing boats of the second class, the property of fishermen residing on Lough Swilly; entrance 3s.

Third day, 3rd July: 8 pounds for sailing boats under 5 tons, the property of any person residing on Lough Swilly, first boat to receive 5 pounds, second boat 2 pounds, third boat 1 pound; entrance 5s.

The *Rathmullan Challenge Cup* to be pulled for agreeable to the article. Won the first time last year by the *Ruby*, Sir James Stewart Bart.

A piece of plate, value 10 pounds, for 4-oared gigs or skiffs, bona fide the property of any gentleman in the counties of Derry or Donegal; entrance 10s.

Fourth day, 4th July: the ladies' flag to be sailed for by yachts, the property of any gentleman residing on Lough Swilly. [Insert footnote: Won by Charles Norman Esquire of Fahan, 1834].

3 pounds for 4-oared boats, to be pulled and steered by women, first boat to receive 2 pounds, second boat 15s, third boat 5s.

2 pounds 10s for a curragh race, first curragh to receive 1 pound 5s, second 15s, third 10s.

NB Various private matches, both sailing and rowing, will take place during the meeting.

Stewards: Sir James Stewart Bart, Captain Boxer R.N, James Wood Esquire, Charles Norman Esquire, Captain Darley R.N, Captain R. Nesbitt, Robert Montgomery Esquire Junior.

Sailing Regulations

1. All boats to come to anchor at the stations appointed by the stewards, as soon as they have paid their entrance money and produced their certificate.

2. Mainsail, gaf-topsail and mizen may be kept set; foresail and jib down, with a single stop on each.

3. The course will be marked out by boats, in each of which a flag will be placed, which are all to be left on the [blank] side.

4. Any boat that touches any of these buoy boats in rounding, or passes them on the wrong side, will forfeit all claims to the prize.

5. All boats on the larboard tack are to give way to those on the starboard.

7. Sails may be boomed out.

8. All boats for rowing or sailing are to be provided with anchor and cable, sufficient to bring to with at their respective stations.

9. Five minutes previous to starting a preparatory gun will be fired; at the expiration of that time a second gun, when boats may slip cables and make sail.

10. All matters of difference to be referred to the stewards, whose decision shall be final.

11. The classification of the boats to be regulated by the stewards; and no prize will be given unless 2 boats start, except in the case of cups already won the first time. The stewards are to withhold any prize if it appears that there is any collusion. The courses for the different races to be laid out by the stewards each day.

12. All boats to be entered, and the entrance money paid, at Mr Trilley's office in Rathmullan, at or before 10 o'clock on each day, a certificate of which will be given and which must be produced to the stewards on placing the boats at their stations.

14. All directions given by the stewards, relative to any of the races, must be immediately complied with: a deviation from this rule will disqualify any boat.

Parish of Kilmacrenan, County Donegal

Replies by Reverend Anthony Hastings to Queries of North West Farming Society, [1820s]

MEMOIR WRITING

Composition of Memoir

Report on the parish of Kilmacrenan by the Reverend Mr Hastings, rector, addressed to the Secretary of the North West Farming Society of Ireland.

ANCIENT TOPOGRAPHY

Tradition concerning Rock

Tradition: Dhuan, about 6 miles north west of Letterkenny, is said to be the birthplace of St Columbkill. [Signed] Charles W. Ligar, Derry, 15th November 1834.

[Insert note by George Downes: This is the Doune rock near Kilmacrenan; see Otway's (Anonymous) *Sketches in Donegal*].

NATURAL STATE

Extent

The parish of Kilmacrenan contains, according to the return made to me, 83 townlands, the names of which I presume it would be unnecessary to enumerate.

NATURAL FEATURES

Soil

The soil is much mixed, consisting of arable, pasture, rocky, a large proportion of bog and heather. In general a wet cold bottom, but there is some very good lands. It is very mountainous, has 1 considerable river, the Lennon <Lannan>, famous for salmon, and many smaller rivers and mountain streams running through it.

Lakes

There are many lakes also, some large and a number of small ones. In general all good for trout fishing and one of them, Lough Fern, is, I may say, almost covered with wild duck and widgeon in winter.

The sea-coast near Milford bounds the parish along the bay of Mulroy.

Woods

There have been considerable woods in the neighbourhood but about 30 years ago they were all cut down and have never been copsed. I know of no plantations except some that I have made on my glebe. I planted about 20,000 trees.

NATURAL HISTORY

Mines and Minerals

I have never observed or heard of any mines or minerals in this parish but I make little doubt that, if there was a proper investigation made, that both might be found. The natural appearance of the country I think warrants the presumption.

Quarries

There are many limestone quarries, the lime of a very superior quality. I know of no other stone except a hard whinstone, very bad for building; but in the neighbouring parish of Mevagh, where it bounds Kilmacrenan, there is a remarkably fine vein of red and white granite which I think might be made very valuable, especially as it runs very close to the sea, from whence it could be easily exported.

MODERN TOPOGRAPHY

Buildings

My own house is the only modern building of any note. I built it about 12 years ago.

Towns and Villages

I cannot denominate Kilmacrenan a town: it is a poor, small village, the only one in the parish, however. I have got a post office in it and a dispensary since I came to reside, which gives it at least a show of consequence.

Gentlemen's Seats

There are 2 or 3 gentlemen's seats upon a small scale, but I am sorry to say they are unoccupied and likely to be so.

Scenery

The scenery from different parts is grand, romantic and picturesque. I cannot conceive a finer view than from the top of Lough Salt, independent of the immediate object itself, the lake on the mountain.

Parish of Kilmacrenan

Inns and Roads

Inns: there are none, but plenty of alehouses.

The roads in the interior of the parish are wretched. Those that lead to the principal towns of Letterkenny and Rathmelton are kept in good order.

ANCIENT TOPOGRAPHY

Abbey

As to ancient buildings, there is an old abbey here near the church, a mere ruin and an ugly one. It seems to have been extensive, is certainly very ancient and held in great repute by the Roman Catholics. There is a large burial place round it, in which all of that communion in the parish bury.

Forts

There are some old forts and one rather curious, having a kind of subterraneous passage round it built with stones.

SOCIAL ECONOMY

Diet

As to the foods generally used, the poorer sort live entirely upon potatoes and oatmeal; those of the better class of farmers always kill a beef at Christmas, besides pigs etc.

Diseases

The only particular diseases I have remarked amongst them are cutaneous eruptions and scrofula, the latter of which is very prevalent indeed.

Habits of the People

I know of no instance of extraordinary longevity. As to the genius and disposition of the people, I believe it pretty much the same as in other parts of Ireland. They are very litigious, great liars and would cheat if possible. I scarcely ever [met] one who would give a direct answer, but I must at the same time do them the justice to say that they are very good-natured, remarkably hospitable, ready to oblige and courteous in their manners.

As to their language, they generally speak English but with a Scotch dialect. Almost all the Protestant families are of Scotch extraction, but there are many of the Irish in the mountainous part who do not speak English.

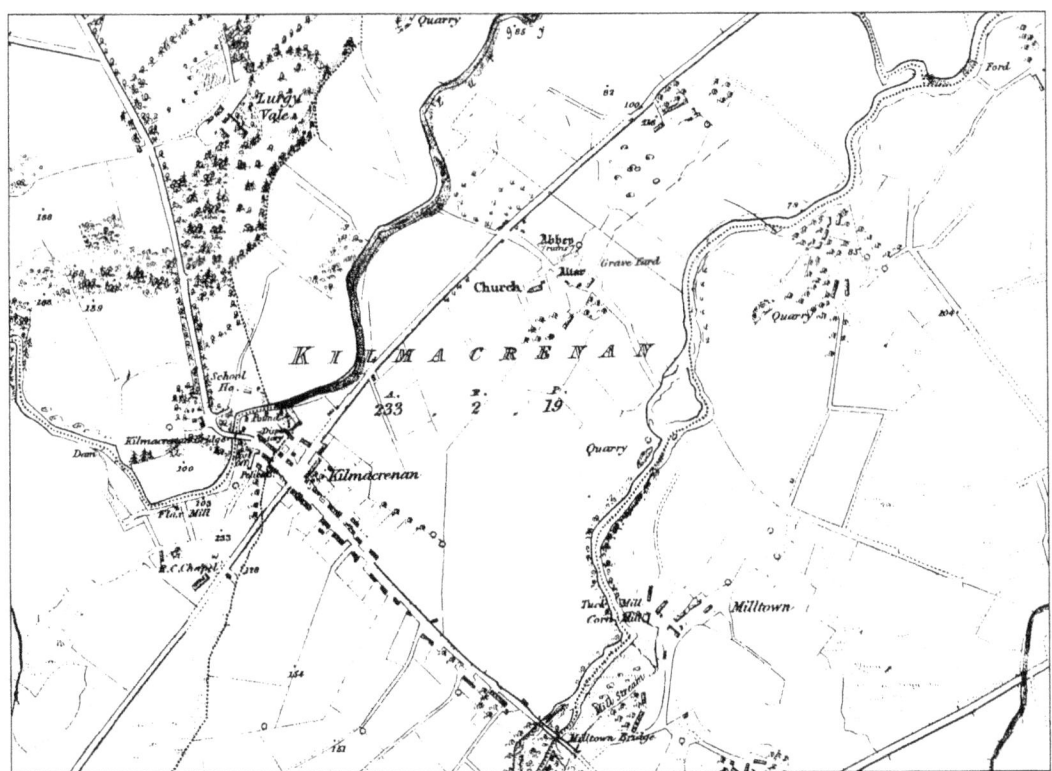

Map of Kilmacrenan from the first 6" O.S. maps, 1830s

Customs

As to their customs, christenings, marriages, wakes and funerals, except in the cases of marriage where the parties generally run away for a day or two before the ceremony takes place, I know of nothing peculiar or worthy of remark. I have never heard the Irish cry at their funerals. They have a number of old traditions but none worth repeating.

Education

There are a number of schools in the parish. The people in general seem very anxious to have their children educated. I have now 2 schools on the Kildare Place establishment and hope to have more as I consider the principle they go on as very liberal: a useful education being, in my opinion, the main object without any attempt at their religious principles.

At certain seasons the children are employed in various ways at home and therefore cannot attend the schools constantly, but in general they are well attended. There are Sunday schools also. I know of no collection of books or manuscripts.

Religion

As to the religious establishment, it consists of the Church of England, the Presbyterian and Roman Catholic. Of these, the Roman Catholic is by much the majority, the Church of England the least numerous. There is a very bad old church, a meeting house and 2 chapels.

As to tithe, I have brought the parish under the Composition Act and have made them a reduction of about 12%.

PRODUCTIVE ECONOMY

Agriculture

Their modes of agriculture are wretched, owing partly to their poverty and much to their sloth. They scarcely do anything in the winter, and even in spring they never begin until the season is far advanced; but the fact is, they have little or no encouragement.

The rotation of crops, where the land allows it, is, I believe, generally barley after potatoes then flax, after that oats twice, then potatoes again.

Livestock

The horses are in general very bad. There are a good number of black cattle and in the mountainous parts plenty of pastures for them. Many send young cattle there in summer. Almost every farmer has a few sheep and pigs.

Fairs and Markets

There is a fair in Kilmacrenan on the 1st of every month. It is very well attended but there is no patent.

Wages

As to wages and the price of labour, I cannot give any direct answer. I am the only person in the parish who keep labourers by the day. I give them 1s in summer and 10d in winter. The farmers hire them by the quarter, which varies, and feed them.

Trades

As to trades, we have all such as are necessary in a country place as carpenters, blacksmiths, shoemakers, wheelwrights etc.

Linen

The linen manufacture is carried on to a good extent. I believe latterly the weavers had constant employment. They also in general make their own cloth, which answers very well, being both strong and warm.

Commerce and Navigation

As to commerce and navigation, we have none. I really look upon Lough Salt or Lough Alt as a very great natural curiosity. It has the appearance of the crater of an extinct volcano on the top of an immense high mountain. It is well worthy of observation.

ANCIENT TOPOGRAPHY

Doon Rock and Well

There is also an extraordinary rock near my house of great size, remarkable in the Irish history of these parts. It is called Doon rock and on it the O'Donnells, who were formerly chieftains here, were always inaugurated. It is a strong natural fortress in the middle of a bog.

Immediately under the rock is the holy well of Doon, frequented by thousands. It would be an endless task to mention all the virtues of this water and all the cures it can perform for the faithful, but it has one peculiar quality which I think ought not to be omitted. It is an fallible remedy against infidelity in husbands: any lady keeping a bottle of it well corked under her bed may rest in perfect security.

Giant's Grave

There is another curiosity in this neighbourhood but I cannot say it is a natural one, being evidently a work of art. It is called the Giant's Grave. I forget the exact measurement of it, but it is at least 20 feet long by 10 wide and is the very shape of a coffin. The sides are built with stone and it is covered with large flags laid over horizontally. It is on the top of a wild mountain and is certainly very curious.

I have never heard of any remarkable occurrences here or of any eminent men or writers.

SOCIAL ECONOMY

Poor

As to ameliorating the condition of the poor, much indeed might be done, nor do I believe there is any part of Ireland where it is more required.

This parish is of great extent, containing above 30,000 acres thickly inhabited. The college estate alone includes 22,000 acres. This property is held under them by Lord Leitrim, a very liberal landlord, who has made a large reduction in rent, but a reduction in rent is of small consequence when not followed up by encouragement and example. Here they have neither, but this is a subject on which I do not wish to enter: it is the business of the landlords more than of the rector.

I shall merely remark that as it is impossible to have a resident landlord on the college estate (which includes almost all the parish), the best thing in my opinion would be to have a resident agent, an active intelligent gentleman residing amongst them, whose situation would entitle him to sit as a grand juror of the county. [He] would soon make an alteration in the country and do more to improve it than any plan in my power to suggest.

[Signed] Anthony Hastings, rector, as may be seen by the report.

Parish of Mevagh, County Donegal

Statistical Report by Lieutenant W. Lancey, 1834

MEMOIR WRITING

Memoir Writing

My Dear Larcom,
This is not a bad Memoir. I wish I had as good of all the other parishes. Yours faithfully, M.M. Waters, 24th November 1834.

NATURAL STATE

Name

Mevagh or Meveigh in English means "Margery's horse" or "my food and my horse," being compounded of Meive and agh(?). The parish derives its name from the townland so called lying on the east fall of the mountain of Granna, but it is seldom called Mevagh by its inhabitants, the whole district being known by the name of Rosguill <Rosgul>, the large peninsula lying north of Rosapenna being denominated "the bottom." Rosguill (Ros-na-gaille) means "the point of the Gaille or Gauls," as Dun-na-gaille means "the fortification of the Gauls." It is now pronounced Rosgull.

Locality

Mevagh is that point of land running into the Atlantic Ocean which separates Mulroy and Sheep Haven bays. It is situated in the north of the barony of Kilmacrenan, in the county of Donegal and diocese of Raphoe; and is bounded on its south by the parish of Kilmacrenan.

Its extreme length from Lough Salt to Melmore Point is 12 miles and its mean breadth about 4 and a half miles, and contains 21,027 acres, 5,933 of which are cultivated, 14,684 and a half uncultivated, 409 and a half water; and paid county cess in 1829, 529 pounds 9s 2d; 1830, 513 pounds 2s 1d; 1831, 393 pounds 8s 6d; 1832, 519 pounds 13s 9d; 1833, 472 pounds 7s 6d; 1834, 462 pounds 17s 9d ha'penny.

NATURAL FEATURES

Hills

The northern fall of Lough Salt (properly Lough Alt), lying on the southern frontier of Rosguill, is a mountain of granite and attains the height of 1,547 feet and, stretching itself on the east and west in lower ranges to the sea, and on the north to the village of Carrigart which stands near the centre of the parish, embraces the heights of Glen, 560 feet, Glenmenagh, 615 feet, Glenhow, 918 feet, and Tullagh, 760 feet above low water mark.

The low sandy isthmus of Rosapenna north of Carrigart divides Rosguill from the peninsula called "the bottom." This is succeeded by a range running north of which Granna, 681 feet, forms the principal elevation, and at Lower Dundoan a second sandy isthmus occurs, north of which stands the rough granite hill of Melmore, 541 feet. At its northern fall a sandy tract separates it from another isolated granite height and again a sandy isthmus divides this from the hill on which stands the signal tower of Melmore.

This district of country, especially the peninsulated part of it, is rough, wild, rocky and sterile, except that part which lies on the shores of Sheep Haven.

Lakes

Lough Salt on the extreme south is 815 feet above the sea and properly belongs to the Memoir of Kilmacrenan. At Lough Nacreaght (675 feet high) this last-named parish, Mevagh and Tullyaughnish meet.

Little can be added to the information under this head to that seen on the plans, as the depths of the loughs have not been ascertained, there being no means to get them. The report in the country respecting Lough Salt is that a fruitless attempt was made to sound it, but no line could reach the bottom. Others say it is as deep as the mountain above it is high, but nothing is known that in such matters can be depended on. (Since the above was written I understand Mr John Stewart of Lough Swilly sounded Lough Salt and found it to be 204 feet deep).

Glen lough, 94 feet high, lies on the south west extremity and is 2 miles in length and 1,300 feet mean breadth. Its direction is north east and south west. It is principally supplied by the Owenreagh river, which drains Glenveagh and empties itself into Sheep Haven bay by the River Lackagh, running from the centre of the left bank of the lake for 1 and an eighth miles in a north west direction.

Table of Loughs

[Table contains the following headings: part [of map ?] and name, content, height, situation].

Part 1: Melmore lough, 11 acres 1 rood 28 perches, 28 feet in height, mearing of Melmore and Gortnaloghog.

Part 2: lough no.1, 1 acre 3 roods 22 perches, 181 feet in height, Derryhassan; lough no.2, 2 roods 12 perches, 44 feet in height, Ardbawn; Rosapenna lough, 6 acres 22 perches, 20 feet in height, Rosapenna.

Part 3: Lough in Aughadehur, 3 roods 22 perches, 68 feet in height, Aughadehur; Lough Coole, 6 acres 20 perches, 38 feet in height, Glanree; Glanree lough, 3 acres 1 rood 18 perches, 26 feet in height, Glanree.

Part 4: Lough Naveeouge, 3 acres 29 perches, 245 feet in height, Aughalatty; Lough Meeltagh, 17 acres 3 roods 22 perches, 421 feet in height, mearing of Gortnatrade and Carrigart; Lough Nabraddin, 7 acres 31 perches, 525 feet in height, mearing of Carrigart in Glenhow; mill-pond, Carrigart, 3 roods 36 perches, Carrigart.

Part 5: Lough Ennerwore, 21 acres 1 rood 11 perches, 92 feet in height, mearing of Cranford, Debhimore, Carmoney and Tullagh; Lough Baughan, 1 acre 3 roods 26 perches, 45 feet in height, Divlinmore, Divlinreagh, Tullagh; Lough Nambraddan, 1 acre 2 roods 37 perches, 136 feet in height, Divlinreagh; Lough Nasmulton, 2 roods 27 perches, 426 feet in height, Tullagh; Lough Anassin, 1 acre 8 perches, 457 feet in height, Tullagh; Lough Amhaddi, 2 roods 7 perches, 614 feet in height, mearing of Downing's bar and Carrigart.

Part 6: Lough Creanmore, 4 acres 2 roods 28 perches, 475 feet in height, Glenhow, High Glen, Gillygraney; Lough Sallagh, 1 acre 26 perches, Lough Sallagh no.2, 1 rood 24 perches, Lough Sallagh no.1, 1 rood 4 perches, Kill; Dunmore lough, 2 roods 24 perches, 34 feet in height, mearing of Kill, Carnagore and Dunmore; Drim lough, 10 acres 3 perches, 45 feet in height, mearing of Kill and Drimditton.

Part 7: Lough Nacreaght, 20 acres 3 roods 20 perches, 675 feet in height, Cratlage, High Glen, Golan; Lough Natooey, 13 acres 3 roods 15 perches, 471 feet in height, Glenhow and High Glen; Lough Maghrymore, 4 acres 23 perches, 921 feet in height, Lough Maghrybeg, 1 acre 3 roods 24 perches, 991 feet in height, Meinformal; Lough Reelan, 16 acres 3 roods 7 perches, 773 feet in height, Meenformal, Meenlara, Meenreagh, Lough Lara, 5 acres 2 roods 29 perches, 540 feet in height, Meenlara, Lower Barnes; Lough Crotland, 1 acre 1 rood 2 perches, 501 feet in height, Glenmunagh; Lough A-Maniofa, 1 acre 3 roods 16 perches, 484 feet in height,

Glenmeenagh and Toragh; Glen lough, 412 acres 3 roods 8 perches, 84 feet high, part belongs to Mevagh parish.

Lough Salt is 204 feet deep and 815 feet in height, in Kilmacrenan parish.

Rivers

The Lackagh just mentioned is the only river. It runs over a rocky bottom for 9 furlongs and is celebrated, as well as the Glen lough, for salmon and eels. Its waters might be easily made to turn as many mills as could be built on its banks, the upper part being a series of rapids about 120 feet wide, backed by the extensive sheet of water of the Glen.

No other streams of consequence are met with, but there are many rivulets flowing from loughs which might be advantageously used for common mills, those mearing the east and west side of Glenhow, those dividing Kill and Toragh, Devlinmore and Devlinreagh, Carrick and Aughaletty being the chief. These all fall to the north and are not more than about 3 miles in length, flowing over stony and gravelly beds. The bottom of Rosguill is deficient in streams and rivulets.

Bogs

There is considerable bog south of Carrigart but not much north of that village. Its depth rises from 18 inches to 4 feet and contains much fir timber imbedded in it, the roots of which stand in many places thickly packed together, the stems having been broken off just above the surface. In some fields the people have ploughed and sowed their crops round these stumps.

Woods

There are no woods now in Rosguill, but evidences continually occur that tend to show this district, in common with others in its neighbourhood, was once an extensive forest.

Coast

The coast from the mearing of Kilmacrenan on the margin of Mulroy runs in a very irregular manner generally to the west, sweeping round to Island Roy near the village of Carrigart. It is all low with a stone beach of small extent and runs into narrow tongues which, forming deep indentations, present a series of harbours for boats and small craft.

In the neighbourhood of Island Roy and the small islands adjacent to it, broad firm strands are left at every tide. From Rosapenna the coast becomes bold but not very precipitous and turns to the north east. From Dundoan to Melmore the sea washes a sandy strand and from thence to Melmore Point round to the west of Melmore lough steep perpendicular rocks generally prevail and, with the exception of the Dundoan sands, extend to the west and south round "the bottom" to Strabeg, east of Downings in Sheep Haven bay.

North of Glenorry are a reef of rocks usually called Slowry. Carrickgull lies to the west of this half a mile and to the west of Melmore, 1 and a quarter miles from the tower, is a low and dangerous reef called the Frenchman's rock.

Strabeg in Sheep Haven bay is separated from Stramore by a rocky height in Rosapenna not yet destroyed by drifted sand, and the low line of strand extends hence to the southern part of Aughadehur. The line of shore extending to the north of the Lackagh is slightly elevated and with occasionally broken strata of rocks.

Thus the coast of Rosguill embraces every variety, from long sandy levels to rocky precipices of various heights and no less than 33 miles in extent. It forms much of the western shore of Mulroy river, water or bay, which is a harbour difficult to navigate, having many shoals, rocks and islands, and is inaccessible for vessels of more than 100 tons past the Hassans, a narrow channel opposite Delvinmore. Vessels meeting the prevailing westerly gales anchor under the lee of Melmore Point, to remain a tide or two, but Sheep Haven bay is the principal place of refuge when Lough Swilly cannot be made.

Sheep Haven, on the west coast of Rosguill, is a dangerous place for vessels to anchor in with the wind from the north west. The usual ground is not far from Downings, where they are beset by a strong shore current from the Atlantic acting powerfully against their sterns that, riding head to wind, one of their cables is of little use and they frequently part, and shipwreck is the inevitable consequence. The shore is, however, so flat that every human assistance can be rendered and the loss of life is not usually great.

On a calm day the flood tide in Sheep Haven rolls in in long broken waves at every half-mile, between which the water is quite smooth; but in a north west gale the waves are very much broken with a strong eddy and long head seas.

The channel in this bay runs on the west side of it, very near to the house of Ards, but a small one of late years has broken through the land on the east side opposite to Stramore, which obliges persons going to Ards to pass over Lackagh bridge instead of crossing the narrow channel at Ards in a boat at low water.

The tide rises at Downings 14 feet, at the entrance of Mulroy 15, Island Roy 12 and a half and Milford 5 feet 6 inches.

4-decked vessels belong to Mevagh, of 15, 16, 25 and 45 tons. These all sail from the east coast and are generally employed in the exportation of grain to Scotland.

Island Roy

This group is low, cultivated ground and accessible for carts and passengers at every ebb. Its greatest elevation is 44 feet. A little to the north of it is the channel of the river, which runs between shoals sweeping from the coastguard station in the townland of Mevagh to the passage of the Hassans. The scenery from so much water separated by narrow necks of land is remarkable.

The Hassans is a dangerous passage and requires a skilful pilot to take large vessels through it.

Climate

The climate is very moist and changeable, the parish being mountainous and exposed to vapours from the Atlantic Ocean.

NATURAL HISTORY

Zoology

There are very few fish in Mulroy bay south of Mevagh except sprats, an old bank of oysters and large scallops. At the mouth of Mulroy and in Sheep Haven bay every kind of good fish of those belonging to the coast are met with. There is a fine turbot bank on the opposite shore of Sheep Haven, and sole, flounders, cod, haddock, glassons, razor-fish etc. are continually taken in their seasons.

Towards the head of the bay, at the mouth of the Lackagh river, Captain Hart of Doe Castle has erected a stake-net for salmon, and the river fishing of Lackagh and Glen lough produces 50 pounds a year to him.

There are 2 weirs on the Lackagh, one for salmon, the other for eels.

No wild animals worthy of notice except foxes are met with; hares and partridges abound.

Gulls, shaggs, wild pigeons <pidgeons> but no eagles (they frequent Horn Head and are often seen soaring over the northern part of the parish). The shaggs or cormorants with white feathers on their thighs are seen standing on the rocky isles

Parish of Mevagh

drying their extended wings, it being a part of their nature for their feathers not to abound in oil; and the birds, not being able to remain in the water any length of time, are prevented from gourmandising to too great an extent. Porpoises, the basking shark and seals are seen on the coast and in the bays.

Geology

Mevagh is a primitive formation of black granite, quartz rock, gneiss, talc slate, blue limestone and hornblende rock traversed by porphyritic dykes of greenstone. The granite occupies Lough Salt and its western slopes to Lackagh, and forms also the northern part of the bottom of Rosguill, between which are found quartz rock and dykes of greenstone running north east and south west, being a continuation of that broad series of dykes from Malin Head and Greencastle in Inishowen traced through Clonmany, Desertegney and the Bar of Inch across Lough Swilly to Fanad <Fanet>, Killygarvan and Tullyaughnish, from thence to Lough Fern and Cratlage and on to Glen lough and Glenveagh.

Limestone sometimes accompanies these dykes in Mevagh, as well as in Tully, Killygarvan and Fanad.

The ranges of hills, the valleys, the direction of the larger loughs, the strata and the dykes on the north coast and part of Kilmacrenan run from north east to south west (Lough Fern excepted), and this formation is not restricted to this vicinity but appears to be general in the adjacent parishes.

MODERN TOPOGRAPHY

Towns

The villages of Glen and Carrigart are the only places where fairs are held in Rosguill. 12 are held in the former every year, on the 14th day of each month, and cattle, horses, sheep and pigs are the principal things sold. The village itself is of the meanest description but has the advantage of a penny post twice a week from Rathmelton.

Carrigart is a place, if possible, as bad as Glen. 9 fairs are held annually, at which sheep, pigs and yarn are disposed of. This village belongs to Lord Leitrim and is underlet to Mr Marshal of the Lagan. Lands are dearer about it than at Glen, an acre letting for 30s to 40s.

Public Buildings

The parish church and Roman Catholic chapel are the only public buildings. The church stands close to the village and is a plain building without a spire, capable of containing 150 persons in 16 pews. It was erected in 1774 by subscription at an expense of 600 pounds.

The chapel stands on the sands to the west of Carrigart and is a neat building. It was erected in 1807 by subscription and cost 500 pounds, and can hold 400 worshippers.

Gentlemen's Seats

There is no such thing in Mevagh. The rector lives in Rinalargy in a plain low building built in [blank], but there is no rectory in the parish.

Half a mile west of the rector's in Crucknamurlog is a neat, small, slated house built by Mr Armstrong for a shooting lodge. It is the best private dwelling in the parish but is on a very small scale and requires no description. It was erected in 1821 at an expense of 250 pounds.

Mills

There are 6 corn mills in Mevagh, viz. at Carrigart, Maghremagorgan and Aughalatty, the former being the principal one, being an overshot wheel 9 feet in diameter by 2 feet 6 inches in breadth.

In Ardhane there are 2 corn mills, one in Glenmeinagh and in Devlinmore.

One mill in a ruined state. These are all corn mills on a small scale.

Communications

The main roads run from Kilmacrenan and Milford to Carrigart. The former is of steep ascent and passes along the margin of Lough Salt, and enters the parish on the west fall of the mountain and, turning off at Glen, passes over Lackagh bridge to Doe Castle and Dunfanaghy. The latter runs along the banks of Mulroy and is scarcely passable for spring carriages.

Beyond the rector's, the communications to the bottom of Rosguill are of the worst kind, quite impassable for carts and nearly so for horses. The road over Lough Salt is about 30 feet broad, that from Milford about 20, both being in good repair.

The communication with Fanad is by the ferry of Rawris. The ferryman pays 5 pounds per annum for the privilege of passing cattle and passengers over, for which he is allowed to charge 4d a head for the former and 2d for the latter; 2 boats are kept.

The ferryman at Moress pays 5 pounds for the

ferry, 3 acres of land and charges 2d a head and 4d for cattle.

Bridges

The principal bridge is that thrown over the Lackagh. It is well built, of 1 arch and was paid for by the county. Bridges are also met with at Toragh and Glenmenagh mearing called Piper's bridge; Strahan bridge at Aughalatty of 1 arch, Carrick bridge, Doin Erin bridge.

The above are on a very small scale and require no description.

ANCIENT TOPOGRAPHY

Old Church

The ruins of the old parish church, said to have been founded by St Columba stands in the townland of Mevagh, from whence the parish has derived its modern name. Nothing is known in the country respecting it, but from its narrow windows it appears to have been erected prior to the use of glass. The following is a sketch of its present appearance: [drawing of church, wall 3 feet thick, with annotations and section].

The old bell was suspended at "b." The people believe it was taken to Scotland and was brought back by supernatural agency and was heard ringing underground. The general belief is that Mevagh church was erected by St Columba.

At the angle of the road leading to the church stands an old stone cross of small dimensions.

Drumditton Castle

The ruins of Drumditton Castle are not supposed to be of that class which belonged to the feudal times. It was inhabited by Ralph Ditton Esquire, who is said to have been the proprietor of Rosguill, Doe, Cloghaneely, Boylagh and the Rosses. It is said from his extravagance and the portions he gave his 2 sisters he became embarrassed and left the country. No dates could be obtained and nothing remains of the castle but a rude heap of stones.

Rosapenna House

Rosapenna House is a ruin of more modern date. It appears to have been a large building of 84 feet in length and is said to have been erected about 140 years ago by the then Lord Boyne. The property was purchased by Lord Leitrim's grandfather. Mr Macky lived in the house in 1755 and it was afterwards inhabited by Mr Humphrey Babington and in 1786 by Mr John Dennison. At this period the sand began to drift and to destroy Rosapenna and the low isthmus to the south of it, and the lower storey of the mansion became untenable.

The Revd Mr Porter resided in the first floor up to 1808 when, the sand having buried the lower storey and the garden, it was abandoned and has since fallen into total decay. Sketch of its appearance in 1834 from the south: [drawing with annotations and dimensions, 84 feet long].

Melmore Tower

Melmore Tower was erected by government for a signal station in 1804 by Mr Taylor of Derry. It is 20 feet square at the base, 46 feet high and stands on the point of Melmore which runs into the ocean and commands an extensive view of the coast. In 1815 Lieutenant Giles of the Navy and a corporal's detachment of 3 men were ordered to abandon the tower. [Drawing of tower, 46 feet high, battlements 9 feet high by 3 feet wide, base 20 feet wide].

Danish Forts

Danish forts in Mevagh are situated in Glenmeena, Divlinmore, Downings, Kinalargy, Drumlackagh, Largyreagh, Clondallon, Rawris and Creevy; and a standing stone is found in Crucknamurlog on the top of the hill.

Shuggling Stone

The Shuggling Stone called Cloughnabogaty in the townland of Drumlackagh is of granite with black mica. Its stands on the left side of the road from Glen to the salmon-weir in the Lackagh river, 132 feet west of the turn to the right to Lackagh bridge. Its general sections and elevations are thus: [section, 8 feet high from the ground to centre of stone at top; view of stone from side; general section of upright stone, 5 feet 6 inches high, 8 feet at longest point, 6 feet 1 inch on the ground].

Its mean length is 7.33 feet and its specific gravity, ascertained from 4 trials, runs thus: 2.579, 2.570, 2.524 and 2.633, the mean of which is 2.576; and if it contains 181.05 cubic feet of stone, weighs 13 tons. It is so delicately poised that the little finger of the left hand applied to its eastern end moves it with the utmost ease through its whole arc of about 3 inches.

MODERN TOPOGRAPHY

General Appearance and Scenery

Mevagh is generally a wild, uncultivated and barren region. The scenery of its southern portion is mountainous but not striking in itself, the beauties of Lough Salt lying on the opposite side of that mountain. The northern portion is hilly and bleak and uninteresting, but the adjacent harbours, the ocean, the hills of Fanad on the east, the fine promontory of Horn Head on the west, with Lough Salt, Muckish and Tory Island in the distance, afford a fine and most unusual landscape; and with the beautiful parish of Clondavaddog, yet to be described, would amply repay a tourist or a painter the trouble of a visit to this part of the county of Donegal.

SOCIAL ECONOMY

Early Improvements and Progress of Improvement

If Ros-na-gaille be correct, "the point of the Gauls," the early inhabitants of this country, the situation and outline of the district would support the derivation remarkably well, for the bottom of Rosguill, being a peninsula whose isthmus could be easily defended, is a place more likely than any other for a set of savages to entrench themselves.

The present race are a fine-looking, robust people, subsisting on the produce of the land and seas, but apparently unaided by their landlords, farming societies, government fishing, bounties or private premiums.

There are no ancient customs among them except run and dale, no peculiar tenures or legal disputes about rights of land, but all complain of high rents and taxes (general throughout the north of Ireland); and from what I could learn, appeared to be in a state of excitement "ready (as one of them expressed himself) to rebel, not having any other method left."

Local Government

The rector, Mr Wilkinson, is the only magistrate in the parish and settles most of the petty disputes among the inhabitants. He is not assisted by any constabulary force.

An inferior officer of the coastguard resides in the shooting lodge, having a boat and man at Downings in Sheep Haven and 4 men and 2 boats at Mevagh in Mulroy.

An officer and 14 men of the revenue are stationed in Carrigart but a great deal of illicit spirits is yet made and the people use bold stratagems in its defence.

I was informed by an eyewitness, and one who was officially employed on the occasion, of 3 men having defended their malt from at least 30 armed individuals from the situation they had taken up for their kiln. Half-way down a frightful precipice, with the sea foaming at its base in a large opening of the cliff, they had many sacks of malt which could not be approached by the police unless slung down by a rope. This was attempted but the smugglers, armed with poles, threatened to hurl the suspended policeman into the sea, who was immediately drawn up and the party kept in check for 24 hours. They then withdrew and, suffering the smugglers to escape, afterwards captured their malt.

There is neither dispensary or medical man in Rosguill.

Table of Schools

There are 3 schools in the parish supported by societies and 3 hedge schools.

Carrigart, 40 Protestants, 20 Roman Catholics, 20 males, 40 females, total 60; formerly supported by the Kildare Street Society but now by the people themselves, established 1831.

Rinnalargy, 25 Protestants, 25 Roman Catholics, 30 males, 20 females, total 50; supported by a donation of Colonel Robertson, established 1831.

Aughadehier, New Board of Education, established 1834.

Aughalatty, Kill and Derryhassan, no society.

Poor

There are 25 poor, but no provision for them besides the church collection.

Religion

The Roman Catholic religion prevails; the number belonging to this persuasion is 5,329, to the Church 466, Presbyterians 233.

Habits of the People

They live in stone cottages whose badly thatched roofs are tied down with straw ropes and require to be annually repaired. Few of their habitations are whitewashed, although limestone is frequently met with in the parish. 2 rooms with small glass windows without comfort or cleanliness afford shelter for large families.

They live on potatoes, milk and fish, and wear the commonest clothes, with flannels, druggets and linen of home manufacture similar to those of Killygarvan, Clonmany and the adjacent districts.

"They are uneducated but well disposed, active and hardy, of an irritable temper but forgiving disposition, rather idle, addicted to the use of spiritous liquors, both men and women, owing no doubt to the quantity of illicit spirits made in this parish, its bane and destruction."

Amusements

An annual horse-race on Rosapenna sands, too inviting a spot to be neglected for such a purpose, affords them some amusement, but they are, like the rest of this country, not addicted to public sports. They appear either to have lost or never possessed a taste for feats of activity or manly strength, and all their leisure time is taken up in moping over their misfortunes, real or supposed, and reading the newspapers, looking forward from day to day for some change for the better.

Longevity

By the following list extracted from the tombs in the parish churchyard, some of them appear to live to an advanced age: John Evans died 1706, aged 70, Rebecca Evans died 1719, aged 75, Robert Evans died 1725, aged 38 [insert note referring to first three: arms, 3 fleurs de lis]; George Swine died 1775, aged 83; Revd W. O'Donnell died 1792, aged 28; Revd D. O'Donnell died 1793, aged 93; Susanna O'Donnell died 1813, aged 88; Richard O'Donnell died 1790, aged 40; Robert Mann died 1806, aged 82; William McIlhenny died 1805, aged 78; Elizabeth McIlhenny died 1830, aged 60; Revd R. Mahaffy died 1816, aged 64; C. Graham died 1830, aged 74.

Emigration

Some few emigrate to America and some individuals go over to Scotland for the harvest.

Productive Economy

Linen

There is not much linen made in Mevagh and hand-spinning does not prevail. Druggets, flannels and stockings are made for home use but all these branches of profit are comparatively neglected (?).

Fairs and Markets

The fairs and markets have been noticed under the head Towns, but the linens and agricultural produce are taken to Rathmelton, a considerable quantity of oats being also purchased by Mr Hay of Milford for exportation. He employs his father as an agent, who resides in the townland of Rosapenna, where he has a store for housing it.

Rural: Proprietors

The chief proprietors of Rosguill are Lord Leitrim (agent Mr Cochrane of Letterkenny), Captain Babington (agent Mr Sproul of Rathmelton), Andrew Armstrong Esquire (agent Mr Copeland of Enniskillen), James Watts Esquire (agent the Revd Mr Hastings of Cresslagh), Mr Hamilton (agent the Revd Mr Hastings) and William Stewart Esquire (agent Mr Black of Letterkenny).

All the proprietors and agents are non-residents. The latter, it is supposed, are paid as usual 5 pounds per cent on the money levied. The size of the holdings runs from 2 to 25 acres but not more than 20 exceed 10 acres. The average rent is 20s an acre for good land and 10s for middling and 2s 6d to 8s for bad.

Agriculture

The farmers appear to be poor but here as elsewhere, when they say they cannot pay their rents, they can give large sums of money for the free will of a farm. The cultivated lands are laid out badly in run and dale or with crooked stone fences and the whole appears to be, as a farming district, in a very low state.

The soil is coarse, of a gravelly nature, shallow, with a hard bottom and, being unprotected from the prevailing north west winds, does not yield an abundant produce.

Implements of Husbandry

Seaweed is the usual manure; lime may be occasionally used but not abundantly. Few iron ploughs or carts are met with. Horses, slide cars and wooden ploughs prevail for agricultural purposes.

Rotation of Crops

The rotation of crops is simple: first potatoes, then oats, then barley followed by potatoes. No flax grows in the northern part of the parish.

The prices of produce are regulated by those of Rathmelton market and it is said the inhabitants destroy more barley than is grown in the parish in illicit whiskey. A Cunningham acre of barley is worth 6 pounds, an acre of oats 4 or 5 pounds and about a third of the land is under potatoes, which may be valued at 8 pounds an acre.

Parish of Mevagh

Grazing

Farms expressly used for grazing are unknown. Each person, according to his wealth, feeds a few cows and sheep which, from the bad nature of the fences, require constant herding.

Improvements

Irrigation is not practised. The northern part of the parish is adapted for mountain sheep-walks, the southern for pasture for cattle.

Cattle

The usual country mixed breeds of cattle, small hardy ponies, pigs and poultry are common. Green feeding is not practised and no jobbing except at Glen and Carrigart fairs, the former of which is well attended. A pony sells from 3 to 10 pounds, a cow from 2 to 5 pounds and sheep from 3s to 10s a head.

Uses made of Bogs

The bogs are grazed and cut for fuel for the uses of the parish. The tenants generally have not the free use of turbary, the turf bogs being in some parts of the country very scarce. No attempts have been made to drain the bogs. Umricam and the adjacent towns in Fanad are supplied with turf from the eastern coast of Rosguill at [blank].

Planting

There are few trees in Rosguill and no trials have been made to improve the wastelands by planting. Unless proprietors of wastelands had tracts in their own possession, the system of planting could not be successfully carried on, as the tenantry, having now the privilege of grazing their cattle on these wastes, would resist any supposed encroachments on their rights and destroy or damage the young trees.

Sea-Coast

Large flocks of sea birds do not build on this shore, Horn Head being the general place of resort for them. Formerly 100, now about 20, tons of kelp, at 3 pounds per ton, are made in Mevagh and employ about 100 persons periodically.

Fishing

There are 45 boats and a great number of corrachs in Rosguill. The boats are built at the expense of families or small companies and are of a common description, not at all fitted for rough weather.

The corrachs are 10 or 11 feet long, 3 feet wide, very shallow, made of a wooden frame and wicker-work covered with hide or double canvas with tarred paper between them, and cost 1 guinea each. In one of these apparently frail vessels 2 fishermen ride over very rough seas and pursue their occupation. When once seated, they can scarcely dare to alter their position and in case of accidents, a turf or a jacket is made to stop the leak whilst they, with 2 pairs of short oars, make for land.

The villages of Downings and Doagh are the principal fishing places. Some few persons give themselves up entirely to the trade, not having any land, and send their fish to Letterkenny and Derry on ponies or asses. The fish usually taken are cod, ling, skate, flounders, turbot, glassons, haddock etc.

Previously to 1831 at least one Dublin wherry with a crew of 4 men came to the banks off Tory Island to fish, making Downings in Sheep Haven their rendezvous. The usual take of cod, ling etc., commonly called in the north "whitefish," was about 70 dozen a tide which, being brought to Downings, were salted by the crew who then returned to the banks. The small fish were their perquisite, but the speculation failed not from the want of fish but from the bad management of the owners, who ought to have had a separate establishment on shore for salting the produce and checking the labours of the fishermen, who were, in many instances, very unfaithful to their employers.

The banks at Tory Island, Malin Head and Insterhul lighthouse would amply repay the expenses of a fishing company if good decked vessels and faithful crews were sent to them. This branch of profit is sadly neglected by the inhabitants of the adjacent coasts, their poverty and the want of markets tending to prevent any exertion on their parts to reap advantages from it.

The only river fishing is the Lackagh, already noticed under the head Rivers.

General Remarks: Coast

The highest spot cultivated is in [blank], 600 feet above the sea, and the average elevation of the cultivated lands is about 133 feet. Situated between 2 seas or harbours, Mevagh is much exposed to every wind except the south, but the north west gales do incalculable injury to the crops. The devastation of the lands of Rosapenna and other large tracks in the parish by the drifted sand arose from the force of these gales about

1786, when the sand-hills on the shores began to break up and were carried, and are still proceeding, into the interior.

Various reasons are given for this great change in the lands along the north coast of Ireland, but none of them are satisfactory unless it be allowed that the north west winds have blown with greater fury the last 45 years than usual. Fields of drift sand occur at Donegal, Rutland, Horn Head, Rosguill, Fanad, Clonmany, Magilligan, Portstewart and Portrush.

In Clonmany the banks, now nearly destroyed, have been indurated and appear like a sandstone under decomposition. The same thing occurs in Fanad and it is the general report that these sands have altered their appearance materially in the memory of man; and in those parishes to the westward the sand is said to have drifted more the last 12 years than the last 40.

In the sand-fields on Stramore the formation of sand-hills is very conspicuous. The drifted particles are arrested by a blade of bent, around which they accumulate until the wings of the little heap mix with those adjacent, which now, affording greater resistance to the wind, run into one hillock perhaps a foot in height. These again extend their flanks and several of them, forming into one, raise the sand-hill perhaps to a yard. The bent shoots through the sand or is deposited on its surface, and by continued repetition of the above long large hills are formed of many yards in height, which surprise a person when he is told that in the memory of man the whole was a level plain under cultivation.

The bay north and west of Carrigart is rapidly filling up with sand, a space of at least 20 acres being now uncovered at high tides over which the sea flowed in 1828.

There is no doubt Mevagh might be much improved, as there is plenty of seaweed and some limestone in the parish. Many parts of the southern end might be made into good agricultural districts, but the north is generally wild and rocky except that part of it on the shore of Sheep Haven, where limestone is more general and where the crops are considered to be more early than usual.

The products of the coast are not neglected, the seaweed being used in tillage in preference to kelp; but the seas, I have stated, are neglected.

Ports sufficiently convenient invite commercial enterprise. Nothing is exported but grain, which is sent in large quantities to Scotland.

Seed and Harvest

The average seed time is from the 1st March to June and the harvest from the beginning of September to the end of October.

DIVISIONS

Townlands

There are no divisions in this parish except townlands. That part of the parish to the north of Rosapenna has a distinguishing name already noted. [Signed] W. Lancey, Lieutenant Royal Engineers, 22nd January 1835.

MEMOIR WRITING

Letter concerning Shuggling Stone

Rathmelton, 11th November 1834.

The Shuggling Stone called Cloughnabogaty stands in the townland of Drumlackagh. [Diagram showing densities of stone, 7 feet long and approximately 18.5 to 19.7 inches wide; section drawing with dimensions on A to B showing stone upright].

This stone is of granite and weighs, as nearly as could be ascertained, about 13 tons. It can be moved by the pressure of the little finger of the left hand through an arc of 4 inches with the greatest ease. Its specific gravity by 4 trials equals 2,576. The calculation is thus 16.7 face of triangle, 8.0 offset, total 24.7 by 7.33 length, equals 181.05 cubic feet.

181.05 cubic feet by 2,576 specific gravity equals 466,256 oz., equals 13 tons. AB is the watershed line of the stone, Epsilon is the point at which I moved the stone. Note there is a logging stone in Dunfanaghy. [Signed] William Lancey, Lieutenant Royal Engineers.

Rocking Stone in Island Magee

Rathmelton, 11th November 1834.

The Rocking Stone, called also the Yellow Stone, is in Brown's bay at the north end of Island Magee <McGee> [insert note: county Antrim]. The cubic measure of this stone is at least 280 feet and its specific gravity is 2,800, which would make its weight nearly 22 tons. It requires about 30 lbs' force to move it through an arc of one-quarter of an inch, and has a curious effect when a person stands on it and rocks the mass by alternate pressure of the feet on either side of its centre.

The rock is basalt, its greatest length is 9 feet and width 6.5. Plan of the upper surface: [sketch giving depths or densities]. The motion is diagonally from point to point as below: [section showing stone and position].

There are 4 points of contact, 2 on each side under A.A.A.A. The foundation appears to be in a state of decay: fragments are easily removed. The same sort of stone is found close by, but the rock on which it stands does not appear to be exactly of its description.

The Rocking Stone stands on the brow of a cliff 30 feet high, and not far from it a person may step from the flat rocks into 25 feet water. [Signed] William Lancey, Lieutenant Royal Engineers. Note information obtained in 1826.

Geological Table by Lieutenant W. Lancey, January 1835

NATURAL HISTORY

Table of Minerals

[Table contains the following headings: name of townland; type of rock [abbreviation given]; simple minerals: none; metallic ores: none; fossils: none; economical products: limestone and granite; market or place of consumption: none except on the lands where the lime is met with; modes of conveyance: horses' backs and cars; price on the spot; charge for conveyance; remarks].

Ardbane: rocks, Q; Aughadehur: rocks, GmA; Aughaletty: rocks, Gm; Ballyoughagan: rocks, Q:A; Carnagore: rocks, G; Carrick: rocks, Gm; Carrigart: rocks, GM; Cloontullagh: rocks, Q; Creevy: rocks, Q; Crucknamurlog: rocks, Q:Lg; Derryhassan: rocks, Q; Devilinmore: rocks, Gm:A [query]; Divlinreagh: rocks, Gm; Doagh: rocks, Q.Lg; Downings bar: rocks, Q:Lg; Downings: rocks, Gm; Dunmore: rocks, Gm; Drumdutton: rocks, G; Drumlackagh: rocks, G; Finvor: rocks, Q:A; Glanree: rocks, Q:A; Glebe: rocks, Q; Glenhow: rocks, G; Gleneeragh: rocks, Q; Glenmeenagh: rocks, Q; Glenmeenan: rocks, G; Glenoory: rocks, Q; Gortnabeade: rocks, Gm; Gortnaloghog: rocks, G:A; High Glen: rocks, Q; High Glen, Gillygranny: rocks, Q.

Island Roy bar or Drumfin: rocks, Q; Island Roy: rocks, Q:Tp; Kill: rocks, Q.Lg; Kinlargy: rocks, Q:A; Largyreagh: rocks, Q; Largyreagh bar: rocks, Gm; Lower Dundooan: rocks, G:A; Magherbeg: rocks, Q:A; Maghremagorgan: rocks, Q:A; Melmore: rocks, G:A; Meenformal: rocks, Q:Lg.Tp; Meenlaragh: rocks, Gm.Lg; Mevagh: rocks, Q:Lg; Rawris: rocks, Gm:Lg; Rosapenna: rocks, Gs:A; Teerlaughan: rocks, Gm:Lg; Toragh: rocks, Q; Tullyagh: rocks, Q; Umlagh: rocks, Gm:Lg; Upper Dundooan: rocks, Q.

Remarks: 19 specimens sent to Dublin. The parish of Mevagh is a primitive formation of granite, quartz rock, talc slate and blue limestone, with dykes of porphyritic greenstone running north east and south west, being a part of the series of dykes from Inishowen through Fanad, Killygarvan and Tullyaughnish parishes. The granite has black mica and is found at the north on the coast and at Lough Salt on the southern frontier of the parish.

In Doagh bay the granite on the high water mark has large, black, circular spots about a foot in diameter. When broken, it appears they arise from a greater quantity of mica than elsewhere. The whole district is wild and rocky. [Signed] William Lancey, Lieutenant Royal Engineers, 22nd January 1835.

[Insert footnote: "To specify the most valuable mineral productions; to ascertain their relative importance and aptitude for economical uses; and to fix the principles which should guide adventurers in quest of them is the pleasing duty of a practical geologist" (Philip's *Geology of Yorkshire*); circulated by order of Lieutenant-Colonel Colby, Royal Engineers, superintendent].

Parish of Mintiaghs or Bar of Inch, County Donegal

Statistical Report by Lieutenant W. Lancey, May 1834

GEOGRAPHY OR NATURAL STATE

Name

The 5 townlands called Mintiaghs, pronounced by the peasants meenchaus, means in English [insert note: could not obtain the English meaning of Mintiaghs].

It derives its second name, the Bar of Inch, from the island in Lough Swilly to whose inhabitants it was formerly given by the late Lord Donegall for grazing and fuel. Lord Donegall, being in gaol <jail> for a gambling debt, sold a considerable part of his property, by which means Lord Templemore got possession of part of Mintiaghs, Inch etc. [insert note: could not obtain further information].

Locality

It is situated in the county of Donegal, barony of Inishowen and is bounded on the north by the parish of Clonmany, on the west by Desertegney, on the south by Lower Fahan and in the east by Donagh towards the west side of the barony. Its extreme length east and west is 4 miles and north and south 2 and a half miles, and contains 3,255 acres; about one-sixth is cultivated, five-sixths mountain and rocks, in which is enclosed [blank] acres of water in 4 loughs. Its valuation to the county cess amounts to 25 pounds.

NATURAL FEATURES

Hills

The principal hills on the east are Little Slieve Snaght, 1,193 feet, Bannin, 1,044 feet, Ballintraire, 705 feet being the western part of the Slieve Snaght range; and on the west Minicliffe, 1,390 feet and Glassmullan, 761 feet, the eastern foot of the Bulbin range.

Loughs

These meet at Mintiaghs lough, which is about [blank] feet above the sea and lies in the centre of the parish. It contains [blank] acres and is about 23 feet deep. The north east mearing of Ballinlough passes through an island in Lough Nomin which is situated in Mintiaghs and Clonmany. Its depth is about 20 feet and its height above the sea 498 feet [insert note: refer to plan]. There are 2 rocky islands in it which do not exceed half an acre each: Dirty lough on the west is divided between Glassmullan and the parish of Lower Fahan, it contains [blank] acres; and Glassmullan also contains a small portion of the north end of Lough Dhu in Lower Fahan.

Rivers

The principal brook is that which bounds the north west side of Ballintrave lying in the glen by the side of the main road to Carn. It rises in Glassmullan and flows to the north east through Mintiaghs for 190 chains, receiving the drainage of Minicliffe, when it joins the left of the Carn road. Its source is [blank] feet above the sea, its depth at the Clonmany mearing a few inches and its breadth 20 feet, and discharges itself into the ocean to the west of Bannin.

Several small rills of water fall into Mintiaghs lough but the longest, to the north of Bannin, is only 5,500 links in length and is nearly dry except in rainy weather.

The southern mearing of Corroughel is bounded by a brook for 140 chains, which then passes into Lower Fahan and meets the stream from Mintiaghs lough and the parish mearing of Glassmullan, flowing towards the south.

These streams are well adapted for draining the adjacent lands but are not powerful enough for machinery. The only thing worthy of notice is that part of the drainage of Glassmullan falls to the south and empties itself into Lough Swilly at Buncrana and part to the north, and falls into the ocean by the Clonmany river.

Bogs

It is difficult to state the extent of the bogs when it is mixed up with rocks and wasteland. The best are in Ballinlough, varying from 3 to 12 feet in depth. The height of these are about [blank] feet above the sea. Bog firs and black oak are constantly found, especially the former which appear to have fallen principally towards the east. [Insert addition: The usual direction in the adjacent country either east or south east, blown down by west or north westerly gales]. Some are broken off, others lie across each other.

Parish of Mintiaghs

Woods

There are no woods. A very small scrog or underwood is situated on the left of the Carn road in Minicliffe.

Climate

The climate is very wet and cold. The harvest commences at the end of August or beginning of September.

NATURAL HISTORY

Zoology

Black trout and eels in the lough but neither salmon or white trout. Foxes with white rings half round their necks, badgers and others, grouse, hares, partridge, woodcock and snipe, with wild duck and teal on the loughs and the more usual common birds in the fields.

Geology

Mintiaghs lies on a primitive formation of talc slate and quartz rock intercepted by the broad porphyritic dyke of greenstone at Bannon, running to the opposite hill of Glassmullan.

MODERN TOPOGRAPHY

Gentlemen's Seats

The only gentlemen's house is that belonging to [insert addition: William?] Harvey Esquire in Ballintreve. It is a small slated cottage in a glen with 3 or 4 fields to the north of it and was built about 12 years ago [insert note: cost not obtained].

Mills

There are no mills in Mintiaghs. The inhabitants take their corn to the adjacent parishes.

Communications

The high road from Buncrana to the east of Clonmany runs through Mintiaghs for 155 chains and the leading roads to Carn by the lough for 140 chains. There are 2 other roads to Carn not now made use of and one from the Clonmany road to Owenirk in Desertegney.

Their average breadth is 28 feet, made with gravel or broken stone at the expense of the county. The roads to Carn and Clonmany are in good repair and are the best I have seen in Inishowen.

ANCIENT TOPOGRAPHY

Antiquities

There are no ruins or any remains of antiquity in Mintiaghs that I heard of.

MODERN TOPOGRAPHY

General Appearance

Mintiaghs is a wild district of mountains, rocks and bogs surrounding the lough which lies in its centre. The hills rise on each side of the high road to Carn which passes through the valley. The hill of Bannon on the right, composed of greenstone, is broken and bare; between it and the lough lies Mr Harvey's cottage.

The opposite hills of Glassmullan and Minicliffe are wild and rocky, and there is a belt of cultivation running in the low ground contiguous to the highland road.

SOCIAL ECONOMY

Early Improvements

The principal reason of Mintiaghs being located can only be traced to the facilities of cultivation offered by the low grounds about the lough.

Obstruction to improvement: none but those proceeding from want of capital.

Local Government

There is no magistrate nearer than Carn or Buncrana. Illicit distillation is very much on the decline, as the present system of police is far better adapted to its suppression than the old one.

Dispensaries: Buncrana and Carn dispensaries supply the medical wants of the poor.

Schools

There is no school: the children are educated at a school in Lower Fahan near the mearing of Carroghel, at a place called Crooky's.

Poor

There are many poor but only 2 travelling beggars belonging to Mintiaghs.

Religion

There are 56 families, all Roman Catholics except Mr Harvey's. As there is no chapel they usually go to that at Cock Hill at the Priest's bridge in Lower Fahan.

Habits of the People

Their cottages are 1-storey high and built of stone, the roofs thatched and bound down with straw ropes. One, 2 or 3 rooms, usually 2 with glass windows, very uncomfortable and dirty. The food of the people is potatoes, milk and a little meal. Their fuel, turf and bog fir.

The man's dress of home manufacture of woollen and linen cloths; the women add cheap cottons purchased in Buncrana and elsewhere. The usual number in a family is about 6. Many have 10 children. They speak Irish and English; the latter is increasing. They do not marry so early as the people of Desertegney, usually from 20 years of age to 30.

They have no amusements or saints' days peculiar to themselves and the celebration of St John's Eve is going into decay.

Emigration

Very few emigrate from Mintiaghs.
Remarkable events: none.

PRODUCTIVE ECONOMY

Linen

There are 4 looms; the linen cloth is sold from 4d ha'penny or 5d to 10d a yard, woollen cloth from 6d, 8d to 9d a yard undressed. A weaver earns 2d a yard for linen and 1d ha'penny for woollen webs, and can weave about 6 yards a day.

Hand-spinning is general in the cottages. The price of the cloths show their quality to be of the coarser kind.

Fairs and Markets

There are none in Mintiaghs. The produce is taken to Carn or Buncrana.

Proprietors

The proprietors are: Mr Ferguson of Burt, who holds Glassmullan under Mr Harvey, its rent is 60 pounds; Lord Templeton [Templemore] possesses Ballinlough and receives 80 pounds; Carroghel is held by the Revd A. Cary under Mr Harvey and receives 32 pounds; and Ballintrave, at a rent of about 42 pounds, and Minicliffe, at 45 pounds, belongs to Mr Harvey, the total rents being 259 pounds British. Mr Harvey resides and is his own agent. Glassmullan is received by John Dysart of Burt and Ballinlough by Mr Kennedy of Derry, who are paid 5 pounds per cent.

Holdings

The usual size of the holdings is about 4 acres arable with grazing for 2 head of cattle. There are 2 farms of 10 acres arable and about 10 of 5 acres. A farm of 10 arable and 50 pasture pays 14 pounds rent; one of 5 acres arable and grazing for 2 cows pays 5 or 6 pounds.

The lands are held by lease of lives except in Ballinlough, where they are tenants at will. The fields are not laid out with much respect to appearance and the fences are of stone.

Taxes

The only tax is the county cess, as the Bar of Inch does not pay tythe to any parish.

Farm Buildings

The farm buildings are very indifferent, with little exception. They are built and repaired at their own expense.

Soil and Manures

The soil is not very good. The manure used is that from the farmyard and sea-sand, with a little lime from Carn. The sea-sand is brought in the empty carts from Buncrana when returning from market. The lime costs at the kiln at Carn 1s a barrel. 3 barrels can be conveyed on 1 cart which, if hired, would cost 2s 6d a day.

The farmyard manure is the cheapest that can be obtained, as it is on the spot.

There are about 20 carts in Mintiaghs each drawn by 1 horse, but no iron ploughs.

Crops and Produce

The rotation of crops on a lea field is potatoes or oats. Of the former, 64 stone an acre are required for seed; then oats which take 24 stone; then flax or oats again; if flax, 24 gallons of New York seed are sown on an acre, then potatoes again.

The produce of potatoes is 50 to 60 sacks of 24 stone; 3 to 5 sacks and sometimes 6 sacks from an acre of oats; and an acre of flax on the ground sells for 5 to 6 pounds.

Buncrana and Carn markets are the outlets for the produce. Potatoes sell for 5s a sack, oats for 7d ha'penny a stone and undressed flax 5d a lb. A very little forced grass is planted in Mintiaghs. Bad clay slate was occasionally quarried and its produce sold at 1 pound a thousand. It is not now worked as the people are too poor to purchase them.

Grazing

The people of Mintiaghs rent some acres in [blank] in Clonmany, [insert marginal note: some Irish name I cannot tell where, probably in Mindoran], for which they pay 5 pounds to enlarge their capabilities of taking young stock to graze. About 70 head are annually received into the Bar from the liberties of Derry and the vicinity of Burt from May to October, at the rate of 3s to 4s 6d a head. Each farmer has a certain number of cattle on his own account, varying from 2 to 8.

The hills are too rough for sheep except the half-wild country kind and there are few fences to keep them within bounds.

Wages

The wages of male servants are from 4 to 5 guineas a year with board and lodging, those of females about 50s.

Cattle

There are a few Yorkshire cattle but usually they are of the common mixed breed of the country. They sell from 3 to 5 pounds a head. The horses are the small kind used in Inishowen, worth from 5 to 8 pounds. Pigs sometimes weigh about 9 score. Poultry of the common breeds are about the farmyard. The average number of horses is 1 to a family.

Use made of Bogs

The bogs are grazed and used for fuel. The inhabitants have free rights of turbary and the imbedded timber is used for fuel or, if large enough, for building.

Drainage

Each farmer drains his own land and the falls of the hills render this an easy task.

Planting

There are no plantations but a few young trees about Mr Harvey's, and one or two farmhouses which thrive well.

Fishing

The black trout and eels are occasionally taken in the loughs in the usual manner, more for pleasure than for profit.

General Remarks on Economy

The highest point cultivated is in the townland of [blank], [blank] feet above the sea.

Irrigation and drainage are easy. The former might be useful, the latter is not much required except at Mintiaghs lough, which might be drained for 60 pounds [insert marginal note: estimated by the principal farmer who lives near Mr H's house]. As the cultivated lands lie in a deep valley which runs north and south, they suffer if either of these winds prevail.

The soil I do not feel capable of giving an opinion of, but those which usually lie on talc slate I have always observed are not very productive. Lime and seaweed would be of use but they are too far off to be generally used. There are no streams fitted for machinery nor anything in Mintiaghs which invites commercial enterprise. The roads to the market towns are good and the effect has been that 20 carts are used in this small district.

DIVISIONS

Townlands

There are no other divisions in Mintiaghs than the following townlands: Ballinlough, which lies east of the Carn road; Ballintreve, which lies east of the Carn road; Carroghel, which lies east of the Carn road; Glassmullan, which lies west of the Carn road; Minicliffe, which lies west of the Carn road. [Insert addition: Distance from markets etc. cannot be accurately stated without adjacent plans].

[Signed] William Lancey, Lieutenant Royal Engineers, 19th May 1834.

Parish of Moville, County Donegal

Statistical Report on Lower Moville by Lieutenant W.E. Delves Broughton, May 1833

GEOGRAPHY OR NATURAL STATE

Situation

The parish of Lower Moville, situated at the north east extremity of the barony of Inishowen, in the county of Donegal, is bounded on the north by the ocean, south by Lough Foyle, east by the sea forming the entrance to the lough and west by the parishes of Culdaff and Upper Moville.

Townlands

Townlands: Ballybrack, Ballynelly, Balleighan, Ballymacarter, Ballymagarahy, Brody Glen, Eleven Ballyboes, Carrahue, Carratrasna, Carnagariff, Carrablagh or Leakamy, Carromenagh, Carrobeg, Drumawier, Glenigiviny, Gullado, Mossy Glen, Meanlettorbale, Shrove and the detached townlands of Carrablagh, and contains 16,950 acres, about a third of which are cultivated, the remainder being bog, sand and rocks.

MODERN TOPOGRAPHY

Towns

Principal market town: the town of Bonyfoble or Moville is situated in the townland of Ballynelly. It has a market on a Thursday, chiefly for grain and potatoes, being otherwise but badly supplied. The market place is a square space walled in with lean-to open sheds on 2 sides and a thoroughfare opening on the road. The shops are small and bad and few of any sort.

This is a police station and the magistrates hold their sessions in a room adjoining the market place.

The town is nearly new and is becoming more important every year as a bathing place for the wealthier inhabitants of Derry, who resort to it during the summer months.

The houses chiefly built of the stone of the country, being a coarse clay slate which, splitting in lamina, is easily procured and rendered fit for the purpose of building. They are, however, small and generally ill-contrived and inconvenient.

The post office is about quarter of a mile to the north west of the town.

The stream forming the boundary between Upper and Lower Moville runs below the town, from which a corn mill is supplied.

There are 4 fairs during the year for cattle.

A small steam-boat offers a daily communication with Derry.

Schools and Church

There are 2 schools in the town under the direction of the clergyman (vide report of schools).

The parish church is built on a bank forming a prominent object in the townland of Drumawier.

ANCIENT TOPOGRAPHY

Forts and Castle

There is a fort commanding the entrance of the lough and very extensive remains of an old castle. Adjoining these are also 3 remains of old Danish forts, 2 on the roadside leading from Bonyfoble to Shrovehead and 1 on the north of the parish in Glenigiviny.

NATURAL HISTORY

Geology

The geological structure of this parish is exclusively clay slate with occasional traces of hornblende passing in gradations into slate.

PRODUCTIVE ECONOMY

Cultivation and Produce

Being essentially part of a mountain district running from south east to north west, as is usual in such cases every patch to the south between rocks or bog is cultivated. The chief produce is oats, potatoes and a small quantity of rye and flax. Seaweed forms the chief manure.

Subsistence and Employment

The inhabitants exist almost entirely on potatoes, oatmeal bread and the produce of fishing, which forms a large portion of their employment and means of subsistence (vide Statistical Report on the Fisheries).

Coast and Harbours

The coast on the north side is precipitous and in

many places inaccessible. To the south, however, and on the borders of the lake, are many small inlets and sandy bays which form harbours for their boats.

There has also been lately erected at the expense of Fishery Board a pier at Greencastle, as also one at Moville for the accommodation of the steam-boat.

SOCIAL ECONOMY

Schools in Lower Moville

[Table contains the following headings: name of townland, number of pupils subdivided by religion and sex, remarks].

Ballynelly, Moville daily, 22 Protestants, 24 Catholics, 42 males, 4 females; was under the Kildare Street Society.

Ballynelly, Moville daily, 17 Protestants, 16 Catholics, 33 females; the London Hibernian Ladies' Society give 8 pounds per annum to the teacher.

Ballynelly, Moville Sunday school, 25 Protestants, 25 males.

Drumawier, Greencastle daily, 26 Protestants, 19 Catholics, 38 males, 7 females; was under the Kildare Street Society.

Drumawier, Greencastle Sunday school, 114 Protestants, 54 males, 60 females; taught by ladies and gentlemen of the neighbourhood.

Carrobeg, Sunday school, 23 Protestants, 23 males; was under the Kildare Street Society.

Carrobeg daily, number of pupils variable; under the new Education Board.

Glennigivinny daily, 10 Protestants, 35 Catholics, 30 males, 15 females; under New Education Board, salary 8 pounds per annum.

Gullado daily, 1 Protestant, 19 Catholics, 14 males, 6 females; under new Education Board, salary 8 pounds per annum and 1s per quarter from the children.

Since the Kildare Society has been broken up, the schools are not at present on any established footing, with the exception of those under the new Education Board. The number of scholars they have varies with the season of the year. [Signed] W.E. Delves Broughton, Lieutenant Royal Engineers, May 1833.

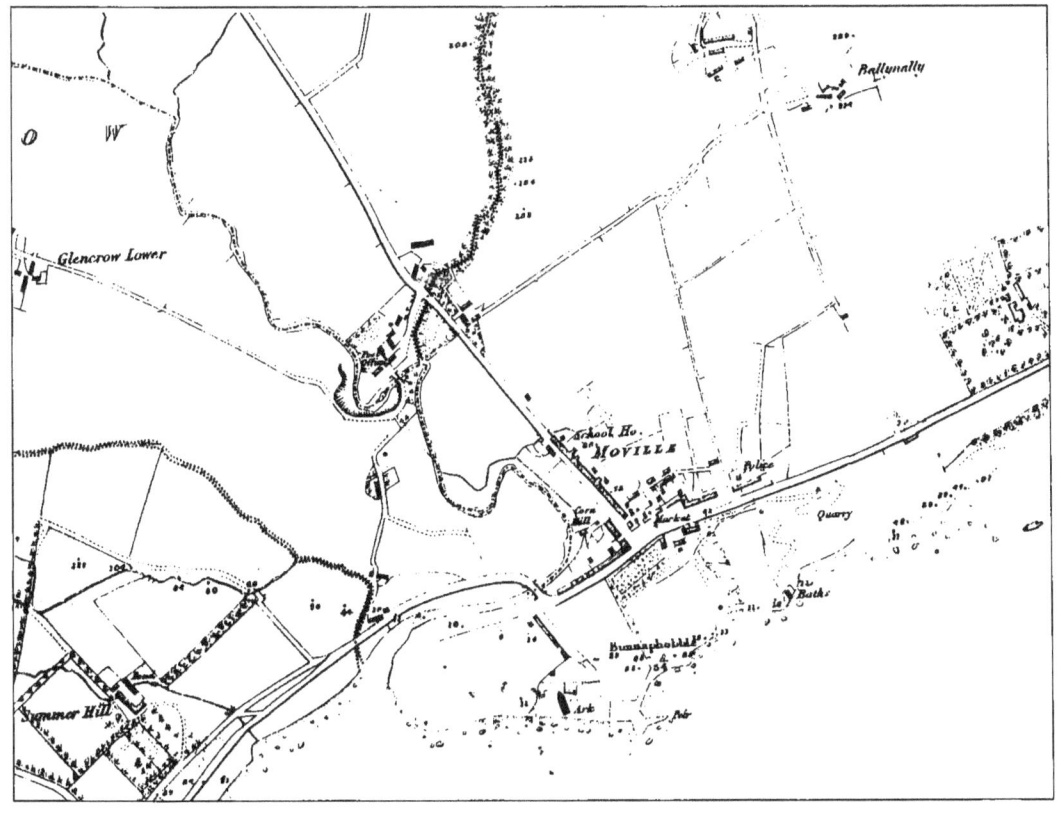

Map of Moville from the first 6" O.S. maps, 1830s

Replies to Queries on Lower Moville from North West Farming Society, July 1825

NATURAL STATE

Name and Extent

Section 1st. Name, townlands, soil, mountains, rivers, lakes, sea-coast, plantations: the parish of Lower Moville is situated in the barony of Inishowen, in the county of Donegal and diocese of Derry; is bounded on the north by the Atlantic Ocean, on the east by the North Channel, on the south by Lough Foyle and on the west by the parishes of Upper Moville and Culdaff.

It contains 18 and a half quarterlands, viz. Shrove, Carratrasna, Carrihew, Ballahar, Ballymacarton, Eleven Balliboes, Dramaween, Ballybrack, Carmagarve, Ballynally, Galladuff, Brady-glen, Carrowblaw, Carramenagh, Carrowbeg, [?] Murlitterbral, Mossy Glen, Glenagivney and Ballymagarahey.

NATURAL FEATURES AND NATURAL HISTORY

Soil

The soil varies from light gravel to stiff clay. It contains several mountains and is well supplied with streams of water, but with the exception of the Breda, which separates it from Upper Moville, not one of those streams can be called a river. There are no woods and but few trees, and these only around the seats of the few gentlemen resident in the parish.

Mines and Minerals

Section 2nd. Mines and minerals, quarries, different kinds of stones: neither mines nor minerals have been discovered. Building stones are to be had in every townland and slates of an indifferent quality have been raised in different parts of the parish.

MODERN TOPOGRAPHY

Modern Buildings

Section 3rd. Modern buildings, towns, gentlemen's seats, scenery, inns, roads: a regular fort has been constructed by government at Greencastle near the entrance of Lough Foyle, and a handsome row of houses has also been lately erected at the same place for the accommodation of the different persons employed in the service of the customs.

Villages

There are 3 villages, viz. Moville alias Bonyfabb and Green-castle. The first mentioned is a daily post town. The following-named gentlemen have seats on a small scale, viz. Mr Walker, Shrove; Mr McEntire, Greencastle; Mr Curry, Ballybrack; Mr Reynolds, Carnick; Mr Montgomery, Newpark; Mr Grierson, Moville Lodge; Dr Irvine (dispensary); and Mr Anderson, Galladuff.

Scenery

The southern part of this parish commands a beautiful view of Lough Foyle, parts of Derry, Tyrone and coast of Antrim, and on a clear day Rathlin Island and parts of Scotland. The northern side commands a view of the ocean, island of Inistrahul <Eristrahal>, Glengad Head, and on a clear day parts of Scotland and the Antrim coast.

Inns

There are several licensed public houses but they cannot be called inns; they, however, afford accommodation to the humbler classes.

The parish is well intersected by roads which are in general kept in good order.

ANCIENT TOPOGRAPHY

Ancient Buildings

Section 4th. Ancient buildings, churches, castles: there are the ruins of an ancient castle at Greencastle which tradition says was built by the Earl of Ulster in the 13th century.

SOCIAL ECONOMY

Food and Fuel

Section 5th. Food, fuel, diseases, instances of longevity: potatoes, oatmeal, fish, milk and butter constitute the food of the lower classes. The first, however, is the article most in use. Turf is used for fuel.

Consumption, pleurisy and indigestion are the most prevalent complaints.

Instances of longevity are not frequent. A man of the name of Loag died in 1821 at the advanced age of 100 years.

Habits of the People

Section 6th. Genius and disposition of the inhabitants, language, manners, customs, christenings, marriages, wakes and funerals, traditions: the inhabitants are intelligent, well disposed and civil in their manners, speak the English language. Some of them understand Irish but it is seldom spoken.

Education

Section 7th. Education and employment of children, schools, collections of books, manuscripts: the children are not generally educated. Their parents are poor and unable to pay qualified masters. No proprietor of a quarterland, with the exception of the rector of the parish, is resident. There are at present 2 schools, viz. the parish school, to the master of which the rector pays an annual salary, a Sunday school supported by him. The masters of the other schools derive their incomes from the payments made by their respective scholars.

There is no manufacture to employ male children.

Their first employment is attendance as herds upon the cattle when they get forward and are able to bear fatigue. Many of them are taken into boats and taught the art of fishing, and in some cases that of piloting vessels on Lough Foyle. Others are hired out as servants or assist their parents in the cultivation of their farms.

The female children are taught to spin linen yarn at an early age and generally continue that industrious pursuit to the end of their lives.

Religion

Section 8th. State of religious establishment, tithes, churches, meeting houses, chapels: the parish of Lower Moville is a rectory. There are no lands tithe free, nor is any particular crop discharged by custom or otherwise. The parishioners generally compound for their tithes for a certain number of years.

The parish church is situated near Greencastle, is in good order and, although the great bulk of the population is Roman Catholic, is attended by a respectable congregation. There is a Roman Catholic chapel in the parish but no meeting house.

PRODUCTIVE ECONOMY

Agriculture

Section 9th. Modes of agriculture, rotation of crops, stock, horses, black cattle, sheep, pigs, fairs and markets, wages and price of labour: agricultural improvement has made little progress in Lower Moville. The lands are split into such small portions that the occupants ought rather to be styled cottiers than farmers. The grounds are in general unenclosed and in some places they hold in rundale.

Rotation of Crops

The arable land is almost constantly under crop. The rotation of crops as follows, in land of best quality: 1st potatoes, 2nd barley, 3rd flax, 4th oats. Sometimes oats are sown often early and then follow flax and oats. The same rotation again commences.

In land of an inferior quality: 1st potatoes, 2nd oats, 3rd flax, 4th oats and, in some instances, a second crop of oats. The rotation again commences with potatoes.

Livestock

Horses, sheep and black cattle are small. They graze on the mountains and coarse lands. Pigs are in general of a good description.

Fairs and Markets

There are 4 fairs held in Moville in the course of the year, viz. on the 28th January, 28th April, 28th July and 28th October. There is also a market held in the same place on every Thursday.

Fairs are also held in Greencastle in the months of February, May, August and November.

Employment and Wages

Stout men at the present time, as labouring servants, receive about 6 guineas per annum, a younger description about 4 guineas. Labourers are paid in winter 10d and in summer 1s per day. Female servants as spinners are paid by farmers about 2 pounds 8s per annum; when hired by a higher class as general servants, from 3 to 4 pounds.

Trades and Manufactures

Section 10th. Trades, manufactures, commerce and navigation: the usual tradesmen are in sufficient number to minister unto the necessities of the population. Manufactures, with the exception of linen yarn, can scarce be said to exist. Linen, however, and even woollen cloth are made for home consumption. A small quantity of linen manufactured in the parish is sold in Moville market, although surrounded on 3 sides by water.

Commerce is not in a flourishing state. Quantities of yarn are shipped every week at Moville and Greencastle, landed at Magilligan Point and from thence carried to the market of Coleraine.

Grain is also occasionally conveyed to Londonderry by water. Indeed, there is a constant communication by water with the last-mentioned place. A large portion of the fish sold there is supplied by the Moville fishermen. There are several shops on a small scale in the parish and they both seem to extend and improve.

Improvements

Section 12th. Suggestions for improvement and means of ameliorating the condition of the poor: the enlargement and enclosure of farms, investment of capital in the improvement of now unprofitable lands, extension of the linen manufacture, encouragement of fisheries and a well digested system of education would give employment to the poor, inform their minds and consequently ameliorate their condition. But it is not easy to discover how these objects can be accomplished without the residence, exertion and encouragement of the landed proprietors. 1st July 1825.

Printed Statistical Enquiries on the Coast Fisheries in Lower Moville

NATURAL FEATURES AND PRODUCTIVE ECONOMY

Fisheries

That the inhabitants of the maritime districts of a country, or even of the shores of its great lakes or banks of its rivers, should habitually seek, and subsist principally on, the fish obtained in the adjacent waters, must appear a natural supposition to every one; and yet, reasonable as in theory it does appear, in practice it is so greatly modified by the habits of the people, their inclination or disinclination to the life of the fisherman.

But whilst in some places we find the inhabitants of the coasts, as of many parts of England and Scotland, fishing with ardour and perseverance, at all times and in all seasons, in others, as in some parts of Ireland, they only flock to the ocean at those epochs when the periodical arrival of large shoals of herrings or other fish kindles a momentary enthusiasm. It becomes, then, a fitting subject for statistical enquiry, how far the advantages of a productive ocean have been overlooked or profited by, and from what cause fishing has hitherto languished, or by what means it may henceforth be stimulated and made to constitute a source of national wealth and individual comfort.

Fishermen may be divided into 2 classes, constant or periodical: the first being those who follow fishing as a leading pursuit and depend on it principally for their subsistence; the second, those who, engaged ordinarily in agricultural or other occupations, fish only when the great visitations of herrings or other fish offer them an immediate and certain recompense for their labours.

To the constant fisherman the absolute possession of boats, nets, hooks, lines and other tackle seems indispensable. To the periodical fisherman the occasional use of those implements of fishing is sufficient, and the property in them might be vested in the landed proprietor, who could easily, during the unemployed intervals, shelter the boats from the weather and keep the nets etc. dry and in proper repair, ready to be used at a moment's notice.

In both cases it would be desirable, and evidently beneficial to all parties, that the landed proprietors should erect proper sheds, at convenient points, for curing fish, and keep an ample stock of salt and staves on hand, so that no portion of the supply, afforded so liberally by nature, should be lost, or, as a last resource, applied as manure to the soil.

The following questions and the appended table are formed on the preceding principles.

Question 1. Do many of the inhabitants of the maritime coast of the parish of Lower Moville apply themselves to fishing? Answer: About 600.

Question 2. Are they constant or periodical fishermen? Answer: Constant.

Question 3. Are the boats and tackle employed the absolute property of the fishermen, or hired as occasion may require? Answer: Absolute property, none hired.

Question 4. Are there any banks adjacent to the coast well stocked with fish? Answer: several, viz. Isle bank, Dunmore bank, South Isle bank and Ton bank.

Question 5. Are the deep waters near the shore generally well supplied with fish? Answer: Yes.

Question 6. Are the shores rocky and precipitous, or do they afford good landing places for nets and convenient spots for drying fish, either in bays or along sandy beaches? Answer: On the north side the shores are extremely rocky and precipitous, but there are several sandy bays between Shrove Head and Moville perfectly adapted to the purposes specified.

Question 7. Is the fishing limited by insufficiency in the number of boats? Answer: More certainly might be employed. There is no scarcity of fish.

Parish of Moville

Question 8. Is the fishery limited by the want of salt, or other means of curing the superfluous fish? Answer: The fish is cured but for private use except salmon, which fishery is a monopoly and is confined to the lough and river. In fact no salmon are taken so low down as Lower Moville.

Question 9. Is fishing a favourite pursuit of the people or is it uncongenial to their habits and feelings? Answer: It is congenial and a favourite pursuit, in some degree a necessity, for by no other means could they pay the extreme high rents demanded for eligible situations.

Question 10. Does the fish taken form a large portion of the food of the inhabitants of the coast; is a considerable portion of it sent to inland parts of the country or to any principal market? Answer: Fish with potatoes may be said to constitute their sole food. It is sent in the seasons to Derry, Coleraine and Belfast occasionally.

Question 11. Can you enumerate the edible fish which most abound at all times in the deep water or on the banks and those which visit periodically the shores of the parish? Answer: Codfish from March to May, very fine, average 6d each. Turbot remarkably fine, from 1s to 2s and sometimes 3s, according to the number caught, from May to the latter end of July. Codling from July to Christmas. Herring in vast shoals from middle of July to Christmas.

Question 12. Can you state the periods at which the great shoals of fish arrive and the ordinary length of their visit? Answer: Generally in July and remain till end of August.

Memorandum. From experiments tried last year by Hugh Lisle Esquire, it was found prawns, shrimps and soles could be obtained on the borders of the lake and mud-banks, but it is questionable whether they will ever be taken in such quantities as to become part of the fisheries.

[Insert note: Answers are requested to be addressed to Lieutenant-Colonel Colby, Royal Engineers, Ordnance Survey Office, Dublin].

Notes on Fisheries

The boats average from 4 to 5 men and boys each, 4 on ordinary occasions and 5 during the great seasons. They have each their nets and tackling separate. They grow their own flax which the women spin and make into nets.

The fishery received a severe shock by the loss of nearly 30 lives one day by a sudden squall coming on when they were out fishing and which upset them before they could reach the land, leaving nearly 20 families destitute in the year 1831 and which has rendered them cautious of going out to the farthest banks ever since. This is the information I have been able to obtain. The boats are of about 1 and a half tons burden, open in the shape of whale boats.

The population round the coast may be said to be entirely fishermen, each having his 2 or 3 acres of bad land among the rocks and banks on which his hut is situated. [Signed] W.E. Delves Broughton, Lieutenant Royal Engineers, 8th May 1833.

Statistical Report on Upper Moville by Lieutenant W.E. Delves Broughton, October 1833

GEOGRAPHY OR NATURAL STATE

Situation

The parish of Moville, situated to the east of the barony of Inishowen, in the county of Donegal, is bounded on the north by the parishes of Lower Moville and Culdaff, south by the parish of Muff, east by Lough Foyle and west by the parish of Donagh.

Townlands

It is divided into the townlands of Ballyargus, Ballylawn, Ballyratten, Cabry, Carrickmaquigley, Carrokiel, Carinaff, Clare, Clegan, Cooley, Cross, Creehennan, Cruckglass, Cruckahenny, Cooley (detached part), Cullaneen, Drung, Flughland, Glebe, Glencrow, Glencaw, Gortanny, Gort no.1, Gort no.2, Keeranbaan, Leamacrossan, Magheralan, Meenaleavin, Meenavanaghan, Meenabaltin, Terryrone, Trumity, Tullyally, Tullynavin, White Castle, Ronskey, and contains about 19,092 acres.

MODERN TOPOGRAPHY

Towns

The principal market town for the produce of this parish is Bonyfoble, which is situated in Lower Moville on the verge, being only divided by the small stream forming the boundary between the parishes of Upper and Lower Moville which has been already described in the remarks of that parish. It may here be observed that formerly these 2 parishes were united, in which case this town would be nearly central.

There is, however, a cattle market held quarterly at Carrickmaquigley but is inferior in every respect.

Post Office and Schools

The post office is also in Lower Moville. There are 7 schools under the National Society (vide report on schools).

MODERN AND ANCIENT TOPOGRAPHY

Parish Church

The parish church is situated in the townland of Tullynavin and is nearly central. The remains of the old church and yard at the time the parishes were united, however, still exist in the neighbourhood of the glebe in the townland of Cooley.

There is a curious old cross still remaining at the entrance gates.

Forts and Altars

The other antiquities of this parish consist in the remains of old Danish forts scattered about and 2 druid's altars situated one in the townland of Drung and the other in Carrokeel.

NATURAL HISTORY AND NATURAL FEATURES

Geology

The geological structure of this parish is coarse clay slate in which is interspersed in many places lumps of quartz nearly white and portions of freestone.

A vein of coal is said also to have been discovered in an old quarry about 4 chains to the north of the road leading from Derry to Moville, on the boundary between Cabry and Cruhennan but was closed up. It never worked.

A specimen of clay and freestone found in this quarry has been transmitted, as also one of the quartz and clay slate alluded to.

Soil

The soil is of a cold gravelly nature and the produce proportionally light, the inhabitants being too poor to obtain the necessary manure for its improvement. In fact, the only means they have is by collecting the seaweed thrown up on the coast, at considerable toil and labours.

PRODUCTIVE ECONOMY

Produce

The chief produce is oats and potatoes and a small proportion of barley and wheat, for which latter the soil appears but ill adapted.

Fishery

Along the coast the chief means of subsistence is obtained by oysters drudging [dredging] and the herring fisheries, the banks offering commodious sandy inlets for their boats (vide Statistical Report on Fisheries). 30th October 1833.

SOCIAL ECONOMY

Schools

[Table contains the following headings: name, townland, number of pupils subdivided by religion and sex, remarks].

Cabry, 44 Protestants, 6 Catholics, 26 males, 24 females; national school, salary of teacher 8 pounds per annum and 1s 3d per quarter from each child.

Crehennan, 47 Protestants, 13 Catholics, 31 males, 29 females; national school, salary of teacher not fixed and 1s per quarter from each child.

Carrickmaquigley, 3 Protestants, 60 Catholics, 40 males, 23 females; national school, salary of teacher 10 pounds per annum, average 1s 3d per quarter from the children.

Cooley, 34 Protestants, 86 Catholics, 80 males, 40 females; national school, salary of teacher 15 pounds per annum, 1s per quarter from each child.

Ballylawn, 15 Protestants, 22 Catholics, 18 males, 19 females; national school, salary of teacher 10 pounds per annum and from 1s to 1s 6d per quarter from the children.

Drung, 26 Protestants, 44 Catholics, 32 males, 28 females; salary 10 pounds per annum, average 1s 3d per quarter from the children; this is also a national school.

Trumity: this schoolhouse has been built but has not been yet opened.

[Signed] W.E. Delves Broughton, Lieutenant Royal Engineers, 31st August 1833.

Replies by Stewart Marks to Queries on Upper Moville from North West Farming Society

Memoir Writing

Answers to the statistical questions of the North West Farming Society by S. Marks, curate of Upper Moville.

NATURAL STATE

Situation and Proprietors

County of Donegal, barony of Inishowen and diocese of Derry, parish of Upper Moville; the Revd John Molesworth Staples, incumbent.

Parish of Moville

4 townlands, Glencrow, Timeroane, Cooley, Cavanaff, commonly called the Churchlands, Earl of Caledon, proprietor, non-resident; townland of Ballylawn, William Thorpe Esquire, Samuel Carmichael and [blank] Gilmour, proprietors; William Thorpe only resident.

Clare, Robert Young, non-resident; Tullyally, Carmaquigley and Cullaneen, Revd Lucius Cary, resident occasionally.

Ballyorgus, Drung, Whitecastle, Chreheenan, held by the heirs of the late George Cary Esquire; Cabry, held by the heirs of the late George Cary Esquire and the occupying tenants under the Marquis of Donegall; Carrokeel, Revd Lucius Cary; Trumity, William Thorpe and Mrs Brumhall, resident.

All 18 quarterlands held by the proprietors under the Marquis of Donegall except the Churchlands, Clare, Tullyally, Turlevin, Carroquigley and Cullaneen. I do not know what number of acres the above townlands contain.

PRODUCTIVE ECONOMY

Farms and Improvements

5. The farms all various in size, but in general all small and scarcely any enclosures at all, as the greatest part of them are occupied in rundale. The method of cultivation is such as might have existed 2 or 3 centuries ago. The succession of crops are potatoes, oats or barley, flax and oats.

I consider that the first great step to improvement would be to divide the farms into reasonable sizes, say from 10 to 20 acres, according to the ability of the occupier, and to cause the tenant to enclose his farm with a good clay ditch planted with thorn quicks and to build his house upon his own farm, as the cabins at present are generally built in a cluster which is a continued source of contention, from their cattle, fowls etc. trespassing on each other.

By adopting this plan and giving the tenant reasonable encouragement by giving him a lease (as it is the policy of most middlemen in this place to give no leases at all), I think that the country, in place of bearing the appearance of a deserted wild [country], might become enclosed and highly improved.

6. [Grazing] The pasture-grounds are only mountains.

NATURAL FEATURES

Mountains

7. The whole parish of Upper Moville is bounded by a continued range of mountains on the west. They are not capable of being cultivated to any height as they return to their regional sterility, notwithstanding the greatest expense in cultivation. They are therefore only fit for pasture.

Bogs

8. The whole range described in no.7 is mountain or bog. There is some timber found in the valleys of the mountains commonly called bog fir, at various depths from 6 to 16 feet.

Plantations and Woods

9. No plantations except a little about the gentlemen's residences and a little natural wood at Redcastle and Castlecary, of no great extent but seems to be thriving pretty well.

10. Various species of trees thrive well if protected, as larch, Scotch fir, ash, oak, birch etc.

PRODUCTIVE ECONOMY

Rents and Farms

11. [Rents] I cannot say, as the land is in most places set by the lump so that the tenants cannot [say] what number of acres they possess; but have heard of some arable as high as 3 guineas and so low as 15s. When there is green or moory pasture convenient, the tenants have a portion of it thrown into their arable.

12. I have not heard of any charge for turf bog being made in my neighbourhood.

13. I have not seen any improvements made by the generality of landholders.

14. [Fences] No description of fence whatever; I have detailed at length what I would consider best adapted to the place in no.5.

Employment

15. Employment does not seem to be wanting, as those of the labouring classes who have not small portions of ground of their own are occupied in fishing etc. It is of course more abundant in spring and harvest than at other times.

16. [Wages] Various, from 3 guineas to 2 pounds in the half-year when the servant is kept in the house. Labourers who get constant employment have 1s per day.

Crops and Drainage

17. [Green crops] In very few instances.

18. [Artificial grasses] Very limited: rye grass, white grass and some little clover.

19. I have seen very little draining in this parish.
20. I have scarcely seen any clay burned for manure.

Irrigation

21. There is very little meadow in this place, but where it has been laid down in proper order and watered in a proper manner, it seems to do very well. The common people never think of watering their meadow if they have any.

Farm Techniques

22. [Dairies] I know of none.
23. [Oxen] I have seen none used for that purpose.
24. [Spade husbandry] Very rarely, unless where ploughs cannot be used.
25. [Grain crops] Barley and oats; the price is regulated in general by the Derry market.
26. [Unit of measurement] The Marquis of Donegal computes his land by the Irish acre. Those who derive from him let the ground by the Scotch acre.

Livestock

27. The common small Irish cattle.
28. Young heifers, bullocks and beef cattle.
29. The common Inishowen small sheep. They seem to be very well adapted to the mountainy pastures. South Downs are reared by the gentlemen and seem to thrive well. Some Merinos have been reared by Sir Arthur Chichester, but do not seem to be thriving too well; and [I?] consider the climate too cold for them.
30. The small Scotch pony with the generality of the common people; with gentlemen and the better sort of farmer, good horses of the Irish breed.
31. The common Irish swine; they are not numerous from want of enclosures.

Improvements in Stock

32. I cannot say: stock has been greatly reduced in this parish by the last dear summer and the impositions practised under the still-fine system, but seem to be increasing very fast. Any description of small black cattle seem well adapted both to soil and climate.
33. [Improvements in breeding] I cannot say, as I have not been resident so long.

NATURAL FEATURES AND NATURAL HISTORY

Rivers and Lakes

34. No rivers of any magnitude; Lough Foyle, Moville bay, Greencastle ferry. All the parish lies on the shore of Lough Foyle, the productions of which are herrings, cod and different descriptions of flatfish etc.

Minerals and Mines

35. I have heard of no mines being discovered.
36. [Quarries] There is no limestone in this parish and no quarries except one of freestone.
37. [Limestone] At Whitecastle, which does not seem of a good quality. It is not wrought.
38. [Coal] I have heard of none being found.
39. I have heard of no mineral springs.
40. No marl has been discovered in this parish.

SOCIAL ECONOMY

Condition of the People

41. Poor to a great degree; their domestic comforts are very limited. They are inclined to industry. The only means of making money is by fishing, except what they make by their small farms.

Houses and Fuel

42. [Houses] Miserable to a degree and very dirty, without any comforts. I mean the cabins of the common people in general. Those who have large farms have their houses tolerably comfortable.
43. Fuel is plenty as the mountain is convenient, which produces abundance of turf.

Food

44. [Farmers] Potatoes and, when they fare better, herrings, as they seldom, I believe, taste animal food.
45. [Manufacturing class] There is no manufacturing class distinct from those connected with farming in this place.
46. [Labourers] I believe the fare of the labouring classes is very poor indeed.

Education

47. There seems to be a general desire among the lower orders to educate their children, as appeared obvious from a Sunday school lately established under the auspices of Mr and Mrs Staples, and which was well attended by children of every denomination until the Catholic clergy forbid any of the children of their flock from attending the school, though there was not the least inference [interference] with any of their religious tenets by any person connected with the school.

No place seems to require education more, as the people are in general very ignorant, I mean, the lower classes.

48. I believe children pay 2s 6d for reading and 3s 4d for writing and accounts; any of the higher branches are seldom required. There is a schoolhouse built at Cooley, in Earl Caledon's property, and in Mr Cary's property, patronised by the Hibernian Society, besides several other schools in diverse parts of the parish.

49. [Improvements] Wherever education prevails, a difference in the state of the people is obvious; but it is so limited in this country that I cannot say I see any.

Health

50. The state of health is generally good. Fevers and other occasional diseases prevail, which I consider might be remedied in a great measure by cleanliness.

Friendly Societies and Towns

51. [Friendly societies] I know of none.
52. [Towns] Carrickmaquigley.

PRODUCTIVE ECONOMY

Improvements

53. The people seem inclined to improve if encouraged; but from the land being all overlet and in general the people having no leases, they are deterred from making any improvements. But if the land was let at a fair value and sufficient encouragement given by granting leases for a reasonable time (say 21 years), I consider the country might become highly improved as the land along the shore is generally good.

54. I know of no practical farmers in this neighbourhood.

55. [Linen manufacture] There is nothing in this place that deserves the name of manufacturing.

56. [Bleach greens] None.

Flax

57. [Sown on?] the land after barley or oats and sometimes the second crop after barley or oats, and sometimes the second crop after the ground has been ploughed twice, though some people sow after ploughing once. The farms are so very small that little can be spared for exportation; scarcely any seed is saved.

58. [Preparation of flax] Some by mills, but most by manual labour; fire is always used. I have often seen flax on the grass in the morning and turned into yarn before night. I think they lose the half of their flax by not handling it properly.

Yarn

59. [Linen yarn] Very coarse: I believe 2 hanks grist is considered fine, as they spin it all, flax and tow together. They sell it at from 1s 8d to 2s, so that if the spinner has to provide the flax, she must make very little indeed.

60. [Price of yarn] As above; some used for home consumption and some sold for exportation.

61. Most of the poor people have a little flax of their own.

62. [Double wheel] It has not been introduced.

63. [Preparation of yarn] The weaver, I believe, purchases the yarn green and prepares it himself. I do not know the expense of preparation, but it is, I believe, trifling.

64. [Yarn greens] There are none, nor would the establishment of such greens be any use until some person can be introduced who understands manufacturing linen.

65. [Quality of webs] Very coarse: there is a description made commonly called stinting. It cannot be finer than from seven to eight hundred. It is sold at from 8d to 10d per yard. There may be a little finer manufactured which I believe is disposed of in Derry market.

Wool and Cotton

66-68. No woollen manufacture.
69. [Knitting] I know of none.
70. I have not heard of any shearing their sheep twice.
70-71. No cotton manufactory.

Kelp and Fisheries

73-75. No kelp of any description is made here.
76. [Fisheries] Herring, cod etc.
77. Open boats, to the number of 300 or 400; the boats are but small.
78. Cod to a great extent. The fishermen go in the summer season to the distance of from 20 to 30 miles to a place called the High bank. In the winter season they take them in Lough Foyle.
79. [Numbers employed in fishing] I cannot say: a great number.
80. [Curing of fish] I have heard of none; Derry market is supplied with fresh fish and a great quantity sold in carts, carriers.
81. [Improvements] The fisheries might be very much improved by building boats of a large

description which would be able to go to sea at every season of the year, as boats of the present size can only go to sea in the summer.

NATURAL STATE

Description of the Parish

Parish of Upper Moville, situated from 9 to 14 miles north of the city of Derry, barony of Inishowen and county of Donegal, bounded on the north by the parish of Lower Moville, south by the parish of Muff, east by Lough Foyle and west by a range of mountains extending from the churchlands north to the mountains of Eachiheen south, together with part of the parishes of Culdaff, Donagh and Lower Fahan, extending from 8 to 9 miles and greatest breadth from 4 to 5 miles.

The first stream of any consequence is called Bonifoble river, which divides the parish of Upper and Lower Moville; rises in the mountains of Greencastle and discharges itself into Lough Foyle convenient to Bonifoble.

MODERN TOPOGRAPHY

Gentlemen's Seats

The first place of any consideration is Summer Hill, the residence of A. Murray; the grounds well enclosed and cultivated. The rest of the grounds in that neighbourhood unenclosed and badly cultivated.

The second small stream is called Glebe river and falls into Lough Foyle convenient to the glebe of Upper Moville, the residence of the Revd John Molesworth Staples; the grounds well enclosed and cultivated with a considerable portion of young planting which seems to be doing very well.

The next residence is that of William Thorpe Esquire; the grounds well enclosed and cultivated, and convenient to the farmhouse of Samuel Carmichael. The farm well enclosed and the only one which seems to be cultivated in anything like a practical farmer's in that neighbourhood, the rest of the ground being badly laboured and having occupiers without capital and means of improvement.

The next gentlemen's residence is that of Sir Arthur Chichester, denominated Castlecary, near to which is the small stream called Clare river, at the mouth of which there is a secure anchorage for vessels of all descriptions.

The next seat of consideration is Claremount, the property of Robert Young Esquire, at present unoccupied; the ground belonging to the house tolerably well enclosed but not cultivated either for benefit or beauty. The lands convenient is the same as the rest of the country, unenclosed and badly cultivated.

Public Buildings and Gentleman's Seat

The meeting house of Clare is near to this place, being but a small building with a small congregation; and a little farther on is the parish church of Upper Moville, a good building and in very good order, convenient to which is the village of Carrickmaquigley; and convenient is Redcastle, the stately mansion of the Revd Lucius Cary, with an extensive demesne situate upon the very shore of Lough Foyle. The demesne is well laid out and enclosed with a little natural wood which was cut down some years ago but is now thriving very well.

The ground in this neighbourhood is mostly unenclosed and badly cultivated.

NATURAL FEATURES AND MODERN TOPOGRAPHY

Cataract and Gentleman's Seat

The next stream is that of Drung <Doung>, near the mouth of which is a remarkable cataract at least 30 feet high.

The next place of note is White Castle, belonging to the heirs of the late Tristram Cary Esquire, which has lately been highly improved and a good quantity of young trees put down which seem to be thriving very well. The ground attached is well laid out and enclosed.

Cabry

There are no streams of any consequence near the place and convenient is the townland of Cabry, held by the occupying tenants in a great measure under the Marquis of Donegall, and who alone seem to enjoy any comforts on their farms, although they have now enclosed their grounds much better than their neighbours, notwithstanding a long lease caused, I presume, from the want of emulation and a good example.

The next stream is that of Carrokeel, which falls into the sea near Quigley Point, and last residence is that of Mrs Brumhall.

Natural Curiosities

There are few natural curiosities in this parish: a small lake in the vicinity of Carrickmaquigley [which] produces char, trout and the high waterfall mentioned above seem the only things worthy of notice. [Signed] Stewart Marks, curate of Upper Moville.

Printed Statistical Enquiries on the Coast Fisheries in Upper Moville

NATURAL FEATURES AND PRODUCTIVE ECONOMY

Fisheries

Question 1. Do many of the inhabitants of the maritime coast of the parish of Upper Moville apply themselves to fishing? Answer: Only those adjoining the banks of Lough Foyle.

Question 2. Are they constant or periodical fishermen? Answer: Periodical.

Question 3. Are the boats and tackle employed the absolute property of the fishermen or hired as occasion may require? Answer: Absolute property.

Question 4. Are there any banks adjacent to the coast well stocked with fish? Answer: Yes, with oysters.

Question 5. Are the deep waters near the shore generally well supplied with fish? Answer: Not so far up the lake.

Question 6. Are the shores rocky and precipitous or do they afford good landing places for nets, and convenient spots for drying fish either in bays or along sandy beaches? Answer: The shores are not precipitous and there are several inlets affording safe harbours for boats.

Question 7. Is the fishing limited by insufficiency in the number of boats? Answer: No, but the fishing is confined to the lough.

Question 8. Is the fishery limited by the want of salt or other means of curing the superfluous fish? Answer: No: herrings and occasionally a few cod are the only fish cured.

Question 9. Is fishing a favourite pursuit of the people or is it uncongenial to their habits and feelings? Answer: It is a source of profit to those who engage in it, and is their chief means of paying their rents.

Question 10. Does the fish taken form a large portion of the food of the inhabitants of the coast; is a considerable portion of it sent to inland parts of the country or to any principal market? Answer: The fish taken that are not consumed, and particularly the herrings and oysters, make a ready sale at Derry.

Question 11. Can you enumerate the edible fish which most abound at all times in the deep water or on the banks, and those which visit periodically the shores of the parish? Answer: Herrings, oysters, a few cod and salmon. This latter fishing is confined to the rector and one other resident gent[lemen].

Question 12. Can you state the periods at which the great shoals of fish arrive, and the ordinary length of their visit? Answer: Oysters from September to April; herrings from August to October in vast shoals; salmon from July to August; cod from November to February.

Table of Fishermen

Fishermen: periodical 200 men, 40 lads, 40 boys; boats, nets, lines, hooks etc.: periodical 70 boats, 280 tons, about 5 pounds each, value of nets variable.

Key: lads 12 to 17, boys under 12.

Comments on Fisheries

From the above, it will be observed that the fisheries of this parish are confined to Lough Foyle; that only a small part of the population are engaged in it and that only periodically. Their nets and tackle are absolute property. With regard to the salmon fishery, it will be seen that only 2 individuals engage in it and their rights are, at this time, being disputed by the Fishing Company of Ireland. [Signed] W.E. Delves Broughton, Lieutenant Royal Engineers, 21st November 1833.

Parish of Muff, County Donegal

Replies by William Stanay to Queries of North West Farming Society

NATURAL STATE

Situation

The parish of Muff in Donegal, being a division of Templemore, separated from it in the year 1809 by an act of parliament called the Primate's Act, contains the following townlands: Autmore [insert alternative: Ardmore], Muff, Craig-sapperg, Carnamarl [insert alternative: Carnamail], Ishahien [insert alternative: Iskahien], Drumshellan [insert alternative: Drumskellen], Ture, Aught, Threetrees and Calfiey [insert alternative: Calpey], the Treien [insert alternative: Trien] of Trimmily.

NATURAL FEATURES

Soil

The soil is rather fruitful where well cultivated, but the want of limestone or marl and the monopoly <menaphaly> of sea manures by the farmers whose farms are washed by the Foyle is injurious to them that are less favourably circumstanced.

Mountains and Rivers

The mountains are Threetrees, Glashmere, Aught, Iskeheehen hill and the Rarky hill. These mountains form a chain from the south west to the north east.

The rivers, or rather brooks, are those of Muff, Drumsallin, Ture, and Aught, as the mountains already mentioned form the north western boundary.

Plantations and Quarries

The principal plantations is that of Kilderry. There are different kinds of stone quarries in this parish. Iskaheen and Drumskellan abounds with excellent building stone. In the latter there is plenty of middling freestone. There is also a freestone quarry in Ture and an excellent quarry of paving stone on the sea-shore. The soft white freestone of the latter place is carried to Londonderry, by which several poor families are enabled to make a livelihood.

There is a slate quarry in Glashmere mountain which, if sunk to the proper depth, would be of value.

MODERN TOPOGRAPHY

Gentlemen's Seats

The mansion house of Kilderry, the residence of Lieutenant-General Hart, M.P. for the county Donegal, is the principal modern structure in the parish; next in order, the mansion house of Ture, the residence of Captain Valentine; and thirdly Muff Lodge, built by Dean Barnard when Dean of Derry, are the only buildings of notice in this parish.

Town of Muff

Muff is the principal town, another village in the parish which is neither very compact nor regular but in a state of improvement.

Scenery

The scenery is much enlivened by the River Foyle, whose western shore bounds the north east extremity of the parish, the navigation of Derry etc. Latterly the unique appearance of the steampackets plying from Glasgow to that city contribute their part to render the scene both agreeable and delightful to the north west. The range of mountains already mentioned, at seasons attracting the vapours exhaled from the northern or western ocean, render the scene rather gloomy.

Inns

The inns in the village of Muff are 4, that is Rimer's, Barr's, Dougherdey's, Johnstons; in Drumscillen McGonegal's [crossed out: McClonegals]; in Ture McColgan's.

Communications

The great road leading from Londonderry to Greencastle intersects the parish from west to north, leaving a small segment along the shore of the Foyle. The next road of note commences at John Remus' [Rimer's] in the village of Muff, running in a north western direction passing the church, the meeting house, hence to Birdstown, Burnfoot church, town of Fahan and Buncrana. There are several other roads of much importance, the chief of which branches from the great leading road at Ture and, stretching westward at a mile and a half, passes the mass house of

Iskeheen and, about 3 miles further, unites with the second road at Burnfoot, about half a mile further north in the townland of Threetrees.

Another road branches off the great road leading to Greencastle, ascends the hill and passes the police barrack from hence through Glentaker to Carndonagh <Carendonagh> and Malin, and hence to the celebrated bathing place called Malin Well, where the sea water appears to have a petrifying quality virtue, as sundry sea shells have been seen by the writer in a state of proximity to become Malin pebbles.

Muff Lodge

On the old road from Londonderry, entering the parish at the bridge of Muff on the right hand, stands the neat building of Muff Lodge built by Dean Barnard about 50 years ago with a small plantation of forest trees.

MODERN AND ANCIENT TOPOGRAPHY

Old Church

The only ancient building in the parish is the old church or rather ruin of Iskeheen.

There is 1 church, 1 meeting house and 1 mass house in the parish.

SOCIAL ECONOMY

Food

Potatoes with a little oatmeal forms the principal support of the lower class. Those who have middling beneficial farms or trades enjoy a little more of the comforts of providence. Turf is the only fuel made use of by the inhabitants, except in very few instances.

Health

As the people are generally [too?] poor to indulge the various passions, there are very few diseases. Sciatica in the old men and rheumatism pains in elderly persons of the other sex, with the diseases common to children, are most of the evils we have to complain of in that respect.

There have been several instances of persons living to 90 years, and within these last 10 years one to 103 years.

Habits of the People

As to the genius and dispositions, there are certainly several individuals who manifest considerable acuteness and penetration, and would be susceptible of great improvement if the means were offered.

In Dishalier [insert alternative: Dishlier] the people are tolerably friendly to each other and willing to assist in any case of emergency.

The language is rather a pure dialect of the English tongue, being clear of the western brogue and southern twang.

The manners of the people are generally plain and unaffected, considering their education, and they are rather agreeable.

Amusements

Christenings and marriages are generally conducted with becoming hospitality and hilarity. The wakes and funerals in most cases are conducted among the more respectable with a gravity suiting the occasion; but very generally the custom of giving liquor at the funeral of Protestants has had an injurious effect on the circumstances of the families of the deceased persons.

Education

There are 5 or 6 day and 3 Sunday schools in the parish and no established schoolhouses, so that the education of youth depends in a great measure on the precarious liberality of a few farmers.

Books

There are several private collections of books in the parish. The principal is that of Kilderry. Edward Mulherin of Ture has some papers relative to the doctrine of magnetism and the variations of the magnetic needle. He thinks he has succeeded in penetrating the mystery of the magnetic phenomena and is willing to exhibit his papers to examinations. The same person has also some papers on the theory of the weather.

His aim in the papers on magnetism is to give that systematic view of the subject mentioned in the supplement of the *Encyclopaedia Brittanica* and *Magnetism* (where see the importance of such work, article America); and from his abilities and penetration a good deal certainly may be expected.

Religion

As to our religious establishment, the principal part of the more opulent are either of the Established Church or Presbyterians. There is, however, a few exceptions but in point of number the Roman Catholic populations is equal if not superior to both. The tithe, having been raised the one-third within a few years, is considerable, on account of the cheapness of markets, as rather dear.

There is 1 church in Muff, a meeting house about a quarter of a mile and a mass house about 1 mile from Muff.

PRODUCTIVE ECONOMY

Crops

To begin: with respect to potatoes, in the winter seasons the ground is sometimes trenched and then ploughed. The potatoes at the proper seasons is then put in by what is called kibling and then laying on the manure any time before the bud appears above the surface. Some are put down in the drill way as requiring less labour, but is rendered not so favourable for the ensuing crops.

After the potato crop next comes barley then oats and flax, lastly oats, when the land requires to lie fallow, which produces very poor grass and only fit for the small Inishowen breed which is put on in [blank].

The better sort of the farmers have commenced sowing red clover and grass seed with tolerable success.

Livestock

The horses are perhaps superior to those of most other places, considering the state of the soil.

Cows are most of the old Irish breed, which on trial are considered equal, if not superior, to that of any other.

Sheep are of the small mountain breed, not well woolled and generally difficult to keep enclosed in parks.

Pigs, being mostly of the common breed, thrive well enough and are generally a profitable stock.

Fairs and Markets

We have only 1 fair in the year in the village of Muff worth mentioning, which is held on the 11th of December, where there is commonly a large show of cows and pigs, some horses and sheep, which being the last fair in the barony is frequented a good deal by butchers and those wanting beef cattle.

Wages

The wages of menservants is found to vary in proportion to their respective merit from 2 to 4 pounds per half-year, and that of women servants from 1 pound to 30s for the same time. Day labourers without diet get from 10d to 12d a day, and if fed from 5d to 6d by the day.

Trades

As to trades, we have sufficient to supply our own demands and cartmakers who also supply the neighbouring parishes.

Exports

Under the head of commerce and navigation we have no imports, and our exports are only that of the paving stones of Ture shore which largely supply the streets of Londonderry and Liverpool.

ANCIENT TOPOGRAPHY

Standing Stones

The only curiosity worth mentioning is a line of standing stones from the shore to the mountain through the townlands of Ardmore and Iskeheen, some of which are 8 or 10 feet above the surface and were doubtless designed as a line of demarcation between some of the ancient feudal chiefs.

SOCIAL ECONOMY

Remarkable Events

The most remarkable occurrence in the memory of the writer of these was an extraordinary gush of electric fluid in a thunderstorm that killed a boy and a mare in the townland of Ture. The boy was remarkable for profane swearing.

Remarkable Men

The only eminent man amongst us was Dean Barnard, who built the Lodge of Muff.

The different branches of the Hart family have filled important stations, the most so of any other family in the parish. The father of the present General Hart was the Revd Edward Hart and a magistrate. The Revd George Hart for several years resided in the parish. Captain Hart of the Royal Navy, afterwards commodore and I have been told latterly admiral, for several years resided here.

And in elder time the Revd Thomas Torrens, father of the present Judge Torrens, also lived some time in Ture. He it was baptized the writer of this note. A Captain Smyth and a Captain Skipton also resided here.

I should also have mentioned above the only son of Captain Hart, Henry, a fine interesting youth who lost his life in the Royal Navy in the late protracted struggle for empire with France.

Education

Previous to the establishment of Sunday schools in 1813, the education of the poor was much neglected; but since that time, among the Protestant children at least, gradual improvement has become visible. Grants of books and religious tracts to those schools by the Sunday School Society is also diffusing information through the families, and a taste for reading is rapidly advancing, while the sabbath day is respected.

To follow up the system of education already in use and render it permanent by the erection of schoolhouses and the appointment of proper masters with competent salaries would tend much to improve the morals of the rising generation. [Signed] William Stanay.

Parish of Tullyaughnish, County Donegal

Statistical Report by Lieutenant William Lancey, 1834

NATURAL STATE

Name and Locality

Read January 1835.

This parish derives its name from the union of 2 parishes called Tullyfernon and Athenish, the derivations of which are not known (see Dr Reid's *History of the Presbyterian church*).

It is situated on the left bank of Lough Swilly and is bounded by the parish of Aughanunchin <Aughenunchen> on the south, by Conwal and Kilmacrenan and the bay of Mulroy on the west, by Clondavaddog on the north and Killygarvan on the north east. Its extreme length north and south is 11 miles and from the parish burn to Lough Nacreaght this parish is 7 miles in breadth. That part lying south of the River Lennon was formerly Athenish, that part north of it was formerly Tully and the Roman Catholic Church still keeps the old boundary.

The union paid county cess in 1829 1,103 pounds 16s 7d, in 1830 1,090 pounds 15s 2d, in 1831 850 pounds 7s, in 1832 1,101 pounds 2s 11d, in 1833 974 pounds 3s 9d, in 1834 977 pounds 13s 8d.

NATURAL FEATURES

Hills

There are no mountains of consequence in Tullyaughnish except Glenalla, already described in Killygarvan parish. The undulations of the country seldom exceed 600 feet and usually do not attain the height of 500 [feet]. Knockalla range in Clondavaddog terminates in the north of Tully at the margin of Mulroy bay, that part of the shore to the north of it being in gentle slopes and to the south of it in rough rugged steps of small elevations.

Lough Swilly on the south and east, and the bay of Mulroy on the north and west tend materially to enliven the parish. There are considerable tracts of uncultivated and rocky ground with some levels of bog or wasteland capable of improvement.

Lakes

There are a great number of lakes at different altitudes marked on the plan: Lough Nacreaght, 675 feet above the sea, being the highest. The most remarkable thing noticed in connection with these lakes, as well as those of Killygarvan and the opposite shore of Inishowen, is the almost constant accompaniment of a basaltic dyke on their margins.

Most of the loughs have eels, some trouts, no salmon; Lough Columbkill contains very fine trouts.

Lough Fern is the principal sheet of water. It contains 460 acres and lies on the north west of the parish. The River Lennon passes through its southern end. It is 6 to 8 feet deep and rises about 4 feet at the Lammas floods. It is said the salmon do not rest in its waters but proceed at once to the Gartan loughs.

The depth of the other loughs are not known in the country and there are no means of ascertaining this information.

The islands of Mulroy belonging to this district are either dykes or strata of hornblende rock which have resisted the general destruction; and lifting their heads above the surface of the water, exhibit a chain of small isles of low elevation, the highest being 41 feet above low water mark.

The islands of Lough Swilly present nothing worthy of remark. They are 5 in number and are situated at the mouth of the Rathmelton river, all of them being accessible at low water. Aughnish Isle is 81 feet above water mark and contains 66 and a half acres (see Coast).

Rivers

The Lennon is the principal river. It flows from the Gartan loughs into Lough Fern at its southern extremity and leaves it for the sea at 1,142 feet from its entrance. It is a slow black stream about 40 feet deep at Clara bridge and, with the exception of a rocky ford above Tully bridge for half a mile, and a few deep holes, this may be taken as a mean. It flows for 5 and a half miles from Lough Fern to Rathmelton bridge into Lough Swilly in a very circuitous direction to the south east, being about 80 feet in breadth and nearly filled to the edge of the banks, being kept up by the dam of the flour and bleach mills in the townland of Bridge-End.

Opposite Rathmelton it is affected by the tide, which rises at spring 15 feet and becomes capable of receiving, at high water, vessels of 100 tons;

Parish of Tullyaughnish

but at low tides a boat cannot float from the town into the Swilly. [Insert note: The largest cargo ever brought to this port was an American one of 300 tons of timber. There is only 1 vessel of 50 tons belonging to Rathmelton].

The Lennon turns 1 flour mill, 1 bleach green mill, 2 flax mills, 2 corn or oat mills and 1 small churn mill for making butter, and might be used to any extent in machinery. It now overflows its banks at Lammas but it is said that formerly this was not the case and is attributed to the dam built at the flour mill. The land through which it flows is level and its inundations leave a rich deposit.

The parish is tolerably well watered. The chief stream next to the River Lennon is that which, after draining Glenalla and Lochrus Glebe, in 2 branches unite in Ballyconnelly and empties itself under Ray bridge into Lough Swilly. This, however, is so inconsiderable that it has been necessary to unite the 2 streams by a lead to turn the mills in Drumherve which lie below their junction.

The stream at the March burn is described in Killygarvan and there are no others of any consideration.

Bogs

Bog is becoming scarce in Tullyaughnish. It is generally of good quality and is found from 100 to 500 feet above the sea. Fir and birch, especially the former, are usually found in it broken off on the surface. Sir James Stewart's agent receives 10s a dark and Mr Darcus' agent 5s from the tenant, but Mr Watt makes no charge for fuel to his tenants.

Woods

There are considerable traces of woodland and large woods still exist. The principal is that of Glenalla and Ray, where art has added to nature and produced a very interesting woodland scenery. The Revd Mr Hart has planted a considerable number of acres about his house and demesne, where the abrupt rocky steps of Glenalla rise at high angles, and, being judiciously embellished with trees, has rendered his estate decidedly the most finished place in the neighbourhood.

Ray wood was cut about 2 years ago. Sir James Stewart's demesne is planted with fine trees and is highly ornamental to the country.

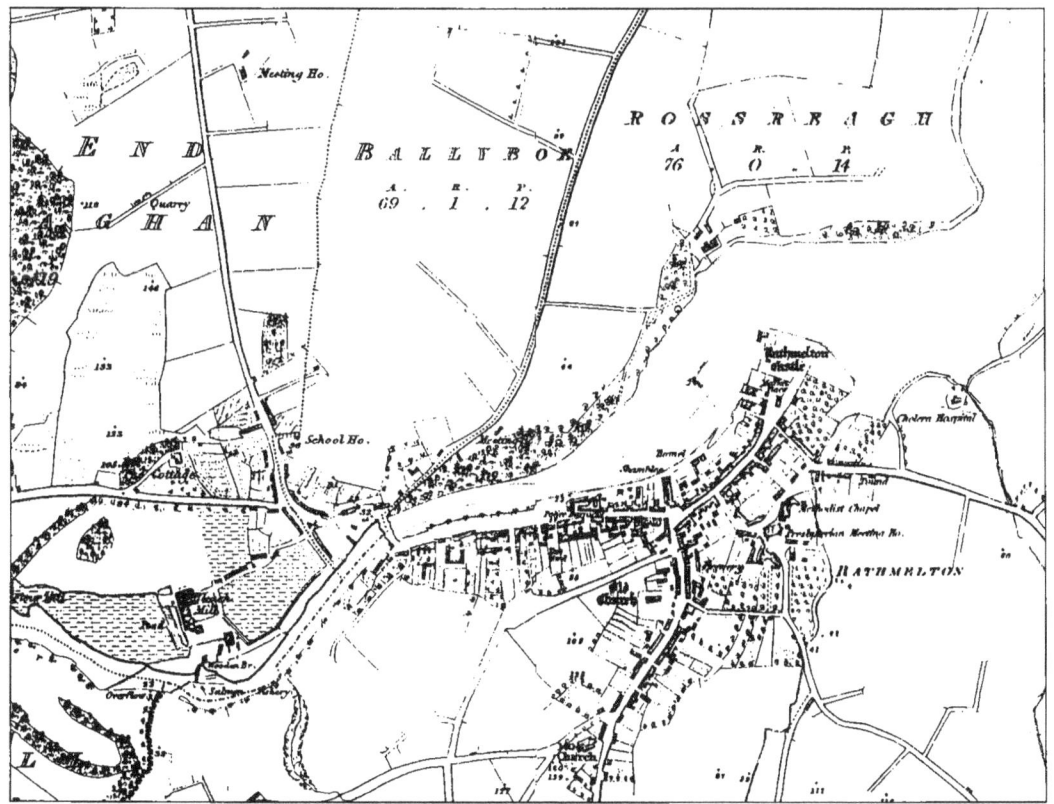

Map of Ramelton from the first 6" O.S. maps, 1830s

The other localities where woods exist are at Bridge-End close to Rathmelton, and Ballyar, 2 and a quarter miles west of it. In the latter there are 42 acres of birch, holly and alder, and in the former 77 and a half acres of oak. This wood was cut 20 years ago.

Traces of wood are found at Cratlage and other parts of the parish.

Coast

The eastern side of the parish lies on the left bank on Lough Swilly, the direction being north east and south west and, following the indentations of the shore, extends 16 miles. The principal bay is that of Rathmelton, but numerous smaller ones for boats are met with. These are only accessible at high tide, as a broad muddy strand runs round the whole coast at low water; the rise of the tide is usually 15 feet.

The largest island, called Aughnish, contains 66 and a half acres and stands at the entrance of the bay of Rathmelton; it is 81 feet high. 3 small isles, called Craig's Isles, each 16 feet high, lie between Aughnish Island and the town, and immediately north of these, on the opposite coast, is a rocky island belonging to Brown Know. All these islands are accessible from the mainland at low tide.

The shore is low, rising in gentle undulations to the interior and adorned by Sir James Stewart's mansion and demesne, Shelfield, Killydonnell Abbey, Fort Stewart, Rathmelton, Cairne, Salt Pans, with many good farmhouses, and has a general appearance of industry and comfort.

Mulroy bay on the west of the parish extends 4 miles and is the extreme end of its much varied waters. Its shores are generally accessible at high and low tide, and it contains 24 rocks and islands belonging to Tullyaughnish. Very narrow strands are exhibited at ebb tides and in consequence of the confined entrance at the Hassans in Fanad <Fannet>, larger strands are left dry at neaps than at springs. The general rise of the tide at the entrance of Mulroy is about 15 feet, at Island Roy 12 and a half feet and at Mr Hay's store at the head of the bay at Drumberne 5 feet 6 inches, and vessels of 100 tons can navigate it.

The scenery of this lough is striking and picturesque, being a fine piece of placid water studded with islands and surrounded by high and broken hills. Fishing is not practised by the inhabitants: a death-like silence pervades its shores.

About 34 Cunningham acres have been added to the townlands of Ardnaree and High Cairne, 14 of which belong to Mr Stewart and 20 to Sir James Stewart. The work was executed last year by a Scotch engineer, who received 100 pounds for his trouble.

The bank is from 30 to 40 feet thick and from 14 to 10 feet high by 1,190 feet in length and cost 400 pounds, executed by the tenants who pay 3s an acre rent on a short lease of 18 years and are not allowed to lease it for more than a guinea an acre.

Climate

The climate is very moist and changeable. The usual seasons for cutting the harvest vary from the 14th August to the 30th September.

NATURAL HISTORY

Botany

The woods are composed of oak, ash, birch and fir. Wild camomile grows at Rughan and the yellow geranium grows wild at Rathmelton ruin.

Zoology

The species of fish caught in Lough Swilly have been detailed in the Memoir of Killygarvan and comprise turbot, sole, cod, herrings. There are very few, if any, fish in Mulroy except sprats, oysters and scallops. These latter grow to a very great size and sell from 12d to 14d a dozen. The Rathmelton or Lennon river is celebrated for its salmon, which continues in season all the winter. Freshwater mussels abound in this river and produce fine pearls, which have been sold as high as 2 or 3 pounds apiece; and in one instance one was valued by a competent judge at 20 pounds.

Badgers, foxes, hares, weazels, polecats, rats etc., with the usual birds, are met with in Tullyaughnish.

Geology

The district is composed of primitive rocks of quartz, talc slate and gneiss intersected by porphyritic trap dykes running in a north east and south west direction. The strata generally rise at high angles from 70 degrees to 90 degrees. Talcose flags near the Dean's Road in Tierhoman dip 21 degrees. There are also 2 or 3 veins of flinty limestone in the parish, but they are of bad quality and very limited extent. The lime of Mullacheap burns yellow. The usual supply of the district is brought from Cranford in Kilmacrenan.

Modern Topography

Towns: Rathmelton

Rathmelton is the only town and derives its name from rath "a fort" and "mill town." It consists of 3 streets meeting in an open space in which the market is held and contains 2,026 inhabitants. It is 118 miles north of Dublin, in the diocese of Raphoe and north west circuit, and lies on the right bank of the Lennon river at its confluence with Lough Swilly. The main road from Rathmullan to Letterkenny passes through it. Its length is about 3 and a half furlongs, being prettily situated on a hill with its church on the highest point.

General History

"Sir William Stewart first obtained lands here in November 1610. They formed part of the forfeited estates of O'Donnell, of which Sir William Hansard was the first patentee. In 1618, according to Pynnar, Sir William had erected at Rathmelton a large and strong tower 80 feet square, 16 feet high with 4 flankers, and a fair strong castle, being 3 and a half storeys high, and had made a large town consisting of 45 houses, in which there are 57 families, all British. He had also begun a church of lime and stone which is built to the setting on of the roof. There is also a water mill for corn. It is a market town and standeth well for the good of the country and the king's service.

Rathmelton and its church were burned and pillaged by the Roman Catholics in the beginning of the rebellion of 1641, but the Lagan forces under Sir William recovered possession of the castle; and a few monthes after the elder branch of Sir William Stewart's descendants were ennobled with the titles of Viscount Mountjoy and Earl of Blessington, but became extinct in 1769 when the baronetage reverted to a younger branch and is now enjoyed by the present baronet, Sir James Stewart of Fort Stewart, Rathmelton" (see Dr Reid's *History of the Presbyterian church*).

The walls of the church alluded to above are yet standing, but of the castle nothing is left but a corner of the building near the mouth of the river. [Insert query: Is the castle described above that of Fort Stewart or Rathmelton?].

Present State of Town

Rathmelton is still an inferior town but is rising into prosperity. The houses have been principally rebuilt and are well covered either with Welsh or Lagan slates. Wharfs are being built on the bank of the river and some good storehouses are erected. Encouraging leases have been granted by Sir James Stewart and a new and commodious church built about 7 years ago. There is a large Presbyterian church in the town and 1 on the other side of the river, a Methodists' chapel, a brewhouse, an inferior inn, a shambles and reading room, 3 schools, and a few respectable private dwelling houses.

It is also a market town, held every Tuesday, and 2 annual fairs are held in it on 4th May and 17th July. The town is well supplied with the common necessaries of life. Messrs Watt <Watts>, Hazlett and Dunlap stall-feed cattle and good townparks are let for pasturage from 2 pounds to 3 pounds an acre. Good slates are brought from Dooish hill in the Lagan across Lough Swilly, timber from Norway and America, and lime from Cranford in Kilmacrenan parish.

There are no insurance offices in the county and in Rathmelton such means of protection are scarcely ever pursued.

A mail car leaves for Letterkenny every day at 9 o'clock, a daily running post to Rathmullan and 3 times a week to Rosnakill in Fanad. Messrs Grier, Love and Clark have post cars for hire.

The dispensary, schools, provision for poor are described under their respective heads. A cholera hospital on the bank of the lough below the town is a modern brick building capable of holding 25 patients.

Rathmelton also possesses a reading room, the members being admitted by ballot, the annual expense being 20s; also a library, the subscription to which is a guinea per annum.

Trade in Rathmelton

The trade of Rathmelton for its size is considerable. About 6 tons of dressed flax are taken weekly to Derry for about 8 months of the year, the present value of which, being 60 pounds a ton, is equal to 12,240 pounds per annum. About 3 pounds of spun yarn are sent every week to Armagh and from 80 to 180 webs sold in the market every week, according to the season in the year. About 420 weavers are employed in supplying Rathmelton, which is the best linen market in Donegal. A considerable number of webs are bought and taken to Derry to be resold. Hogs abound in the seasons.

Custom House

There is no custom house. The imports are about

1,000 tons of timber, 100 tons of salt, 500 barrels of herrings, 150 tons of slates, 200 tons coals.

The exports are about 1,000 tons of oats, 300 tons barley, 400 tons wheat annually.

Village of Milford

This village stands 4 miles north west of Rathmelton, near the southern end of Mulroy bay. It consists of 1 street on the slope of a hill, at the southern foot of which stands a large mill from whence the place derives its name. It is an ancient village and has been much improved in late years. Several good substantial houses have been built on the churchland property.

It contains a barrack for the revenue police, a tannery, a timber and coalyard, a school on Erasmus Smith's foundation, and the mill is the finest I have yet seen, having an iron wheel of 18 feet diameter and 4 feet in breadth supplied by a chain of loughs to the east of the village. The mill has lately been rebuilt and the metal wheel put in motion this year.

Mr Hay, the chief exporter of grain, resides in Milford and imports timber, coals. [Insert marginal note: Mr Hay exports about 600 tons of oats, 350 tons barley annually, valued at 12,000 pounds].

Mr Levens holds the mill and a tannery which dresses 500 hides worth 15s to 20s green, 2 pounds 2s 6d tanned; 400 calfskins worth 1s green, 2s 6d tanned.

2 stone tigers' heads at his gateway were brought from Rosapenna House in Rosguill, once the residence of Lord Boyne but now totally destroyed by drifting sand.

There are 8 fairs in Milford annually.

Public Buildings: Rathmelton Church

The new church was built in the year 1837 at an expense of 2,500 pounds and is, next to Derry Cathedral, the most complete place of worship I have seen in the north of Ireland. It contains 366 sittings. The centre is fitted up with forms with backs and cushions. The sides are pewed and there is a gallery at the west end. The service is well attended and performed by 2 ministers. Mr Nixon of Strabane was the architect and he took 12 months to build it.

Presbyterian Meeting House

This meeting house was erected in 1798 by the congregation at their own expense; it cost 1,000 pounds. It is double-roofed, is about 80 feet long and 50 feet wide, with 3 galleries, and can contain 1,400 people in pews. The congregation consists of 2,400; stipend 80 pounds, regium donum 100 pounds per annum.

Seceding House

Seceding house stands in Rossreagh, half a mile from town, on the road from Rathmullan. It was built in 1807 by the congregation at a cost of 280 pounds, is 55 feet long and 25 feet wide, and can contain 350 persons in pews. The congregation consists of 774 persons; stipend 50 pounds, regium donum 70 pounds.

Methodist Chapel

This building was erected in 1801 and cost 180 pounds, and can hold 200 people. There are, however, few Methodists in the neighbourhood.

Covenanting Meeting Houses

That near Rathmelton stands a quarter of a mile south of the Seceders' house in Rughan. It was built in 1810 and cost 250 pounds. It is 55 feet long and 25 feet broad, and can contain 400 persons. The inside is not yet completed. Divine worship is performed in this house only every third sabbath, as there is but 1 minister and he has to officiate at Letterkenny and Ballygay near Milford.

The Ballygay house was erected in 1794 at an expense of 220 pounds and is of the same dimensions as Rughan. The aggregate number of Covenanters who attend divine worship in these 2 houses is 874 individuals. Several of them live in Killygarvan and Fanad. The minister does not accept the regium donum. His stipend is 70 pounds.

Carrowkeel Meeting House

Carrowkeel meeting house lies at the north west end of the parish. It was re-erected in 1777 and cost 430 pounds, and can contain 700 worshippers. The house is 56 by 46 feet without a gallery.

Roman Catholic Chapels

About 1 mile from Rathmelton, on the road to Fort Stewart in the townland of Killycreen, stands Killycreen chapel. It was built in 1833 at the expense of 230 pounds. Its dimensions are 68 feet by 30 feet, having an aisle of 26 by 24 feet, and can contain 1,300 persons.

In Lochrus Glebe, in the Roman Catholic parish of Tully, stands the Lagg chapel, erected in 1829 at an expense of 300 pounds. The building can contain 1,200 worshippers, the congregation of Tully being about 3,000.

There is also a chapel in Cratlage where mass is occasionally performed.

Gentlemen's Seats

Fort Stewart, the house and demesne of Sir James Stewart Bart, is the principal residence in Tullyaughnish. It stands on the banks of Lough Swilly and was built by Mr Brooke <Brooks> and called Brookhall for a considerable time. Sir James holds it for lives renewable forever at a rent of about 150 pounds, the lease having been obtained by his grandfather from H.V. Brooke, the member for the county. The house is whitewashed, is 3-storeys high and contains a good library. The demesne comprises about 200 acres of land with good gardens and the income of the proprietor is upwards of 4,000 pounds a year.

The Glebe House was built by Dr Ussher, the present incumbent, about 8 years ago and cost 6,000 pounds. It contains the best library in the county. The house is a stolid mass of building with good stables, garden and orchards, standing about 220 feet above the sea, in about 120 acres of ornamental grounds. Dr Ussher's income is 1,100 pounds and 4 glebes, worth about 400 pounds more.

Glenalla, the property of Revd Mr Hart, was built 20 years ago by Dr Hume, the Dean of Derry. It belonged to General John Murray's family, and this townland and one in Fanad were purchased by Mr Hart for 2,000 pounds. Glenalla pays 200 pounds a year to the proprietor. The house is now being enlarged. It is well situated in a romantic spot but its architecture is of the most common kind. It stands in 180 acres of ornamental ground and woodlands, and commands a fine view of Lough Swilly and its adjacent shores.

Ballyar House belonged to a bleach green and is a good whitewashed house of 2 storeys high.

Ballyar is a slated house of 1-storey high connected with the adjoining bleach green.

Shelfield is pleasantly situated on the bank of Lough Swilly, north of Sir James Stewart's demesne.

Carnisk is a neat cottage and farm with orchard, and requires no detailed description.

Claragh is the residence of Mr Watt of the bleach green. The house is 3-storeys high, has 2 orchards and the grounds are extensively farmed and well planted and fenced. It was built by Mr Watt's father in 1796 and cost 800 pounds.

The Lodge in Bridge-End, the residence of Miss Watt, was built 20 years ago, cost 200 pounds. It is a neat cottage.

Bleach Greens

The green on the Lennon river is the only one at present at work in the parish. It employs 12 individuals, being only one-third of the number formerly at work when this branch of trade was in a flourishing state. It is in Sir James Stewart's estate and is conducted by Mr Watt. He bleaches about 1,200 pieces a year, about one-fourth only of the work of the mill in 1826.

Brewery

A good ale and beer brewery in Rathmelton employs 7 men and brews about 1,200 barrels of ale and beer annually.

Mills

Above the bleach green there is an excellent flour mill belonging to Mr Watt. It has an undershot wheel of [blank] feet in diameter and turns 3 pairs of stones. It is the only flour mill in the country.

[Table contains the following headings: situation, type, diameter and breadth of wheels, remarks].

Bridge-End, flour, undershot; Carrowkeel, corn; Drumherve, corn and flax, 14 feet by 18 feet, 12 feet by 22 feet; Moyle, corn and flax; Rubbleshinny, corn; Milford, corn; Aughnish, flax; Cashel, corn; Newmills, corn, 18 feet by 4 feet (iron), 3 pairs of stones, 2 grinding, 1 shelling; Ballygay, corn, flax; Cratlage, flax; Tullyhall, corn, flax, 10 feet by 2 feet, flax 7s a cwt if unbroken, 5s if broken; Ballyar, corn; Castleshanaghan, corn, 12 feet by 24 inches.

A good pair of millstones are [were] brought from Donegal and deposited in this parish by Mrs Walker for 4 guineas.

Communications

The principal road is the mail line from Letterkenny through Rathmelton to Rathmullan. It is kept in tolerable repair, is about 45 feet in breadth and, like all the roads of this parish, is paid for by the county.

The leading roads from Rathmelton by Milford to Kilmacrenan and Fanad are also good and generally the roads are kept in very tolerable repair.

Bridges

Ray bridge was built in 1764 and cost [blank]. Tully bridge was built in 1800 and cost [blank].

Drummond bridge was built in the year [blank], cost [blank]; it has good arches. Rathmelton bridge was built in the year 1894 [sic] and cost [blank]; it has 3 good arches. Bridge-End bridge was built in 1808 at a cost of 200 pounds. All these bridges were paid for by the county.

Claragh bridge was executed by Mr Watt in 1807 at his own expense for the accommodation of the bleach green and cost [blank]. Besides the above, there are bridges called Drummond, Crooked, Glashock, Headly and Walker's, which do not require particular description.

Ferry

Fort Stewart ferry, the property of Sir James Stewart, is well conducted and worth 400 pounds per annum. Laden carts, carriages, horses, cattle and passengers are passed over with the greatest expedition. The tolls are collected on the Tully side, 3d for a man, 5d for a horse. Good cattle and other boats are constantly ready on each side [of] the water.

ANCIENT TOPOGRAPHY

Killydonnell Abbey

[Drawing of north east window in wall, with decorative stones, overall height 19 feet by 6 feet, with gravestones within the walls; detail drawing of window with decorated head].

Killydonnell Abbey, south of Sir James Stewart's, is beautifully situated on the left bank of Lough Swilly and commands from its eastern window a striking view of the lough to Inch Island and the mountains of Inishowen, seen over the woods of Fort Stewart. Killydonnell has been the burial place of the Stewart family since they possessed the estate.

Of its past history, not having the works of reference to examine, I am enabled to say little. It is, like any other old church in the north of Ireland, said to have been founded by Columba [crossed out: Columbkill]. The O'Donnells endowed the abbey and buried their family in it. It also is supposed to have been a monastery, but of what order of friars I have not heard.

The ruin consists of a large church with a handsome eastern window, a return or chapel to the south. To the north are the remains of the dwelling apartments built on arched crypts, 2 of which only remain, one being the Stewarts', the other a cowhouse.

The architecture is Gothic, the materials of the walls rough, the pointed arches turned with thin slates and the windows of cut freestone and limestone. The cornices and chiselled work are in good preservation and some of the plaster still adheres to the interior walls.

It is still used as a burial place for the Roman Catholic population and is esteemed a place of peculiar sanctity.

[Drawings: profile of moulding at Killydonnell in blue limestone; detail of pattern of vine leaves on stone springers of east window].

Old Churches

The old church of Aughnish stood in the island of that name at the entrance of the bay of Rathmelton. The tradition respecting it, extant in the country, is that it also was founded by Columbkill and fell into the hands of the Protestants at the Reformation, and divine service performed in it till 1618. It is reported by Bishop Knox in 1610 to have been then in ruins and then only accessible by water. This is still the case at high tide, but there is a road over the strand to it at every ebb.

The trace of the building is now only visible. About 40 years ago it stood 3 feet from the ground but was destroyed to procure building materials. Half the churchyard was added to a circular field, once the only grazing park in Aughnish. The most remarkable feature connected with this burial place is the remains of bodies lying in white cockle shells, similar to the shells of Killygarvan bay.

Bodies are sometimes found in stone-built coffins which evidently, after their introduction into them, have been filled up with shells. A piece of an old bell (sent to Mountjoy) was dug up in this yard lately.

Tully old church was erected, as tradition states, by St Columba. It was in ruins before the Reformation, but after that date the Protestant church was erected on its site and divine worship performed in it until about 80 years ago, when the union of the parishes of Aughnish and Tully took place and the church of Rathmelton became the parish church. No vestige of the building is now to be seen.

Glenalla Church

In the Down Survey a church is shown in the townland of Glenalla, but no tradition of its having ever existed remains among the inhabitants. Its locality, however, can be traced by the name of the mountain of Glenalla, which is also called Mass hill, and a large stone 10 feet high by 8 feet long, said to be the place of performing the ceremony in Elizabeth's time, and called "a church stone," still exists in Glenalla. There is also an altar at which the Roman Catholics performed penance, prayers etc. about 2 years ago.

Rathmelton Old Church

This church alluded to [above] was unroofed when the new one was completed and the 4 walls are standing in good preservation. The eastern window is said to have been that of the old church at Aughnish Island and tradition states that one of the stones could not be found at the time of its removal, and its place was supplied in re-erecting the window. Some years ago the lost stone was discovered amidst the ruins in the island.

Burial Grounds

There are old places of burial in Drumatrummon, Kilwary and Milford.

Rathmelton Castle

At the north end of the town, and close to the entrance of the river, stands the ruins of an old castle said to have belonged to the O'Donnells, baronial princes under O'Donnell, King of Donegal. This family is said to have resided here from the 5th century to the accession of James VI of Scotland to the throne of England and in the rebellion of Ireland had their lands confiscated which, together with the castle, fell into the hands of the Stewart family in 1610.

Nothing remains of this castle but an angle of the building near the entrance gate. [Drawing of castle, dimensions of walls at right angles 24 feet by 12 feet].

Dr Hunter of Rathmelton, in whose field the ruin stands, informed me he dug up the foundation of the walls and gave me the subjoined plan: [drawing]. He stated the walls were grouted, having first layers of sand laid between the stones. The cement in the ruin is shell-lime. Evident traces of fire were discovered on the burnt timbers.

A modern attached cellar contained a number of burnt bottles, and some bones, said by Dr Hunter to be those of deer, were dug up within the walls of the castle.

In the small window which flanked the gate are the remains of the lead which held 3 iron bars.

The blue limestone window, stools and cut stone are probably from Rathmullan.

Dr Hunter stated the description of the castle given [in] Dr Reid's work is intended for Fort Stewart and not for Rathmelton.

[Insert note: The family of Stewart is now intermarried with the legal descendants of O'Donnell. Lady Stewart's father's (Mr Mansfield's) great-grandmother was O'Donnell, whose mother lived in the lands now Sir James Stewart's. The nearest male heir of the O'Donnell family is Sir Neal O'Donnell of Lakefield in Connaught].

Fort Stewart

The drawing of the round tower on the sheet opposite represents the remains of Fort Stewart on the shore of Lough Swilly near the ferry. I have no information respecting it: [drawing of tower].

[Drawings of cromlechs in Gortnavernon and Trumpadisha, dimensions of the latter 5 feet 7 inches high, 4 feet wide].

Danish Forts

2 exist in the townland of Gortnaverne, 1 in Tierhomen, called Ballyboe Fort, 1 in Kerrowkeel, Ranny, Ballyarr, Aughnish, Fort Stewart, Killydonnell, Ardnaree, Claggan, Killwary Rae, and 2 in Glentidally. The Granny's Bed in Gortnaverne consists of 5 stones thus: [drawing].

Other Remains

A giant's grave in Claggan, with standing stones in Glenalla, Glentidally, Lochrus, Dunmore, Lower Glen, Claragh, Carrowcastle, Fort Stewart, Cornarnd [Cornarnel] and the celebrated stone of Trumpadisha in Ranny, and the chair of St Columb near the lough of his name in Kilwary, complete the antiquities of Tullyaughnish.

Trumpadisha is the stone from whence St Columbkill "banished" the rats from Fanad, and none were known to live there until this stone unfortunately was removed in 1765 [insert note: Captain Skipton and Andrew Patton through mere wantonness]. The chair of the saint is a rude stone on the margin of the lough.

MODERN TOPOGRAPHY

General Appearance and Scenery

This parish is very extensive and presents various aspects in the landscape, from cultivated to wild, from level to precipitous. Its general features are long sweeps of land of uniform slope broken occasionally by rough ridges of rock, which in this neighbourhood rise at high angles and run for considerable distances through the cultivated country. The old parish of Aughnish does not attain to any great height and lies in gentler undulations than that of Tully, where towards Moyle hill and the bay of Mulroy the land becomes much broken and the ridge of Glenalla rises into almost perpendicular steps to the height of 1,132 feet.

The number of lakes and the shores of Mulroy and Lough Swilly vary and enhance the beauty of the scenery, added to which the woodlands, rivers, residences and town, with considerable tracts of cultivation, tend to embellish it, but there are many wastes, tracts of rocks, bad drainage, with much poverty, which show this district has not attained to that state to which it might be brought.

Social Economy

Table of Schools

[Table contains the following headings: name of townland, number of pupils subdivided by religion and sex, how supported, income of master, when established].

Tyrhoman, 74 Protestants, 26 Roman Catholics, 68 males, 37 females, total 100; supported by London Hibernian Society, the payments of children; the society grant varies according to number and progress of children; established 1828.

Milford, 61 Protestants, 24 Roman Catholics, 44 males, 41 females, total 85; supported by Erasmus Smith's fund, from which teacher gets 20 pounds per annum, besides a yearly gratuity as above, and pay of some of the children; established 1814.

Rathmelton parish school, 44 Protestants, 31 Catholics, 53 males, 22 females, total 75; supported by Robertson's donation of 11 pounds 1s 6d per annum and the payment of children, about 12 pounds per annum, and a house; established time immemorial.

Rathmelton, 84 Protestants, 36 Roman Catholics, total 120, all females; supported by London Hibernian Society, the payments of children; the society grant varies according to number and progress of children; established 1824.

Rathmelton, 56 Protestants, 19 Roman Catholics, 63 males, 12 females, total 75; supported by pay of children, formerly under Kildare Street Society; established 1820.

Brown Know, 77 Protestants, 43 Roman Catholics, 58 males, 62 females, total 120; supported by London Hibernian Society, the payments of children; the society grant varies according to number and progress of children; established 1827.

Glenalla, 103 Protestants, 84 Roman Catholics, 76 males, 111 females, total 187; boys' teacher receives 5 pounds per annum from Mr Hart, girls' mistress 8 pounds from Ladies' Hibernian Society, and a gratuity according to number and proficiency of children, who pay nothing; established 1810.

Glentidally, 51 Protestants, 18 Roman Catholics, 46 males, 23 females, total 69; supported by pay of children, formerly under Kildare Street Society; established 1826.

Glenlary, 93 Protestants, 38 Roman Catholics, 77 males, 54 females, total 131; supported by Methodist Society and pay of children; established 1833.

Kerrokeel, 62 Protestants, 14 Roman Catholics, 51 males, 25 females, total 76; supported by London Hibernian Society and pay of children, house in bad repair; established 1821.

From the curate of the parish.

Early Improvements

The small bay of Rathmelton, so capable of defence, with the fisheries of the lough and the River Lennon appear to have been the chief causes of the site having been chosen by its ancient proprietors for the erection of their stronghold; and in the settlement of Ulster Rathmelton was planted with 57 British families.

Local Government

There are 3 magistrates in the parish, viz. Sir James Stewart, Dr Ussher and Mr Hazlett, aided by an officer and 4 police constables. There are 20 revenue police under an officer at Milford. Petty sessions are held in Rathmelton every alternate Thursday, but court leets formerly held for the manors of Rathmelton, Fanad and Fort Stewart have been discontinued for the last 5 years.

The crimes of the district are those considered of a common nature and on the decrease. The country is remarkably quiet: illicit distillation is decreasing; but little, if any, other kind of smuggling is carried on. The coastguard station of Mevagh prevents the introduction of contraband goods by sea via Mulroy, and that of Crowris in Fanad and the Rathmullan station watch the line of coast in Lough Swilly.

Dispensary

There is only 1 dispensary, established on the 8th

Parish of Tullyaughnish

December 1813. Its officers are a treasurer, secretary and surgeon. The custom is to give a ticket to a patient for 12 months, which is of great advantage to the poor. The diseases are typhus, fever, pulmonary consumption, fevers, indigestion and the usual complaints of the country. The present surgeon is Dr Hunter of Rathmelton, who receives 50 pounds a year.

Schools

There are 10 schools under the patronage of societies (see table) and [blank] schools not receiving this advantage. About one-half of the people are Presbyterians, who usually educate their children in the elements of religion; and as the endowed schools all use the Bible there is no doubt that a perceptible improvement in the moral habits of the people must continue to take place.

Poor

There are no almshouses or places of refuge for the poor. The ladies of Rathmelton conduct a poor shop and a loan fund on the usual principles. There is also a temperance society and religious lending library.

Religion

Of the 2,026 inhabitants of Rathmelton, there are 284 Church, 678 Presbyterians, 124 Seceders, 940 Roman Catholic worshippers. The general census of the parish, by the last year's enumerators' lists, is for Aughnish, 458 Church, 1,530 Presbyterians, Seceders and Covenanters, and 2,638 Roman Catholics; for Tully, 267 Church, 2,342 Presbyterians, 849 Seceders and Covenanters, and 2,638 Roman Catholics.

The rector receives 1,500 pounds a year, the Presbyterian minister a stipend of 80 pounds and regium donum of 100 pounds, the Seceding minister a stipend of 50 pounds with 70 pounds regium donum and the 2 Roman Catholic priests of Tully and Aughnish (the union not having taken place in the Roman Catholic Church) are paid in the usual manner by the people.

Habits of the People

Cottages of 2-storeys high are not uncommon, but the general appearance of most of them is far from clean or comfortable. The tenantry of Sir James Stewart appear to be highly respectable and far superior to the general run.

Stone cabins of 2 rooms, seldom slated, of 1-storey high with glass windows, constitute the usual habitations. Their food is potatoes, milk and oatmeal with fish occasionally in those families who live on the coast and have boats. They live to a good old age.

Beal Tinne is kept up and the people resort to the bridge at the March burn described in the Memoir of Killygarvan. They go 3 times a year to a well near Tully churchyard, go round it 3 times and hang rags on the bushes as memorials of their cures. They also frequent Doon Well in Kilmacrenan.

Emigration

The number of individuals who left this parish in 1834 cannot evenly be determined, but in addition to those who emigrated from the left bank of Lough Swilly by way of Derry, no less than 500 between Letterkenny and Fanad took their passage for America this season at the offices of Letterkenny and Rathmelton.

A good many go to England and Scotland for the harvest, leaving part of their family at home to take care of their crop.

Remarkable Events

There are no remarkable events, persons or occurrences connected with Tullyaughnish that I have heard of.

PRODUCTIVE ECONOMY

Manufacturing or Commercial

Flax, hand-spinning and weaving are common but are fast falling into decay, in consequence of the little encouragement and small prices. Yard-wide linen is usual and sells in the market from 14d to 2s 6d a yard, at an average rate of 200 pounds a week. Druggets are manufactured for home use and bring 2s a yard and flannels from 13d to 14d.

There are 2 brickfields in Breachy on a limited scale for country purposes.

A great quantity of salt was formerly manufactured at the Salt Pans in Ray, but in consequence of the duty having been taken off that article of commerce, the works have fallen into decay.

Rural: Proprietors

The names of the landed proprietors will be found in the Name Book. The principal are Sir James Stewart, Lord Leitrim (who possesses the Trinity College lands) and Mr Irvin. Sir James collects his rents immediately around Fort Stewart and Mr Sproul those of his other estates. Mr Sproul resides in Rathmelton and collects the rents of other proprietors, receiving 5 pounds per cent. About 20 persons hold farms above 50 acres, the average size from 10 to 15 to 20 acres, at rents varying from 8s to 24s the Cunningham acre.

Mr Fullerton of Glencairn holds under Sir James Stewart 150 acres, 60 of which are arable, the tenure being 60 years and 3 lives. Church property is let in the usual term of 9 years.

Farming

The soil about the town is of a middling quality and is not generally good in the parish. About one-tenth of the farmers are respectable in their circumstances and a few independent yeoman. Mr Dill lets land on the conacre system for 4 pounds an acre. The fields are moderately well laid out and larger than usual, but badly fenced with stone walls or banks without hedges. County cess and tythe are the only local taxes.

The farm buildings are neither good nor commodious and are kept in repair by the tenants. There are no farms as examples to the people.

Shells from the banks in Lough Swilly with compost are the usual manures, but they do not answer well for the nature of the soil and are getting into disuse. Lime is not much employed and there is no stone nearer than Cranford <Cranfort> in Kilmacrenan. Seaweed is common but seldom purchased.

One-horse carts are usual. There are a few iron ploughs and oxen are harnessed by Mr Watt of Claragh. There are no threshing machines in the parish.

Seed and Produce

The average seed and crops of farm produce are thus: potatoes, seed 15 measures, produce 200 measures, value 11 to 15 pounds, at 1s 6d a measure.

Wheat, seed 15 stone, produce 180 stone, value 8 to 15 pounds.

Barley, seed 12 stone, produce 140 stone, value 8 pounds.

Oats, seed 18 stone, produce 126 stone, value 5 to 6 pounds.

Flax, seed 36 gallons Riga, 28 gallons York, 30 gallons Dutch, produce 40 stone, fit for hackling, average value 10 pounds; potatoes again.

Produce and Exports

Agriculture is improving. The produce is taken to Rathmelton and Letterkenny, and a considerable quantity is bought on commission for exportation. Mr Hay of Milford annually forwards to Greenoch, Campbelltown <Campletown> and Glasgow no less than 600 tons of oats and 350 of barley, valued at 12,000 pounds. He has a sloop of 47 tons continually employed during the season and hires others. His stores are in Drumberne in Mulroy bay.

Mr Moses Spencer of Rathmelton exports grain in considerable quantities to England, bringing back goods and using his sloop of 60 tons in the Scotch herring fishery during the winter.

Farmers

Many farmers have small fields of clover and keep from 2 to 8 cows each, enabling them to sell 60 or 70 lbs of butter in the season.

Farmers are getting poorer every year. They complain of rent and taxes generally.

About one-half the population is Protestant. Few kill a beast at Christmas as formerly, some only a fat pig but the generality of the people are contented with an occasional fowl or a few pounds of meat on great festivals.

Mr Watt of Claragh farms about 250 acres of land in a superior style and sends fat cattle to England every year. He employs 40 labourers at 10d a day.

Grazing

Sir James Stewart grazes 30 or 40 head of cattle at 3 guineas a head, but there are no farms exclusively kept for this purpose. Irrigation is continually practised. Sheep are not extensively fed, the increase of grain having diminished this article of farming, and the uplands are too limited and too rough for good sheep-walks. A few are generally purchased in the autumn and sold again in the spring.

Wages

Menservants receive 3 pounds, women 1 pound a half-year and are obliged to work in the fields, spring and autumn. Cowherds receive 20s a season. All these servants are fed at the farmer's expense. Some keep cotters, to whom they give an acre of corn land, a cow's grass, half a rood of flax and 1 day's cutting of turf for 4 pounds a year.

Cattle

Ayr and Devon, with some of the old Irish breeds,

Parish of Tullyaughnish

sadly crossed and mixed, are the usual cattle. The Irish are the best for milk. A good cow sells from 5 to 10 pounds.

Good horses for 20 pounds are to be met with about Rathmelton and numbers of small good ponies from Scotland and the Isle of Rathlin, crossed with the country breed, can be had from 5 to 7 pounds a head.

Uses made of Bogs

The bogs are grazed and used for fuel. The tenants consume it in the parish but turf is becoming scarce. It is conveyed from Glenalla to Ray bridge and boated to Whale Head. It is sold in Rathmelton for 2s 6d a car, with a large box on it called a "box cart." Fir timber is very common and is occasionally used for cabins.

Drainage

Every facility exists for draining the country. Lough Fern might easily be emptied at its normal end and, by making a new channel for the Lennon river for 1,140 feet, many acres of land might be reclaimed.

Planting

Larch grows best but it has been little tried. Mr Watt of Claragh and Mr Hart of Glenalla are the most extensive planters. Much wasteland now of no use whatever might be most profitably covered with trees.

The timber of the district does not supply its demands, but Mr Stewart of Rathmelton imports fir, deals from America and Norway. About 1,000 tons of timber are annually received into the parish.

Sea-Coast

There is no kelp made on the coast of Lough Swilly or Mulroy bay in this parish. Between Ray bridge and Rathmelton there are 38 boats, from Rathmelton to Whale Head 21; from thence to Ballgreen <Ballygreen> 8; from Ballgreen to the Ferry House 33; from thence to Castlegrove 11; and at Aughnish Island 6; making 117 boats, besides a decked pleasure yacht of Sir James Stewart's and 2 or 3 row-boats.

24 boats are provided with 7 herring nets each, which require 120 men and lads to manage the boats, nets and tackle belonging to fishermen or persons who employ them; but the supply of fish is uncertain and this once lucrative trade has fallen into great decay. The price of herrings is about 4s 6d a hundred.

Deep-sea fishing is partly carried on adjacent to the shores of the parish, where small codlings and flounders are taken, but no boats venture out to the banks outside Lough Swilly. Oysters and scallops are occasionally dredged but the trade of fishing appears to be carried on more for the supply of the fishermen's families than for the supply of the markets.

The seasons for the varieties of fish have been enumerated in the Memoirs of Killygarvan and Desertegney. The principal trawling ground in Lough Swilly is opposite Buncrana, but herrings are taken in every part of it from Fanad lighthouse to the head of the lough. Inch Island opposite to Rathmullan is celebrated for small oysters but they are seldom seen on this coast for sale, being principally consumed in Derry.

River Fishery

The Lennon is celebrated for salmon and trout. The former is in season in the winter, when salmon is not to be had elsewhere, and sells from 16d to 17d a lb. The fishery is close to Rathmelton and is superintended by Mr Watts for Sir James Stewart, and produces 200 pounds per annum profit.

General Remarks on Economy

Tullyaughnish requires resident landlords and ready money, consolidated farms, planting and draining. From its natural position it ought to become a valuable district. Lough Swilly and Mulroy present facilities for introducing coals, manufactories and every requisite, and carrying away its surplus produce.

The former is considered to be by naval men one of the best harbours in the British dominions. The Saldanha rock is the only danger to its navigation and vessels of any burden in any weather can ride in safety in it. Smaller vessels can be beached in perfect safety in sand or muddy flats. The navigation of Mulroy is difficult but not dangerous. Machinery could be advantageous[ly] set at work on the bank of the Lennon.

The soil has been already alluded to as indifferent; cultivation has been carried to 734 feet above the sea. The central parts lying between the loughs are much exposed to the north west gales. Roads might easily be made decidedly good.

DIVISIONS

Manors

There are 3 manors in Tullyaughnish, called Fort

Stewart, Fanad and Rathmelton, which comprise the following townlands, viz. statistics of Tullyaughnish, barony of Kilmacrenan, county Donegal. Total cultivated acreage 15,467 acres 2 roods 17 perches, uncultivated 10,501 acres 19 perches, water 286 acres 2 roods 23 perches, total 26,255 acres 1 rood 19 perches. [Signed] W. Lancey, Lieutenant Royal Engineers, 20th April 1835 [to] Lieutenant T.A. Larcom.

Townlands

Rathmullan, 12th August 1834. List of townlands in the parish of Tullyaughnish. [Table contains the following headings: name of townland, proprietor, tenure, manor].

Ballygay, Charles Hamilton, in fee simple.

Loughrus Glebe, Dr Ussher, incumbency while rector of Tully.

Legmuckaduff, Humphrey Babington, fee simple.

Magherydrummon, Solomon Darcus, lease for years under the see of Raphoe.

Aughill, Solomon Darcus, lease for years under the see of Raphoe.

Loughnakey, Humphrey Babington, fee simple.

Glenkeen, Thomas Brooke, fee simple.

Farquar, Nathaniel Stewart, fee simple.

Moyle and Moyle Hill, Mr Hazlett, Mrs Swiney, Mr Watt, leases for years under the see of Raphoe.

Blackland, Mr James Malseed, held by lease from James Watt, who holds under the see of Raphoe toties quoties conversant for renewal.

Moyagh, representatives of the late Daniel Swiney, lease for years under the see of Raphoe.

Tullybeg, the representatives of the late Charles Hazlett, Solomon Darcus, lease for years under the see of Raphoe.

Tullymore, Solomon Darcus, lease for years under the see of Raphoe.

Tully Mountain, Mr Watt, lease for years under the see of Raphoe.

Tully Hall, James Watt, lease for years under the see of Raphoe.

Clooneymore, Solomon Darcus, lease for years under the see of Raphoe.

Drummon, Solomon Darcus, lease for years under the see of Raphoe.

Ballyarr and Glebe, [crossed out: Thomas] Brooke, fee simple, the late Mr Patterson's heirs, fee simple; Glebe, Revd Dr Ussher, incumbency while rector of Tully.

Mullocheap, Daniel McCay, fee simple.

Milford, Earl of Leitrim, lease for years under Trinity College, Dublin.

Aughanurshin, Humphrey Babington, fee simple.

Rossgarrow, Earl of Leitrim, lease for years under Trinity College, Dublin.

Drumbern, Earl of Leitrim, lease for years under Trinity College, Dublin.

Rubbalshinny, Humphrey Babington, fee simple.

Killiveny, Earl of Leitrim, lease for years under Trinity College.

Claggan, Earl of Leitrim, lease for years under Trinity College.

Garrygart, Earl of Leitrim, lease for years under Trinity College.

Tierhomin, Earl of Leitrim, lease for years under Trinity College.

Garamore, Earl of Leitrim, lease for years under Trinity College.

Gortnaverne, Earl of Leitrim, lease for years under Trinity College.

Ranney, William Wray, fee simple.

Dunmore, Sir James Stewart, fee simple.

Drumatrummon, Thomas Brooke, James Foster, fee simple to fee farm.

Kerokeel, Sir James Stewart, fee simple, manor of Fanad.

Gortcally, Sir James Stewart, fee simple, manor of Fanad.

Cratlage, Earl of Leitrim, fee simple.

Clooney, Sir James Stewart, fee simple, manor of Rathmelton.

Breaky, Sir James Stewart, fee simple, manor of Rathmelton.

Rathmelton, Sir James Stewart, fee simple, manor of Rathmelton.

Aughahull, part of the lands of Aughnish, Sir James Stewart, lease for years under the see of Raphoe; the bishop's manor to which the tenants are bound to do service are Court and Portleen.

Ballybokeel, part of the lands of Aughnish, Sir James Stewart, lease for years under the see of Raphoe.

Ballyyelly, Sir James Stewart, lease for years under the see of Raphoe.

Killicreen, Thomas Brooke, fee simple.

Aughanagaddy Glebe, Dr Ussher, incumbency while rector of Aughnish.

Rough Park, Sir James Stewart, fee simple, manor of Fort Stewart.

New Mill, Glenlary, Sir James Stewart, fee simple, manor of Fort Stewart.

Glenlary, Sir James Stewart, fee simple, manor of Fort Stewart.

Parish of Tullyaughnish

Newtownfore, Mrs Brooke, fee simple.

Castle Shanaghan, Mrs Brooke, fee simple.

Ardrumndon, part Captain Mansfield, heirs of the late Thomas Patterson, heirs of the late Hugh Armstrong, fee simple.

Carrowcastle, Sir James Stewart, fee simple, manor of Fort Stewart.

Kern Hill, Sir James Stewart, [crossed out: Mrs Brooke], fee simple.

Prablin, Sir James Stewart, fee simple.

Killydonnell, Sir James Stewart, held by lease for lives renewable forever under Thomas Brooke.

Kerrygalt, heirs of the late Thomas Leckey, held by lease for lives renewable forever under Thomas Brooke.

Aughnish and Aughnish Isle, Sir James Stewart, lease under the see of Raphoe, manor of Court and Portleen.

Ballylin, Charles Norman, fee simple, manor of Fort Stewart.

Gortaway, Sir James Stewart, fee simple, manor of Fort Stewart.

Farmagh, Charles Norman, fee simple, manor of Fort Stewart.

Crohane, Sir James Stewart, fee simple, manor of Fort Stewart.

Fort Stewart (old), Sir James Stewart, fee simple, manor of Fort Stewart.

Ballgreen, Sir James Stewart, fee simple.

Shelfield, part of the lands of Kerrygalt, which see.

Ray, part Henry Irwin, part Andrew Delap, held by leases for lives renewable forever under Archibald Hamilton Rowan, who has the fee simple.

Drumherve, held by lease renewable forever by Andrew Bredin Delap under Revd William Mortimer, who holds them and other lands for the like tenure under Archibald Hamilton Rowan, in whom is the fee.

Ballyhenny, heirs of the late Captain John Stewart, held by lease renewable forever under Archibald Hamilton Rowan, in whom is the fee.

Ballyconnelly, Revd William Mortimer, held by a lease renewable forever under Archibald Rowan, in whom is the fee.

Glentidally and Glentidally Glebe, Henry Irwin, held by a lease under Archibald Rowan, in whom is the fee; Dr Ussher, incumbency.

Glenalla, held by lease for lives renewable forever by the Revd George V. Hart under Archibald Rowan, in whom is the fee.

Drumacloughan, Revd William Mortimer, held by a lease under Archibald Hamilton Rowan.

Longhill, Revd William Mortimer, held by a lease under Archibald Hamilton Rowan.

Tervoddy, heirs of the late John Stewart, held by a lease under Archibald Rowan.

Brownoe, heirs of the late John Stewart, held by a lease under Archibald Hamilton Rowan.

Ardnaree, heirs of the late John Stewart, held by a lease under Archibald Rowan Hamilton.

Cavin, High and Low, Sir James Stewart, fee simple, manor of Rathmelton.

Upper Glen, Blacks Glen and Lower Glen, Sir James Stewart, fee simple, manor of Rathmelton.

Roohan, Sir James Stewart, fee simple, manor of Rathmelton.

Bridge-End, Sir James Stewart, fee simple.

Ballyboe, Sir James Stewart, fee simple, manor of Rathmelton.

Rossreagh, Sir James Stewart, fee simple, manor of Rathmelton.

Ray Hill, Sir James Stewart, fee simple, manor of Rathmelton.

Carnisk, Sir James Stewart, fee simple, manor of Rathmelton.

Claragh, part James Watt, part Solomon Darcus, lease for years under the see of Raphoe.

Gurteen, James Watt, lease under the see of Raphoe.

Conaghrud, Revd William Mortimer, held by lease for lives renewable forever under Archibald Hamilton Rowan.

Loughdow, part of the lands of Ballygay, Charles Hamilton, fee simple.

Tullyaughnish parish: the parish of Tullyaughnish is union of 2 parishes, viz. Tully Aghnish. The Revd Cornelius Ussher D.D. is the present incumbent. The patrons are the provost and the fellows of Trinity College, Dublin.

Fannanoughan, Humphrey Babington, fee simple.

Lough Swilly, County Donegal

Account of Lough Swilly [by Mr Montgomery and Others], 1820s

NATURAL FEATURES

General Remarks on Lough Swilly

Lough Swilly <Sooilly>, though not the most frequented, is the best and safest harbour on the north coast of Ireland. It is, from its conflux with the ocean to Ballyraine bridge, by the ship's course, about 23 Irish miles and a half long. Mariners allow that it would afford secure anchorage to the whole British Navy. It is encumbered with but few rocks without the tide mark and these, except Swilly rocks, are out of the ship's course in and not dangerous. The bottom from the very entrance is clean sand. It holds well and ships may anchor almost anywhere within it, but the most secure anchoring places are under Buncrana <Buncrannagh> Castle or off the river in (according to the size of the vessel) from 2 to 8 fathoms, or at Rathmullan <Ramullin>.

Dunnaff Bay

In Dunnaff bay ships may anchor safely to wait for the stream of flood or for wind for about a mile off Doagherabeen Point in calm weather. Lough Swilly is well described in the following extract from a paper written by Captain Smyth of Rathmullan who, for above 40 years, commanded the revenue cruising cutter on that station.

Fishing Boats

The best places on the lower Lough Swilly for harbours for fishing boats are on the west shore. The first from the entrance of the lough is Doaghbeg, a little above Swilly rock. The second is a creek of Crowrus on the north shore of Ballymastocker bay; a third is Creeve port in Drumhallagh bay, about 3 miles below Rathmullan; a fourth is Killygarvan river at the bridge a mile below Rathmullan; and Kerr's bay at Rathmullan Fort.

Seasons and Fish

The fishing season and fish usually taken off each of these harbours are as follows; off Doaghbeg: cod, haddock and herrings; off Drumhallagh bay: cod, haddock, turbot, plaice, sole and herrings; off Drumhallagh bay and Killygarvan: cod, codling and herrings; and off Kerr's bay and Rathmullan: cod, codling, whiting, rays and herrings.

The cod and herring fishery generally commence in July. Whitings are caught in summer and the others at all times when boats can with safety go off to fish for them. Doaghbeg and Ballymastocker bay are subject to heavy surfs in bad weather which can be only broken off by shelter piers. At Doaghbeg and Ballymastocker bay the time of high water on full and change days of the moon happens about a quarter past 5 o'clock; at Killygarvan and Rathmullan three-quarters past 5; and farther up Lough Swilly about 6 o'clock in the morning.

Ships enter Lough Swilly most conveniently with north or east winds. The ordinary perpendicular rise of spring tides here is about 14 feet. Extraordinary tides, however, have risen to 18 feet and ordinary neap tides to 8 or 9. Winds from south to west raise these tides [insert note: hinder them to rise or ebb (see tides) as at other times, by which the depth remains less altered] and winds from north to east depress them.

A greater number of boats belong to Kerr's bay than to any other on Lough Swilly and the king's boats lie in it when in port. At present all the boats must be hauled up in stormy weather. However, Kerr's bay could be easily sheltered by adding height to the 2 natural rocks which run out into the bay. They bare at every ebb of tide, run well out and may be considered everlasting foundations for such piers. Killygarvan could also be rendered an excellent harbour for boats by only a small pier on the point south east of the bridge.

Seaweed and Manures

The whole shore affords seaweed, and from Killygarvan to 2 miles above Rathmullan there is a great quantity of rotten shells which afford a very strong manure; and on land a large run of limestone is visible for a mile about due west from Killygarvan bridge.

Fanad Point

The doon of Araheery, or Fanad <Fannet> Point, on which Fanad lighthouse stands, forms the west and Dunnaff or Dunnaugh Head, or Kinnacallie, the east entrance of Lough Swilly. Fanad Point, though not exceedingly high, is very rocky and rugged, and so ceaselessly surged that even in fine weather boats cannot approach it with safety.

Carrigachaskim creek souths the lighthouse doon. Between it and Pinchers bay it is considered a very secure spot seldom troubled with surf; the bottom clay holds well, is sheltered from all points but east and south east. To it, boats, smacks or small sloops run for shelter when in danger near the lough mouth.

A few vessels could with convenience occupy the anchorage together in safety when they dare not approach any other creek near it, but the shore being too steep for landing, it could, for a small sum, be made accessible and convenient by cutting steps down the rocks to the water which is pretty deep close to it. It would then be a very commodious, safe little harbour at which the lighthouse stores could be landed. They have now to be brought a long way by land carriage.

Pinchers Bay

Pinchers bay lies a quarter of a mile south west of the lighthouse doon. It terminates just east of Araheery village in a sandy and stony beach, and has pretty deep water off it. It is troubled with a continual breaking surf and not much frequented by boats, but when a boat reaches it, she must be immediately hauled on shore.

Pulleid lies southward of Pinchers bay and for about a mile that way the shore is stupendously rocky, with high upright cliffs called Binh Bustea and Binh-avilvore to the north point of Doaghbeg, where in the mearing between that and Pulleid it lowers into a narrow pebbly creek, into which in calm weather fishing boats venture but must almost be hauled up. Stooeya, a high grassy rock, norths it. This point of Doaghbeg also becomes a partly high irregular cliff with high rocks close under and off it, of which the highest is Stuick-anmore and Brown George; and off Brown George, which is a high black rock always above water, and a little beyond half an Irish mile off Doaghbeg Point, lie the famous Swilly rocks.

The eastmost and largest of these is called Big and the northmost Little Swilly. Little Swilly dries only at low ebbing spring tides but Big Swilly in spring tides dries from 1 to 2 hours before low water and may at all times, even in fine weather, be distinguished by a continual swell or foaming upon it. They are, when seen, easily avoided, for a ship may pass close by the east side of Big Swilly in from 4 to 6 fathoms at low water; but should the swell upon Big Swilly not be visible as soon as the ship enters the bay, in either direction, she must bring Doagherabeen Point to bear on Greenfort Isle. Big Swilly rock will then be right between her and Doagherabeen Point. She must of course be a couple of ship's lengths to the east of that line or course to steer clear of the rocks.

A light in an eligible situation up the bay would be of infinite service to carry vessels safely up past these rocks.

It is hardly doubted but the *Saldanha* frigate first struck on Swilly rock, as Harry Deany of Lurgan-bwee and Ned Kelly of Carrowblagh found a large chain supposed to have belonged to her upon it a few months after her disaster.

Vessels may in calm weather, and with a fair wind, venture through the narrow passage between Brown George and Swilly rocks. Captain Smyth, from whom I received many useful communications, informed me that he sailed through it but that he considered it a foul, unsafe passage.

Doaghbeg Harbour

Doaghbeg boat harbour lies a little south or south west of Brown George and the Point of Doaghbeg. It is a clean dry harbour, sandy and nearly a quarter of a mile long from the Green Island at north to a small island at south. From this latter a ridge of pretty high rocks runs north easterly between the harbour and the sea towards Swilly rock, and are called Callawoo rocks, and towards other rocks that lie southward of Brown George; and the entrance lies between these and the north point of the Callawoo ridge called Carrigatooder.

This passage is pretty wide but is dangerous from a bed of scattered rocks called the Black rocks which I did not see until about or near half-flood. These appear to be, where broadest, about 3 perches over, in other parts not a perch over and probably little more than 4 feet high where highest, with sharp erect points and not more than about 4 or 5 perches long. This entrance is called the Sound, and to clear it of these Black rocks is at present the utmost favour concerning it that the fishermen of its neighbourhood seek or entreat.

There are several crowded villages near it. It is obviously a most excellent situation for a fishing port and near the deep water. The beach is one of the best and safest for hauling up boats, and this these people say they would not account a hardship, when so many live near it, if the sound was once rid of the Black rock[s].

There is also a passage through to the middle of the Callawoo which can in calm times be rowed through. It is useless to speak of raising the Callawoo to complete shelter. A moderate sum would not effect it, nor would any ordinary work endure the pelting of the surges that so often assail this shore; but it could be done. Doaghbeg would probably rival, in men and boats, any fishing port on the coast of Ulster.

Southward the remaining shore of Doaghbeg is rocky. The shore of Drimnacraig forms the surfy sandy beach of Tramore and is ordinary rocky cliffs along both Doaghcrabeen, Lurganbwee and Croughross to Portsalon <Portsallen> in Ballymastocker bay.

Ballymastocker Bay

Ballymastocker bay from Greenfort Isle north east to Carrig O'Donnel rock and head or point of Knockalla mountain, its south east extreme, is a little more than an Irish mile and a half, and from Ballymastocker strand high water mark at west it is almost 4 miles over to the high water mark in Leenan bay into which it looks towards east. The north west and nearly to the south for almost 3 miles and a half the shore is sandy beach [insert footnote: see crops, manures, Ballymastocker sand excellent manure etc.], on which the surf is almost ever up; indeed hardly the finest weather renders it tranquil for even a few hours. Yet there is within it only Portsalon, one small creek capable of being rendered tolerably secure for boats.

Portsalon

Portsalon opens southwards. A rock stands in the entrance only 10 or 12 feet from the south east point of that entrance. If that point and the rock in the entrance were connected and raised a little, it would, it is conceived, shelter the port from the inflowing swell and surf from south east and south. Another very narrow gut through which, when the bay is agitated, the swell forces itself with great violence should be shut, and 2 or 3 low rocks in the port and in the entrance to it should be cleared away to render it convenient, because it is a very small creek but which could be enlarged towards the land.

In very low spring tides it dries to the rock in the entrance, without which it soon deepens to 5 fathoms on a bottom of clean sand, and it is observed that boats can enter Portsalon in safety the times when the surf on the other parts of the bay would overwhelm anything. Another circumstance is that it is the only accessible point between Doaghbeg and Glenvar bay, a direct forward run of about 5 Irish miles. How desirable then to the poor fishermen of Ballymastocker district should it be if sheltered and cleared for their reception?

Glenvar Bay

Glenvar bay lies south eastward of Knockalla. Between it and Portsalon, Boydes Hole under the south angle of Knockalla Fort is the only accessible creek. It is deep but between high rocks, and so narrow that only 1 boat or 2 can enter it, and that only when the bay is calm and free of swell; but Glenvar bay or, as it is commonly called, Glenwar Burnfoot is (though overlooked or forgotten by Captain Smyth) by the fishermen accounted the safest boat harbour on this shore. It is seldom troubled with surf and is well sheltered from north west north and north east west and south west and, as far as concerns boats, from south east winds.

The bay is quite clean. The river enters it at north west by a channel which is separated from the head of the bay by a raised narrow beach of stones and gravel. Boats can make this river mouth any time after half-flood and are then in perfect security; or if threatened by swell or storm, may be easily hauled up upon the beach, or in good weather, boats may be hauled up outside the beach near Doontinny Point, to south of which the shore is rocky, rather high and from which a ledge of rocks runs out that would probably prove a good foundation for a pier. That would answer both for a landing-pier and a further shelter from south east winds.

Wherries and other light vessels anchor across the bay from Doontinny Point towards the eastmost angle of the village east of Bunnentin, Bushy bank (called by the wherrymen the Scraggy bank) in 2, 3, 4 fathoms on a good bottom that holds well.

This anchorage is almost contiguous to Bunnentin village and but half a mile south of Knockalla Fort, from which and the village a good road to Kerrykeel, a fair town on Mulroy, is now in progress.

Dunnaff and Leenan Bays

Dunnaff bay right opposite to Doaghbeg is extremely wide, a rocky, foul beach and perfectly opened north and west and much exposed to swell and surf. Ships seldom anchor here except to wait at tide and though the shore is not steep, it does not anywhere appear to be improvable. It harbours but 2 or 3 boats.

Leenan bay is partly sheltered by Leenan high cliffy point from north winds and also well sheltered from east and south. It is a sandy bay and subject to heavy surf. The mid entrance is clean, though both points, particularly the southmost,

Lough Swilly

are rocky. It has but one or two boats and large vessels don't enter it.

Dunree Bay

Dunree bay is another sandy bay on the bar of which there is, except in very calm weather, always a heavy surf quite across it, although it is open only to north west, being sheltered in east and north by the south west end of Cronkurris mountain and on the south and west by the cliffs of Crummy's Head and Dunree. It harbours only the boat of the preventive waterguards and one or two more.

Buncrana

Buncrana lies near 5 miles up shore from Dunree Fort. This shore is altogether exposed and does not afford an eligible site for either pier or quay; but, off the mouth of the Crannagh river or under Buncrana Castle, there is safe anchorage for vessels of any burthen and boats can enter the river with but little flood-water, and here they bring nearly all the fish caught in Lough Swilly for sale.

The bar or entrance of the Ouncrannagh into the lough is rather over mud than sand. It is very open to the west and north west, where the water is pretty broad, so that to shelter the boats' landing-place a pier on each side of the river appears to be necessary.

Half a mile up the shore, and just south of the Salt Pan point, the boats frequent the Mill river, the situation of which is very similar to that of Buncrana. From this Mill river about 2 miles and a half to Ruinaraa Point the shore is low, with a broad mud bed that dries between it and the deep water, where I shall leave it and return to Glenvar.

Portbuan Anny lies about three-quarters of a mile south of Glenvar anchorage, along a low rugged shore. It is a small sandy creek, the sand of which is celebrated as a most useful manure and particularly for reclaiming heathy and mossy soils. [Insert note: A large proportion of Portbaan sand is powdered shells].

Creeve Port

Creeve port in Drumhallagh bay lies about a mile south of Portbaan. The shore is very rocky and, though low, is inaccessible to boats. It is a creek of Drumhallagh bay not 3 miles from Rathmullan, formed by the shore of Creeve and a high ridge of rocks that run in the same direction without it and at a breadth of about from 6 or 8 to 14 plantation perches from it, and extends from the house at the new bridge of Creeve in that direction and, at the option of an engineer, from 47 to 50 plantation perches. The highest spring tide does not cover the ridge of this rock.

An opening in the middle which faces east will be the entrance into the new port, which must be shut against the sea at north; and for this purpose every material may be had on the spot but lime, which abounds in the neighbourhood. This proposed port dries only with spring tides, and in nearly the proposed new entrance there is 3 fathoms at low water and 2 fathoms within at high water spring tides.

The road from Rathmullan to Glenvar and Knockalla Fort passes it close on the west side, and from half a mile south of it an excellent road to Kerrykeel <Carrykeel> is in a very forward state of progress. What a boon would the completion of this little safety harbour be to the poor fishermen who inhabit the neighbouring country and what a source of convenience to the other inhabitants thereof.

The rocks Mollores, the Bull lie off Creeve port. The Bull seldom covers but with spring tides, but even spring tides don't entirely cover the Mollores, between and around which and the Bull there is 3, 4, 5 fathoms. The rest of Drumhallagh bay eastward to Illananoon is more rocky and shallow, and it terminates at south in a sandy beach.

Observations on Creeve Port

Of Creeve port, Mr Irwin of Drumalla observes, in a letter concerning it, "that it is admirably situated for a fishing station on that part of Lough Swilly, to which it may be considered central, all the country near it being inhabited by persons whose whole occupation is fishing but who, from want of any certain shelter for which they could run, if overtaken by storm when out, never venture off to fish except in calm or fine weather, by which a considerable part of every year is lost to this useful class of the community and the produce and advantage of their industry lost to their country. But as this place appears to be very easily converted into a commodious harbour to shelter boats and light vessels, if any effectual encouragement can be obtained for that purpose, I will (says Mr Irwin), as part proprietor of the place, do all that is practicable for me to facilitate so useful a public work."

Illananoon

Illananoon (the lambs island) is a very rocky spot, and every creek from it southward to Macamish

<Maccawish> Fort and from it to the Salt Pans is either rocky or sandy and in general very small, narrow and too subject to surf to become objects of improvement. But the Salt Pans bay, although a small creek has been long used and cargoes of rock-salt etc. discharged at it, it is open only to east and a small quay would render it useful and convenient. It is within less than 2 miles of Rathmullan.

From the Salt Pans to near Killygarvan Isles and river the shore is composed of low rocks and mounds, and generally too surfy to be approached except in calm or fine weather. The north end of the valuable bed that produces so much rich and excellent manures, mud, shells, sweet grass and other sea vegetables commences here and follows the shore to Rathmullan, Ray bay, Ramelton bay, Ballgreen ridge and Allison's bay.

Killygarvan

Killygarvan Isles, river and bridge occupy the north west angle of Killygarvan or Kinnegoe <Kinnager> bay, which is a clear sandy bay and dries with low ebbing spring tides, but there is 3 and 4 fathoms close off the very edge of the bed.

The isles are 2 small flat isles in the mouth of a creek which, in time of fishing, receives and shelters a great number of boats behind them, but boats cannot get in here until after half-flood. The bridge or river is a little farther up; small sloops and smacks get to it at high water. It would be completely sheltered by a low short pier run out from the point of Kinnagoe south east of the bridge and very little below it. From Kinnagoe bay to Kerrs bay at Rathmullan it is a low, breaking, rocky shore.

Rathmullan

Rathmullan is well known as an excellent anchorage for large vessels, yet it does not afford a good boat harbour; but Kerr's bay close under the east of the fort could be rendered both safe and commodious by building piers on the 2 rocks that form the bay. One of these rocks points eastward from the base of the fort; the other, forming the north east point of Kerr's bay, points south easterly but is broad enough to allow a pier to be erected upon it in the most proper direction. The kings boats, ferry-boats lie here. Small boats hauled ashore, large boats lie off at anchor.

Ray Bridge

Ray bridge is a little more than 2 miles from Rathmullan towards Ramelton. The Salt Pans (the property of Mr Watt, I believe), the only Salt Pans now at work on Lough Swilly, lie but a few perches below it. Here bridgs [brigs?] arrive by the channel of Ray river with cargoes of rock-salt.

This channel crosses Ray banks, the large bed of shells, three-quarters of a mile, by a winding course to the deep water. And the shell-boats, while landing in the absence of the tide, lie in and near it, in readiness to convey their cargoes along it to land as soon as they get afloat on the next filling tide; and this bed continues until it is again intersected by the channel of Ramelton bay.

Some valuable ground could be embanked on the north side, the inner part of Cairr bay, by a line from Rossmona Point to the south east point of Ardnaree; and on the south east, what lies south and east of Aughnish <Aghnish> Isle, a quay on Ramelton Castle point would be a most desirable favour to both the fishermen of the bay, the merchants of the town and all who draw shells and other sea manures by boats to that landing-place, whether for sale or for their own farms.

Ramelton

Ramelton is a thriving post town with a good market. [Insert note: A productive salmon fishery in the River Lennon, a bleach green and a flour mill, the property of Mr Watt, are all within less than a mile of the market place]. Large brigs could discharge their cargoes at the proposed quay.

The channel and its sounding are best understood from the map. The part of the bed between the Whale Head and the entrance of Ramelton channel into the deep is called the Skate Bed, because rays or skatefish are taken upon it; and half a mile above this a landing-pier or quay on John O'Donnel's Point would be of inconceivable utility to the great number of boats of various classes that frequent this landing with fish, slates, sea manures etc., because the road from it extends into the adjacent country and because the deep water approaches very close to the point.

Whenever a good take of herrings occurs in Lough Swilly, the best fishings are looked for from off the Hawksnest on Inch, to Fort Stewart and in the entrance of the Ramelton and Farland channel, and the greatest part of the herrings are landed and sold at O'Donnel's and Fort Stewart ferry.

Ballgreen Point

Ballgreen Point lies half a mile above O'Donnel's Point, and right off it lies that part of the bed called the ridge, composed of gravel, mud and some shells. It extends about 123 plantation perches from Ballgreen Point to the channel which, at its very edge, is deep water.

The greatest depths here are 7, 8 and 9 fathoms low water; at Fort Stewart ferry quays 6 and a half, off Castle Grove and Castle Wray half a fathom, on the ford of Hoods Isles a quarter fathom, and above that to Ballyraine bridge it varies no more than from one-third to half a fathom at low water spring tides.

A little way off Ballgreen kiln a hollow part of the ridge permits an inner passage for small boats over it any time from about half-flood to high water, and it often happens that this passage is very convenient and safe when high winds make it dangerous to sail by the principal channel east of the ridge; and to stand through the inner channel, bring the turret or tower of old Fort Stewart on Shellfield House: that course followed will carry you over the bed.

Above Ballgreen Point, from the ridge to Fort Stewart ferry and the Oak bank, the bed, although originally composed principally of mud, or mud and sand, has been planted in lots with stones to encourage the growth of seaweed, by which it has taken the appearance of a rocky flat and produces that vegetable manure abundantly; and this applies nearly to the beds on the other side of the channel also.

Allison's Bay

Allison's bay, all above the Oak bank on both sides of the channel to Hoods Isle and to above Castle Wray between the shores, is mud or shells or both, but the richest shell-beds are in Allisons bay and near it, and produce this valuable manure in such inexhaustible abundance that they are called the gold mines of Lough Swilly.

And with the above may class the beds under Fahan that belong to the Isles of Inch and Burt and east of these to the Burnfoot and Lisfannon; but except the sweet grass bed off the Mill bay of Inch, I could not, without much squander of time, see these last sufficiently ebbed to enable me to describe or delineate them and the channel that forms them with sufficient accuracy.

I attended to them with spring tides at both a change and full of the moon (in October and November 1822), but they did not (because of stormy weather) dry at either and I was assured that they might probably not ebb low enough for my purpose before next spring.

Bays near Burt

Cole bay, the large inlet between Drumbwee Point and the grange of Burt and south eastward to Castleforward, ebbs dry, is altogether mud and, including the small Coney Island, may be reckoned a square Irish mile or 640 plantation acres, which is more than 800 Cunningham acres or thereabouts; and but 4 or 5 very small rivulets enter it. About half a mile or say 150 perches of embankment from Drumbwee to the Church Grange of Burt would enclose these. Narrow drains necessary for parking it would collect the rivulets to one drain below the Coney Isle, where a drain of large dimensions would receive and discharge their waters by one principal sluice through the banks.

Inlet near Colehill

The little stream from Colehill to Drumbwee so perfectly defines how much of this glar <glaar> belongs to the Earl of Wicklow and how much to Mr Law, that no dispute whatever concerning it could arise between. When the streams that flow into tracts that are to be embanked off the sea are but small, I conceive that it may in many instances be practicable to carry them from where they enter by drains along the high water mark until they pass the embankment. By this, conducting one or more streams to the sea along shore or, if possible, above high water mark, the expense of a large sluice may be saved and the stream will be reserved, always above the level of the embanked ground, to irrigate it if dry seasons should ever make water necessary for it.

Another tract of glar apparently worth attention lies north of Moness [Moress?] and might be embanked by a line from the east of Carrowan to the extreme point of Speenog, north of (Mr Ferguson's) Burt House. And I imagine that about 600 acres could be enclosed by a bank from Tuban or Tooban to Kairnameddy.

The pilot Sam Craig of Aughnish tried many experiments to ascertain the perpendicular rise of spring tides, from which he is convinced that at Ballgreen, Inch, Burt and Drimbwee this rise in settled weather does not exceed from 13 to 14 feet, to know which may be of use to such as would embank off the sea.

Fahan Channel

Fahan channel separates Inch Island from Fahan. To sail safe into it, Captain Smyth directs you in clear weather to bring the drawbridge of Macamish (which appears low or gap-like and terminating the works of the fort next the land) on Binavilnore Head. That course truly followed will bring you safe off Fahan Point in the entrance of the channel and that point laid on Risk's house will place you in the best anchorage there. Or in hazy weather or Binavilnore Head not visible when you arrive off the west point of Lisfannon sandbank or bed, bring the fish-house on Moress Point in Inch to bear on Mr Ferguson's Burt House, which will bring you to the anchorage as above; a pilot will be necessary to take a vessel higher up.

McKenzie shows a bed west of the west part of Inch as if it dried with every ebb of tides. It has not dried for the last 40 years but the Aughnish pilot, Sam Craig, knows a man of Inch who saw a very small spot of it there. McKenzie makes it reach an English mile west of the Hawksnest, with a channel half that breadth between the bed and Inch. The channel is, however, much narrower and a narrow bank with shallow water upon it that runs southward until it ends in the bed that joins Drimbwee with Ballymoney in Burt, where it crosses the entrance to the Farland channel, which deepens towards Farland ferry as you sail towards it.

Rathmullan Anchorage

Rathmullan anchorage lies nearer to Rathmullan than to Inch and nearly in a line between Rathmullan Castle and the Hawksnest on Inch, in from 6 to 8 fathoms on a clear sand. In proceeding up the bay from this, observe the hollow called the White bay between the Whale's Head and the rough point on Ballylin, and a house with 2 chimneys just in that line beyond it and having other houses and a few trees near it.

Steer upon that house or upon the middle of the hollow of the White bay; this will keep you well off McKenzie's shallow bank last described and if bound up Ramelton channel, proceed until you bring the rough point of Ballylin to bear on the north end of Aughnish Isle, and from that place steer direct for the middle between Aughnish Isle and Ballyheny shore as it then appears or shows to you; and when your ship or boat is right in that course, observe by her head a bush or house or some certain object on land that she stands for, and steer for that object until you barely look along the further side of Aughnish Isle, and from that make your signal for Craig the pilot, whose house stands low with a few trees behind it close to the shore and having 2 little islands in the tide. The remainder of this difficult winding channel requires his assistance.

But if bound for Letterkenny, when within from a mile to three-quarters of a mile of the Whale's Head, stand directly for Drimbwee Point until you have Ballymoney Point nearly shut upon Inch Castle which stands low on the shore. There turn a little off Drimbwee up channel until you wholly shut Ballymoney Point on Inch Castle. That course will take you above Fort Stewart ferry quay until you have brought Drimbwee Point to bear about a perch west of Widow Willson's house in Burt.

Keep Drimbwee Point on that mark to carry you up channel to Kerry Castle or Oak bank, and above this it is difficult for any but an experienced pilot of that place to follow the channel after the tide has overflowed it. The best and safest time is (wind permitting) to start from the Oak bank early with the tide as you are afloat upon it, and so proceed with it to Ballyraine bridge or port near Letterkenny.

Tides

The velocity, perpendicular rise of spring tides and time of high or low water in Lough Swilly and Lough Mulroy (Mooil-rooey) seem, from their variableness, to be much influenced by the weather and direction of the wind as well as by the moon. It is well known to all the fishermen and other inhabitants of these shores that while southerly winds, viz. winds from south south east southward to south west by west, prevail, the tides remain less changed, flow with less rapidity and that they do not rise so high or ebb so low as at other times; and that frost has nearly the same effect upon them.

Winds from north west by north, north east and to east south east always produce here the highest tides and lowest ebbs, unless frost happens to prevent it. This fact I experienced at last January new moon spring tides. It was then frost, a little snow and but little wind, yet the beds in Mulroy based or stranded very little more than in ordinary neap tides. Very great tides generally precede storms.

High Tide or Top Springs

On all our coasts we have been taught to expect what is called top springs or highest spring tides, on the days of the change or full of the moon in the morning. High water does happen near the coast and in the mouths of Lough Swilly, Lough Mulroy on the days of change and full, at about from a quarter to a half an hour past 5 in the morning, at Rathmullan and Isle of Inch at three-quarters past 5, and often later at Fort Stewart, generally not until 6 or a little after 6, and later farther up.

At the mouth of Mulroy high water happens at the same hour as at the entrance of Lough Swilly, but on account of the narrows at Aghtem Point and the Hassans at Devlin in the broad water or upper Mulroy, it is not high water until 20 minutes or half an hour later. The stream of flood in these narrows is extremely strong and the fall at the Hassans is such that the tide below it has risen about 5 perpendicular feet before the stream of ebb slackens on the ford. This clearly shows why the upper Mulroy ebbs a considerable time after it is flood of tide in the lower.

It is also certain that the highest tides do not happen on the days of new and full moon but on the second, and often not until the third, day after the new or full moon. This was the case in last January 1823. It [was] full moon on the 26th of that month, afternoon, but the sea ebbed little more than at ordinary neap tides. However, it was frost; it thawed that night and stranded so much on the 28th and 29th that it uncovered several beds and rocks in Mulroy that I could not see at either the new or full moon preceding it.

When, before a change of weather or an approaching storm, a considerable swell from the ocean sets into these bays, a tide accompanied by such a swell appears to rise sooner and much higher than usual. The sea breaks with great violence and foams with impetuous and astonishing fury against all the shore on every rock and on every beach, although it be perfectly calm at the time, or whatever the direction of the wind; but during the continuance of the swell the sea does not ebb or subside in proportion to its rise as it would in fine or moderate weather.

If swell and a strong inblowing wind together accompany the rise of the tide, it is increased still more by that circumstance. In gloomy and stormy weather the tides do not ebb low. This deficiency in the ebbs generally commence with the first storm that occurs in October and continues until the beginning of the following month of March.

Patricksmas Tides

In fine weather it is always expected that high tides will be followed by proportionably low ebbs and the first good tides and strands are looked for with the new or full moon that happens about or next after the middle of March, and are called the Patricksmas springs and are always hailed in the maritime districts as ominous of an approaching scarce or abundant crop, according as the low ebbs and fine weather at the time enable or permit the farmers of these districts to gather greater or smaller quantities of seaweed for manure (as shall be more fully explained when treating of the application of sea manure) and allowing for changes arising from winds, weather etc.

Good ebbs are expected from March to what is called the Michaelmas springs in September. However, the greatest ebbs that occur in autumn aptly happen with what is accounted the harvest full moon, and I have seen very low ebbs or good strands late in October with moderate or settled weather. Want of attending sufficiently to the phenomena of the tides causes many extraordinary losses of vessels of all classes, of lives and of valuable property. Alexander Speer, the owner of a fishing boat in Sheep Haven, related as follows concerning mistaking the true time of high water.

"I considered it so long after full moon and that we had sufficient time to shoot our nets for herrings in Ards channel before the time we expected high water, and that we should have time to accomplish our purpose before the ebb or turn of the tide. Herrings were very numerous all around us and every hand was advantageously employed. We observed a rippling noise against the boat, which we supposed to have been made by the herrings.

It was a darkish night, so that we could not discern our situation by knowing the land near us. The noise increased; our boat very suddenly heaved so exceedingly that all hands were alarmed. The moon appeared as if rising and, to our consternation and terror, we discovered that a strong ebb of tide had carried us 2 miles below where we supposed we were, and that we were almost among the champions (the breaking surf) east of the bar. In so dreadful a situation we had to cut away, our nets and ropes were never after heard of."

This accident proves most plainly that the ebbing and flowing of the tide should be scrupulously attended to in every harbour on the coast. Tide gauges should be erected and when the average perpendicular rise of the tide for the different times of the moon's age are, by observation, known by it, anybody of ordinary capacity could know pretty exactly when it should be any corresponding quarter of the tide; and it is astonishing that hundreds whom it materially concerns hardly ever think about it at all.

Area North of Fanad

Turning out of Lough Swilly westward a little

north west of Fanad Point, and just under the west side of the lighthouse park, is Purtnamuika, into which circumstances sometimes force boats or smacks. A sunken rock just north east of the entrance breaks greatly in rough weather or before storms and agitates it too much to be always entered with safety. And the basin or berth within is partly foul. It ebbs dry, and a rock that covers only with high spring tides lies inside, between it and port Magheraghanive west of it.

Magheraghanive port also ebbs nearly dry; the bottom is sweet grass bed or sandy mud, and clean and holds well. The entrance is about 20 perches from land and opens to north west through Carrigghonel, a high run of rocks in an easterly direction that separates and shelters the port and Portnamuika from the sea. A short landing-quay added to a small rocky point in the south west part of this and a little ridding done to the entrance would make it safe and commodious.

In spring tides boats can enter Magheraghanive through Portnamuika from north east, should it at any time through circumstances of wind or tide be most safe or convenient so to enter it.

Half a mile of the shore from Magheraghanive to Corryhole and Scaltmore is wholly composed of blocks, flags, slabs and scantlings of variegated granite fit for every purpose in building. It polishes or smooths too readily to answer for millstones, but I doubt not stones could be made here (where they are just ready to hand) of excellent quality for bruising flax. Such stones are now much used and could not fail to sell readily if shipped to Ramelton, Letterkenny, Derry, Coleraine etc.

Scaltmore Creek

Scaltmore creek is celebrated for being, except in dreadful storms from the north, always free from surf and of safe entrance. Boats or smacks of 8 or 10 tons can enter at or a little before half-flood. A rock resembling a pillar that stands within it, and that could be blown away for a few pounds, is the only present objection to it. This rock removed would leave it rid, safe of entrance and very convenient for the fishing boats employed off that shore.

Sludden Creek

Sludden is the last and westmost creek of the Araheeries that is useful to the fishery. It is wested by Curreen Point and Carrigachaanrooa, north easted by another rocky point between it and Purtnaraw, and northed by Yeasky large rock, having an entrance on each side but of which the westmost is the best.

Sludden has a safe entrance with 3 to 4 fathoms clean bottom within. A gravelly beach is capable of harbouring a large assemblage of boats and is pretty well sheltered except from north and from north winds. Hardly any place permits boats to be hauled ashore with greater facility. It, however, requires a landing-quay which, if advantageously placed in the south west part of the creek, would prevent injury from even an ordinary northerly wind.

Except these creeks that I have described, the shore from Lough Swilly to Sludden is rocky low shore with points running pretty far out and almost always breaking and surfy, but producing very large quantities of weed, a sufficient quantity of which is used for manure and the residue burned into kelp.

Glashagh and Ballyhernan Bays

Glashagh bay wests Curreen Point and is wested by the rocky point Rhuinmore. It is about three-quarters of a mile wide. Sunken rocks lie off it. Within it is encumbered with rocks and is sandy and shallow. The beach at south east, south and south west is partly pebbles but mostly sand. It is southed by blowing sand and sandbanks, and is productive only of seaweed.

Ballyhernan bay is easted by the low rocky shore of Rhuinmore, southed by sand-hills and a low sandy beach, and wested by the sandy, rocky and cliffy shore and point of Rhuinbwee, and is sufficiently described above in the description of Glashagh bay, like which it is rocky.

Rhuinbwee Point

Rhuinbwee Point is altogether bounded by rocky shore, all pretty high but the point is highest. The whole area between the shores is sandy waste, covered with piles of seaweed, drying for the manufacture of kelp and exhibiting in December the resemblance of a turf bog with its crop in summer, stacks and winning.

Traemore rocky and sandy bay lies west of Rhuinbwee, between it and Rhuinadrinnea, and Traebeg wests it to Rhuinmore.

Bwellaorisky, a low point which terminates in Illaneeyafta, widely surrounded with low rocks and is the westmost point of the bottom of Fanad and Ballyorisky or Bwellaorisky bay, is the whole space, about a mile wide, between Rhuinbwee and Rhuinmore, Bwellaorisky, and comprising Traebeg and Traemore within it. It is southed by sand-hills and a sandy beach, but all the shore beside is rocky. The bay is encumbered with several rocks and off it lie rocks both visible and invisible. Some of the latter break with inconceivable fury.

Inishowen: Lough Strabreagagh

Lough Strabreagagh has been described as far as Cregnadutchagh or "the Dutchman's rock," within which, from Lagsands and Warrens to Stuckanbwee, the Five Finger Point, and insular high rock Stuckanuller into Killoort bay, the shore is high, rocky cliffs along Knockamenny and Dunargus, but thence to Ardmalin it is low and partly sandy.

Killoort Bay

Killoort bay comprises 3 ports or boat harbours. Portaluaghan is the southmost. It receives fishing boats over the Laarlagh or bar of low rocks soon after the first quarter of flood and sloops after half-flood of tide, but they must be hauled up on the beach, which is sand and pebbles, unless in fine summer weather.

The middle ports are Traebwaar and Cloghandooh. The former is the southmost side, is larger than Portaluaghan and sandy and pebbly. The latter is the northmost and is situated at the mouth of a rivulet that meres between Killuort and Ardmalin. The entrance to [?] Traebwaan and Cloghandooh is the same and over a rocky bar, through a passage in between ridges of rocks by which these ports are bounded and in the south side of which the rock Markagh lies and straightens it materially.

The Markagh seldom bares and is dangerous, but permits laden smacks of about 30 tons and smaller craft to enter south of it without any sailing marks to guide them in but the rocks that bound them or the surges breaking upon them, and they cover altogether with high tides. Cloghandooh affords good shelter from westerly and northerly winds. The bottom and beach are sand and pebbles.

Portaronan

Portaronan is the northmost creek of Killoort bay; is northed by the main shore which is rock and of moderate height. It opens towards west and is southed by Rossnamuck. Houton's rock lies a little within the entrance nearest to Rossnamuck and with smaller rocks between them, which leaves but a narrow passage on the larboard hand close under Ardmalin shore at coming in. Common fishing boats enter Portaronan at any time but smacks not until between quarter and a half-flood of tide. Portaronan, although a good safe sandy cove, is too narrow for any large vessel to enter.

Other Ports

Portluaghan, Traebwaan, Cloghandooh and Portaronan are all rather open to gales from west, south west by west, and from west north west, and are not to be approached by strangers or when their bars are much agitated or breaking.

Innuran port lies on the south shore of Ardmalin, about half a mile within the points. On account of its rocky bottom it is not safely deep until about half-flood of tide or later. Boats may then enter it and will be well sheltered by the high rocks and rocky shore that enclose it, except from south westerly winds.

Bay Breslie near Malin Point is dangerously rocky and not used.

Purtakilleran is a close, stony creek of Ardmalin. It opens to almost due north, is very surfy and unsafe to enter except in perfect calm.

Purtabrillian or Alt-terrien is a small pebbly creek enclosed by 2 pretty high rocks, between which stands a single round one in the middle of the port, the beach of which ascends very gradually and permits a few boats to be safely beached upon it. It is frequently filled with surf, although it is called a good port.

Portluargan is a creek of Aasky bay and the station of a party of the preventive waterguard. The entrance is narrow and somewhat rocky, but a boat once within it is safe from every danger. A few small rocks rid out of the entrance and the bottom cleared of stones would leave it both safe and convenient for small boats.

Ports

Sleibaan port or Portmore opens towards north east but, having the group of the Garrive <Garrine> Islands and rocks before it and land bounding it on every other side, we may suppose that it is very well sheltered. The bottom is sand and holds well, and the beach is roomy enough to permit all the boats of Inishowen to be hauled up upon it.

It deepens from the shore towards the Garrive Islands to from 14 to 16 fathoms, and light vessels anchor towards the east side in 2, 3, 4 etc. fathoms, as may be most proper, between the Garrive Islands and the beach of the port, and larger vessels up to 300 tons anchor in deeper water nearer the group. Yet, however securely and naturally it may be sheltered, it is subject to swells from the north west and these swells are heaviest with north east and easterly winds, which could be greatly remedied by raising or increasing shelter on Minuads rocky point. Portmore is a famous fishing port.

The "sand port" [insert footnote: Purtagannive] lies east of Portmore, beyond Carrig-Coeen rocks and point. It is rather surfy and not much frequented by boats except when gathering seaweed.

Cary's port at the foot of the westmost mearing of Ballygorman with Sleibaan or Ardmalin is but little frequented by fishing boats, because of surf and because high tides overflow too much or do not leave beach enough whereon to secure them in case of storm, and because there is no easy road or path to it down its steep banks. It produces a good deal of seaweed for manure.

Other Ports in Inishowen

Mullintragh is separated from Cary's port by a rocky point from which it extends eastwards almost to Malin Well. It is a pebbly beach, between which and the surge there runs a broad bed of rocks through which 2 openings permit boats to reach the beach, when not prevented by heavy surf to which that shore is very subject.

Malin Well port is generally frequented by 14 or 15 fishing boats that haul up on a beach of paving stones, pebbles and coarse gravel headed by the well-house or inn, from which a good road communicates with the adjacent country and with the town of Malin about 5 miles eastwards from it.

The landing-place at Malin Well is not easily approached or entered, on account of the surf which, except with very fine weather, breaks incessantly upon it; notwithstanding that, it appears to be admirably sheltered from the north and north west by the group of the Garrive Islands, the rocks between them and the shore, and by the doon, while the south and south east are covered by very high cliffs so that it is open only to the north east, towards the anchorage recommended by McKenzie between half and three-quarters of a mile from the port, in from 4 to 9 fathoms on a clean sandy bottom.

But this anchorage would not be safe for any delay upon it beyond that of a few hours, to wait for the tide or the change or freshening of the wind, and that delay could only be risked in settled or very moderate weather. Therefore such vessels as find sufficient depth of water in Portmore, Sleiban prefer that anchorage, although not taken notice of by McKenzie in his nautical directions for navigating these sounds.

In the foregoing articles of report, the several fishing ports from the mouth of Lough Strabreagagh to Malin Well are described but the coast or shores of Ardmalin is rather badly noticed or represented in our charts and descriptions of the coast. The charts represent the south shore of Ardmalin as if low and grassy.

But although this portion of the coast is not formed of stupendously high cliffs, it is very rocky under and off the main shore, of which some approach the height and cragginess of cliffs, and other portions of it are fenced against the waves by rows of high upright rocks, of which the highest and most remarkable are Bhinbaan, Cregaghduargs, Cregalnacky and the Ooigrooey, which last stands on the outer extreme of Malin Point, which is the westmost or south westmost extreme of Ardmalin and not more than a rocky point of ordinary height; but beyond Malin Point north eastward the shore of Ballykillien or Malin Head is high and mostly cliffy, but in many places sloping and grassy as far as Doonaldragh which is the most northerly point of Ireland.

Of this portion of the coast, the highest cliff is that called the Trockagh and the highest upright insular rock is the Skelluranmore, between it and Malin Point. Doonaldragh Island shore is but of moderate height and the strait between it and the main shore narrow, rocky and unnavigable.

The signal tower of Ardmalin crests the summit of Ballykillien hill that overlooks or overhangs Doonaldragh. From Doonaldragh eastward to Malin Well the shore of Ardmalin is low and mostly rocky, with a few pebbly and sandy creeks and fishing ports already described.

East of Malin Head

For 5 or 6 miles eastwards from Malin Well, the coast is distinguished by the general name of the Bengorrems or more properly Bhin-gorrems. It has but few accessible creeks and shows itself to distant observers a continued range of very high and impenetrable cliffs closely overhanging the border of the deep.

But that is not the case: there are but few portions of the shore from Malin Well to Glenagaad and Culdaff river or indeed anywhere eastward to Shroove Head in which the real line or circuit of the shore is not somewhat in front of the cliffs, sloping towards the sea and pasturable for sheep and goats, and in a few instances for other light cattle which descend to these pastures by winding paths made for their feeding excursions up and down the Bhinns; and it is confessed that they thrive better in these recesses of the shore, by much, than on any of the neighbouring mountain pastures and that sheep are more secure and better subsisted in them through the most vigorous winters than they would be in any of the mountain glens of Inishowen.

And the inhabitants gather very large quantities of the larger species of seaweed for manure from every little creek below the Bhinns from which they can possibly ascend with even the most trifling quantity of that vegetable, until, having collected it in large quantities, they send it to their farms.

Ports East of Malin Well

The first place that boats land at, eastward of Malin Well and about 3 miles from it by the shore, is Port Bhinagharrell, a creek of the Bhingorrems, about a quarter of a mile eastward of Carrigavel.

It is esteemed by the fishers to be a very safe desirable port and almost always easily approached from sea, being very seldom troubled with surf or swell and having but 1 rock of moderate size near the landing-place, and some loose stones that could be readily cleared away and which would leave a good clean beach for landing upon; and towards sea the port deepens off north eastward on a clean, sandy bottom into 16 fathoms within a quarter of a mile of the beach.

But however good and safe it may be as a port, or however desirable to the hundreds that desire it, it is almost inaccessible from the land, being enclosed by very high and partly cliffy banks or Bhinns, down which a small brook has hollowed itself a deep, difficult, craggy course; but this brook could be turned eastward over the Bhinns from a point sufficiently above the level of where it enters the deep ravine, down which it now flows, to prevent it from ever again returning to that course.

And that present bed or course of the brook could, by filling and cutting, be, by employing the materials it will afford, changed into an eligible road down to the port which, being very productive of sea manure, both weed and sand, should be accommodated with the continuation of a road to it that is now within about half a mile of it, in a very good direction from Malin town and of which near 2 miles would cross a most valuable turf bog.

Here I found the first white coral I met with going eastward from Malin. The sand found here is a mixture of shells, sand and coral, and effervesces very strongly with muriatic acid. It was tried by Mr Harvey of Malin Hall.

Ports at Malin Head

The situation of Portbhinagharrell, had it the advantages of a road from it to Malin town, would make it very important to the fisheries and to the community at large: boats no longer able to remain on the fishing banks could make it with winds and under circumstances that would make it impossible to reach Malin Well or Portmore, and they could land at it with ease when they could not attempt the surfy landing at Malin Well.

It is about 2 miles nearer to Malin town than Malin Well is to Malin town. Land, turbary and water are in sufficient quantity for the accommodation of a few families conveniently near it, and the coast exhibits no better or more convenient a place for bathing.

Top of Inishowen Head

Portluaghan lies beyond 2 miles eastward of Portbhinagharrell. It is northed and north easted by very high cliffs and Carriggannagh lower rocky island, a rocky high point that runs north east or more nearly eastward out from below them; wested by the moderately high shore of Glentoosker that overhangs the beach; and southed and south easted by that high part of Glenagaad Head called the Ross and the rocky low point Roonahinnera thereof. It opens to a little north of east and harbours 2 or 3 fishing boats belonging to Glenagaad, hauled up on the gravelly beach near Carriggannagh in the north west angle of the port. The Ross is the lookout station of the preventive waterguards from Portasantal.

Portasantal is situated at the entrance of a small brook of Glenagaad into the sea. It is but a small creek that runs but very little within the line of the coast between high rocky cliffs, at the foot of which there are on each side [of?] the entrance a few rocks that seldom cover but that always afford it shelter. It opens towards north east and deepens without the landing-place. There is a rock or rather a bed of stones that could probably be removed by crow-irons at low water, which would greatly diminish the spread of heavy surf to which it is subject. It is the station of a party of preventive waterguards who, with the inhabitants, account it a good boat-port.

The beach is paving stones and pebbles, and a grassy bank down which the path to it is steep, difficult and crooked.

Inishowen Head: Ports

Portalung is a sandy port south east of Burt and

under Ballymenagh. It is separated from Portaleen by Coolkill Point or doon. It is all rocky except the landing-place and, although open to only east, northerly and westerly winds always trouble it exceedingly with surfs and swells. Boats seldom frequent it, but its rich sand is carried far into the country for manure and used in reclaiming moor, bog and stiff soil, but is not, as far as I can learn, applied by any particular quantity to the acre. The road to it is very bad.

Portaleen is another creek of Ballymenagh. It looks or opens north eastward, is north wested by Coolkill doon and the Mullindooh rocks, which last do cover and uncover with the tides, and easted and south easted by a rocky shore and a pretty high and mostly earthy banks. The entrance is clean, safe and wide, and the port capable of harbouring 80 or 100 boats, but the landing and beach are too stony for safety and convenience in hauling them on shore; but a brook that falls into it, being low, could, by removing along 2 perches of gravel bed that bars it, receive and harbour about a score of boats at or after half-flood, without the trouble of hauling them up. About 40 or 50 perches of very bad road or pathway leads from it to the great road to Culdaff.

Portamuck and Other Ports

Portamuck and Bhinagawra port lie within a quarter of a mile eastward of Portaleene. They are small but, although very improvable, they are seldom landed in.

Aaltnanuagh port is a creek of Claggan under the west of Gilloovier Point and is by George Davenport reported to be a safe useful boat-port of clean entrance except a few loose stones; is a landing-beach and open to north east only. The landing-ground terminates upon sloping green pasture under moderately high and partly cliffy banks that cover it from south and south west, and is wested, north wested and northed by a ridge or group of pretty high rocks that tides do not overflow and that could be filled between, so as to shut out the effects of north, north westerly storms. Aaltnanuagh is very productive of seaweed but is altogether in want of the accommodation of a road to it.

Purtachack or Portachack is a creek of Bunagoee, a little north west of the bar of Culdaff river. It is formed by rocks that high tides do not altogether cover. It opens or looks a little south of east into Culdaff bay, with water deepening into the bay on a partly sandy and partly rocky bottom from 2 to 10 fathoms before it. It is southed and separated from Culdaff river by the salmon rock and northed by the rock Luec Charrig, which is partly high enough to shelter it from the north.

The lower part of this Luec Charrig next to or within the port could be quarried and built with other materials upon it, so as to form both a shelter and landing-pier or quay convenient for any time of the tide. The inside of the salmon rock could also be similarly treated if thought necessary, and some low weedy rock within the port could at low ebbs be cleared away so as to have it clean and commodious.

The boa of Portachack lies northward of Lecharrig. It is a pretty large rock that covers and uncovers with the ebb and flood of tide, and between which and Luec Charrig lies a second rock (or one that seldom altogether bares) that makes the passage of that sound dangerous until it has at least half-flood of tide upon it. From Portachack a road leads to Culdaff.

Culdaff

The bar of Culdaff river at low water on 26th August 1824 had scarcely a foot of water upon it. It could be easily deepened were it certain that the blowing sand from Culdaff Point and warren would not again fill it up. However, were it of consequence to the country, that objection could be got rid of by confining the river so as to give effect to the force of the stream which would always clear its own course to the ocean without injuring the navigation of the river, which already carries laden vessels of 30 or 40 tons burden up to the bridge.

Culdaff bay naturally comprehends all the creeks or ports and coast that lie eastward of Glenagaad Head to Culdaff river and Dunmore Head, which is the outmost seaward promontory of Mullinasool. The south shore of this bay to about a mile eastward of Culdaff river is southed by sand-hills and is sand, with but 2 remarkable rocks, Corrateebeg and Corrateemore, in that space; but beyond that to Dunmore the shore, although low, is rocky even to Portaheag on the east side of the bay, at the foot of Dunmore hill, and which port is little used but as a place for gathering or landing seaweed in fine spring weather.

About 2 miles and a half of the west side of the bay and about half a mile of the east side shore produce plenty of weed and the middle part abundance of sand for manure, and a good deal of broken white coral is found there also.

Garrive Islands

The Garrive Islands or Garrove Islands lie directly between Portmore, Sleibaan and Inishtrahull or Inishtuahull Islands. They comprehend 5 small, high rocky islands, of which only Inishglass, the southmost, which is hardly a mile north of Malin Well, Inishbulskin, the middlemost, and Inishbaan, the northmost, produce herbage. Carnbaan, the north eastmost, and Daughglass, the north westmost, are high, of ricklike appearance and barren.

Among and around these, near them, are other lower rocks, of which some never cover at all, some never uncover, some cover and bare with every tide, and of one a part never bares but with the low ebb of spring tides; but there is deep water around and between them all, and a stronger stream of tide than is met with on the neighbouring shores and particularly in the sound or leam between Carndreelagh and Rossnabarton in the southward direction from Inishglass to the doon of Malin Well.

In this sound or leam (except in very calm weather) the stream of tide rises in pretty high surges, although in 5, 6, 7, 9 and 10 fathoms; and the like, both north and south of Daughglass, where the depth is from 14 to 20 fathoms and these surgings are by strangers often mistaken for breakers, both here and in the sound of Inishtuahull, for they take quite the resemblance of breakers as often as the stream of tide is met by a gale of wind blowing in an opposite direction; which can be easily known when it is understood that on this coast and near the shore the stream of tide runs eastward from half-flood to half-ebb and westward from half-ebb to half-flood of tide.

But in the sound of Inishtuahull, between it and the Garrive Islands, the stream does not turn to the eastward until between 4 and 5 hours after high water on the coast and its velocity in the sound and in calm weather may be little more than 4 miles or 4 miles and a quarter in an hour in the mid channel, but it appears to run swifter along the shore either of Inishtuahull or of the Garrive Islands. Spring tides on this coast rise about 12 feet perpendicularly, but with northerly winds and calm settled weather this rise is sometimes greater, and with southerly wind, wet and stormy weather, less.

Malin and Culdaff

Lueck Coulin high rock and some others near it that never cover lie about a quarter of a mile north west from the doon of Malin Well and about midway between the doon and Rossnabarton. The sound between Luec Coulin and the doon is from 5 to 5 and a half and 6 fathoms deep, on a rocky bottom; and the sound between Lueck Coulin and Rossnabarton is very foul with low rocks.

Doughglass <Dughglass> is a stack-like high rock about a quarter of a mile northward of the principal group of the Garrive Islands. It has other rocks near it that are lower than it which never cover and others that cover and bare alternately with every tide, and these stand in not less than from 16 to 18 fathoms; and Dougherty's rocks lie from Doughglass. West, north west from about a third to half a mile the eastmost of these bare a little before half-ebb, but the westmost parts uncover with spring tide ebbs only.

There is a breaking shoal a little south of west and less than a quarter of a mile from Doughglass and another, Carrighollap, that lies almost west of it and more than a mile from the shore of Ardmalin off Aalterrine, that breaks furiously in stormy weather. It lies rather near the navigable course through the sound or leam of Carndreelagh and with so little water upon it that the weed is frequently seen upon it among the surges when breaking moderately over it.

It may be avoided when sailing from the westward. If when scarcely a quarter of a mile off the northmost point of Ardmalin, in about 20 fathoms, you lay the Stuckaruddan on Carrickaviwel Head and follow that course until you bring Dughglass on the eastmost end of Inishtuahull and you will then be clear past Carrigkollegh blind rock, and the same course reversed will carry you through if sailing through from the eastward. There is about a quarter of a mile west of Inishglass (the southmost Garrive Island) another shore on which breakers are often seen and between which and Inishglass there are rocks, some of which do not cover.

Inishtuahull

Inishtuahull, commonly written as Inishterhull and Inishtrahull, lies about 4 miles north east from Dughglass, about 5 and a quarter from Malin Well and about 6 and a half miles a little west of north from Rooenahinnera Point, under the Ross and Glenagaad Head. It is about a mile long from east to west. The south east point of the east end is called the Luack, the north east point of the east end is Illanaweelog (a rocky island), the west point Crucknahulla and the south west point is the Rooe of Purtacheerry.

There are but 2 fishing ports in the island. Purtachurry at the south west is so narrow that 2 small boats cannot enter it abreast. It resembles a trench cut a considerable way through a rock of nearly equal height and that covers with high tides. It opens a little south of west, is hardly ever free of surf and should not be attempted but with a moderate steady wind.

Portmore Inishtuahull lies on the north east side of the island. It runs a good way into land, is safe and deep enough for sloops and small brigs, and secure from every wind but north east and but seldom surfy. The landing beach is pebbles and roomy. The breadth of the port or harbour varies but little and a rock about half-way down from the beach, and that seldom covers, shuts it to about 120 feet; and that opening is the present passage into the inner harbour, which could be made very commodious by building shelter on the above-noticed rock sufficient to enclose the port from winds and swells from without, and would leave it capable of harbouring all the craft that frequent the several banks and fishing stations off the north of Inishowen, whenever sudden storms or contrary winds might compel them to seek and occupy it. It is little more than 8 miles from Culdaff river.

Inishtuahull and Landscape

Inishtuahull viewed from the southward appears to be 2 distinct hills separated by a low deep valley that reaches across between them from Portachurry to Portmore; but the island is narrowed a little east of Purtachurry where it is merely an isthmus of connection between its east and west extremes.

The eastmost part of Inishtuahull is the least but highest. When seen from a distance it appears in one round topped hill, the summit of which is beautified with a stately lighthouse and the buildings belonging to it, which are kept in complete repair and perfect cleanliness. The light-keeper's garden is stocked with roots and vegetables, among which turnips and cabbages grow with luxuriant contempt of the sea winds that so materially injure potatoes and many other species when exposed to their fury. But when we arrive on this part of the island we find it comprehending several lots of tolerably regular surface and, excepting the area walled in and occupied by the light-keeper, the lighthouse and buildings belonging to it, none of this east end has been lately tilled.

The other occupants of the island live on the west side of the valley, of which they till a part; but the late sea winds (August 1824) have for this season destroyed their crops, which were but trifling, the whole quantity tilled being but small and the crop often so much fed down by rabbits when young that it produces but little grain in the calmest seasons; but when damaged by summer winds it is of still less value.

I am convinced the island would produce more by either suffering the rabbits to increase as far as the soil would afford them burrows, and adding as many sheep as it would then support; or by stocking it altogether with sheep, save a couple or 3 cows that should be kept necessarily, and a parcel of ground enclosed off the valley with a stone fence of sufficient height to keep out the rabbits, and that a ground should be appropriated to perhaps little else than the cultivation of potatoes for the maintenance of about a couple of families.

And 2 families would, I conceive, be enough to find food on Inishtuahull, of which the tillable and pasturable surface is not probably half so large as it is commonly supposed to be, and because so large a proportion of that quantity is now thrown out into mere skirts or offal around the park granted to the Ballast Office for the accommodation of the lighthouse and which must in future be less fit for any other purpose than for pasture.

Inishtuahull occupies one of the very best stations from which the white fishing can be pursued, having good and very extensive fishing banks in every direction around it; but the few who inhabit it do [not] possess such means, or are not in such circumstances, as can make that station eligible and convenient to them. Their boats are every way too small, too light, too slender and trifling to carry them safely to the banks on which they would fish with success for fish of every superior quality and species. They must then be contented with taking the smaller description of every species that they daily find convenient to their own shore, and this very circumstance determines the continuance of their poverty and their inability to either make good fishings or to avail themselves of the best markets for what fish they take.

I am the more convinced of this circumstance from knowing the fact that Mr Wishart, the light-keeper at the lighthouse, purchased and cured all the fish that the islanders (6 or 7 families) caught this season, along with those taken by his own boat. They admit that he gave them a fair price conveniently on the island and he has sold them, cured and dried (after receiving the bounty), for a very fair profit, and that he this summer, 1824, cured more fish in Inishtuahull in the manner of Shetland than was cured there for many years before. This circumstance should induce others, either individually or in company, to cure fish at all the bays along the coast at which quantities of fish are landed.

The island is not bounded by a low shore as represented by McKenzie's and other charts. The whole shore is, with only 3 or 4 trifling exceptions, high and rocky, and in some places almost cliffy high; and outside the general range of the rocky shore it is surrounded by an irregular border of lower but very rugged rocks, without a foot of sand or pebbles except what is within Portmore.

Fishing Banks

The fishing banks of this neighbourhood have not yet been noticed in our sea charts and maritime descriptions. They are Dunmore bank, the Hill and Hollow, and Hempton's bank, the Giggan bank, the Island bank, Oieternaghollapagh, Oieter-Carrigouver and Oiternamweela.

Dunmore bank affords good summer fishing in from 15 to 20 fathoms. To come on it, open Carriggannagh with Slieve Snaght over Dunmore Head and you leave it when Culdaff trees begin to open westward and Stuckaruddan just appears along the heads.

The Hill and Hollow bank is come upon by laying Stuckaruddan up the valley of Carnmalin, when Inishglass is barely open with Malin Head, when on the middle of the bed you have Slieve Snaght down the valley of Glengaad and you fish north west until you lay Dughglass on Malin Head. You then lose the bank in the sound and get immediately into deep water.

Hempton's bank is, I imagine, a continuation of Inishtuahull bank called Oieter-more, because we have but partial changes of depth upon it for above 20 miles north eastward, for immediately off Illanaweelog, the eastmost point of Inishtuahull, you have from 12 to 15 fathoms upon it.

At about a mile you have very good fishing in from 18 to 20 fathoms. At 5 miles it is not 30 fathoms and so north eastward it shallows until the west end of the Croagth of Glenagaad is brought on Slieve Snaght mountain. When about 8 or 9 miles from Inishtuahull you will again have 22, 20 fathoms, and at 10 to 13 miles from 13 to 15 fathoms.

The late Captain Hempton first noticed this part of the bank about the year 1778 and gave it his name. It continues with soundings between 20 and 30 fathoms north easterly until Dunmore Head is brought upon the top of Slieve Snaght and probably much farther. [Insert addition: Scotchmen say that it reaches nearly to the Scotch shore].

The Giggan bank lies about 4 miles from the coast, in the direction of east and west, from a little west of Glenagaad Head to a mile or 2 east of Glenaguivna port. Fishers from the eastward take station upon it when Binevenagh <Bhinevna> opens with Shroove Point or Inishowen Head and the signal tower of Malin Well open with the Stuckaruddan. They sail westward and are on the middle of the bank when Slieve Snaght bears right up the valley of Glenagaad, commence fishing when Carthage House is brought on with Slieve Snaght, and continue fishing eastward with the tide until Croaghdooh (the east head of Tiermoan bay) bears on the top of Slieve Snaght. They then deepen off the bank.

Oieternagollapagh lies south westerly from the Lueck of Inishtuahull towards Carrigavuoel Head, the bottom mostly shells, with soundings from 12 to 20 fathoms; it is seldom without surf.

Oiter-carrig-ouver runs about 2 and a half miles from off about the middle of the south shore of Inishtuahull towards the Garrive Islands and more westward of that direction towards the sound or Soois Inishtuahull, in which McKenzie says there is a rough breaking stream of tide, although it is upwards of 20 fathoms deep. But I have no doubt that in the mid channel it is in many places 30 fathoms or more. I did not touch bottom with a much deeper line but had no doubt that my lead was too light for the stream.

Mulroy Bay

Lough Mulroy: creation has divided Mulroy into 4 distinct parts, lower, middle and upper, and the detached north east or east lough that almost intersects Fanad in the middle may, for distinction sake, without impropriety, receive the appellation of Lough Fanad. The point of Rhuinmore, Bwellorsky, forms the east and the promontory of Mellgoim <Mevalgoim> the west entrance from the ocean into Mulroy.

The Lower Mulroy will comprehend the narrow part above that to Illanaviaie, Carrigart, Rowrus ferry, Bullogfeam inlet, the inlet of the Naggles and to the Upper Narrows or Hassans. Upper Mulroy will comprehend all above the Hassans eastward and southward from Rosskeady to Ross-garrow and Bunlin. And Lough

Fanad will comprise that branch of Mulroy that enters Fanad by the strait between Melnahardae Point of Ummeracaam and Ross Point, embracing in its way the peninsula and ferry of Moress <Moaris> and several islands, and terminating on Kindrum and Sullynadaol at north.

Lower Mulroy

In Lower Mulroy, about three-quarters of a mile south eastward along shore, on the rocky point of Rhuinmore, lies the little boat harbour Sluddanawashog. It is reckoned very safe and easily entered, because not liable to heavy surf, but it requires to be cleaned of a small rock or two that are within it and it should be enlarged a little on the north west side.

Portaling lies half a mile south of Sluddanawoohog, between Ballyorisky shore and Islandorisky. The island is surrounded with rocks and part of these fill the opening between it and the shore north of Portaling, but are not high enough to shut out the surf; but it rools into Portaling from the northward about the time of high water. This swell shut out and 2 small rocks rid out of the entrance would leave Portaling safe and sheltered. It is always free of surf in the entrance, little troubled with swell, the bottom and beach at north east gravel; the east side or main shore from Rhuinawoogan Point to the harbour is half a mile of rock 6 or 8 feet nearly upright. The entrance opens to a little south of west and it is northed by rocks that crowd between it and the island.

It is the only safety harbour on this side without the dangerous and uncertain bar of Mulroy to which craft could run if caught in the bay by a squall or opposed by a strong ebbing tide or by wind when the bar is up (breaking) too much to be attempted. This and Pullinrooey on the opposite shore of Melmore, also below the bar, rendered safety harbours for boats would encourage them to go off to fish perhaps many times oftener than they now dare to venture out.

Pullinrooey requires only to build a connecting work from its north east point to a rock in the entrance, not 30 feet from it, sufficient to shut out the swell that enters it on that direction. The entrance would then be from south east. The water off it is deep and it does not ebb quite dry and affords good anchorage in from 2 to 4 fathoms close off it on clean sand.

It is but small; yet it and Portaling, both improved, would be of incalculable service to the inhabitants of Fanad and Rosguill. Boats could the[n], under almost any circumstances of wind or tides, feel securein the bay or be able to make 1 of the 2 harbours in safety.

Mellgoim Peninsula

Mellgoim (Mivalgoim) is a peninsula promontory of Melmore, low at south and appended to it by a very narrow sandy isthmus. A signal-tower stands on the summit. The low rocky island, Illanmacaredy, is separated by a very narrow deep channel from the east extreme of Mellgoim.

Illananoon, situated very similarly to Illanmacaredy, lies about half a mile south of it, on the north east point of Trae-mellgoim, a sandy rocky creek west of the isthmus, and Pullinrooey is a little south of it. The sandy creek Traenafagheybwee, which is shallow and partly rocky, east, a small sandy valley that intersects Melmore and in which are 2 lakes. This valley, now a sandy waste, was but a few years ago a very fertile tillage.

Southward of Traenafagheybwee to Aghlem Point at the Lower Narrows the shore is mostly a surfy, sandy beach with only 3 or 4 small rocky points. A bank commences at the south point of Traenafagheybwee, curves from that point to within less than a cable's length of the westmost Black rock of the bar, and from it to Aghlem. On the middle of the north end of this bed a small patch dries with good ebbs; but south of that it has from 5 feet to a fathom upon it at low waters, but northerly and easterly winds always cover it with surf.

The Black rocks in the bar are situated a little south east from Traenafagheybwee, almost due south from the mid entrance of and nearly in the middle of the bay. The westmost of these [?] never covers but with spring tides. The eastmost, which is little more than a 100 yards somewhat east of north from it, covers with about half-flood of tide and bares at about half-ebb, but is almost always distinguishable by a sensible rippling, a swell or foam upon it about rather less than third way between the eastmost Black rock and the mouth of MacGregor's bay.

There is a shallow space, at least shallower than the rest, on which there is always, with north or north west winds, a high breaking surf called the Garranbaans. This, the Black rocks and the beds west of them (already described) form the bar of Mulroy. The 2 rocks Freaghadoone that lie about a quarter of a mile south of Islandorisky bares with half-ebb and a rock at Doaghmore, south eastward of the bar Black rocks, is seen till about three-quarters flood.

Lough Swilly

In Lower Mulroy from Portaling to the Lower Narrows there is not any boat creek that could be proposed for shelter. Shessagh bay and MacGregor's bay are shallow and sandy, and both are subject to surf, but MacGregor's breaks most and is often called MacGregor's bar.

The shore of Shessagh without the bay to Rhuinawoogan, the point between Shessagh bay and MacGregor's bar, and about half a mile of Doaghmore shore is rocky and moderately high, and more than half a mile of the latter to the Lower Narrows is sandy beach bounded to south and south east by sand-hills and blowing sands.

The bar of Mulroy may be passed in 3 places: the westmost channel lies between the westmost Black rock and Gortnalughog bank. It passes the rock close west of it, has about 3 fathoms there but less above and below it. The best channel for vessels of any considerable tonnage is between the Black rocks and east of the Black rocks. 2 channels may be reckoned upon, one near the eastmost Black rock and one rather deeper near the east shore. These are said to be changeable and only safe for persons who know them well, and when the bar is tranquil, boats and very light vessels only attempt them.

Lower Narrows

The Lower Narrows, entering the middle from the Lower Mulroy, are northed by Aghlem Point and southed by Crucknagralery, the northmost point of Glinskin, this sound. The stream of tide runs extremely strong and cannot be safely passed but on the first of flood at high water or on the last quarter of ebb, and so far at least a mile above Aghlem.

The inlet or creek Traenagin runs about half a mile north west from the narrow across the north of Dundoan. It is easted, northed, wested and south wested by blowing sands. It dries at low water and is, on account of receiving large drifts of sand, very much shallowed.

Dundoan Point, Rannagh, opposite to Finford of Glinsk, is south west of Traenagin. From the Rannagh south westward to the north east point of Annaghlin is about half a mile of moderately low shore.

Dundoan rocks, from Annaghlin and almost a quarter of a mile parallel to Dundoan shore towards Glinsk shore, enclose Dundoan harbour. The depth varies from 4 to less than 2 fathoms. The bottom sand and so sheltry that no wind but from south can be felt in it, and even south wind cannot be dangerous because, unless near to or at high water, it has not space whereon to collect a wave and because waves, if formed, are fended off by Dundoan rocks.

The upper creek of this harbour is separated from Knoxes Hole by 3 or 4 perches of land and is very safe for boats. A landing-quay where the boat of the preventive waterguards lies would render it more convenient because, being a good harbour, it is much frequented. Here vessels stop in safety if hindered to go up or down the narrows by a strong stream of tide, or if detained. Manure sand is boated from Traenagein and carried into the country for use by adverse winds.

Knoxes Hole

Knoxes Hole, the fast creek of Upper Mulroy, runs about 50 perches within land. It is easted by Annaghlin Point, northed by a narrow neck of land between it and Dundoan harbour, wested by Clontallagh and opened to south by a narrow entrance. It is a dry harbour capable of harbouring a flotilla of boats or a few small vessels. It could easily be rid of 2 or 3 small rocks within it and a rock close under the south point of Annaghlin must be avoided at going in.

Fanny's Hole or Legnahullian is from Knoxes Hole about a mile up the Mevagh shore, which is moderately low clay banks but lowering to a pebbly beach at this Fanny's Hole, at which and near the shore there is good anchorage in 4 and 5 fathoms in a channel between the Oetter Garroo and the beach.

The navigable channel for brigs or vessels of burthen up Middle Mulroy leads through between 2 of the middlemost and largest of Dundoan rocks, and runs half a cable's length clear of the range of the said rocks to near the west or Mevagh shore. The stream will then guide the channel between that shore and the Oetters and round Mevagh Point to Fanny's Hole anchorage, above which the channel curves a little to enter between Oetter Garroo and Oetter Onah along the north of Islandreagh, Inishfar and Bradan sand towards Coolaward <Coolawed> boat harbour in Glinsk.

Coolaward

Coolaward lies on the south of Glinsk and convenient to the road and to the village it leads to. It is situated in a well-sheltered part of Mulroy, except with a strong south gale, but from south winds it requires shelter. This can be effected by only erecting a low addition to a rock that runs out from the south west side and to which a landing-pier may be inclined from the south east side, so as to enclose and perfectly shelter a fleet of boats. Coolaward harbours more boats than any other creek on Mulroy.

About a furlong eastward of Coolaward a difficult dangerous passage and crooked has been cut through the end of the precipice Barnaduarg, where it meets the shore. As it is, the passage is close along the brink that is 10 or 12 to 20 perpendicular feet high and very dangerous to travellers. 4 or 5 years ago a wall to support this was begun but was not raised high enough to be useful. If about 6 perches long of strong wall was built a little wide of the road where it is narrowest, it would be filled so as to both widen and support it and also preserve travellers from its dangers.

Glinsk

Glinsk is a populous village. Its inhabitants are respectable. Some business is transacted in it in groceries, kelp, deals, iron, herrings, cordage and which I saw in passing through it.

James Hays' quay on Treeagh, within Islandreagh opposite Glinsk, half a mile southward above Fanny's Hole, is also a good situation for a small landing-quay. There is a road from this quay into the country. Herrings and whitefish are landed here, and Hays and his sons, who are merchants, land heavy goods here also.

A light vessel having passed Dundoan rocks may safely enough, upon a good tide, pass up between the Oetters and Glinsk shore until she falls into the first-described westmost channel about one-fifth of a mile south of Coolaward where, if necessary, let her anchor safely in 3, 4 or 5 fathoms. But to proceed, let her steer for any object a ship's length west of the Ballyboe Point, then in view until she can see up the middle of the narrows of Rowries ferry north of it.

Should a vessel in that station or on any occasion require anchorage when thereabouts, let her proceed upon the east end of Fadian's slate-roofed house on Terluaghan shore and anchor about a third nearer that house than Illanaviaie. This is well sheltered except from north and used for light vessels with from 2 fathoms to half a fathom on clean sand.

The Oetters

Oetter Cluig begins near Glinsk shore and opposite the entrance of Knoxes Hole, and forms the west channel to a little above Mevagh church, Burn foot, where it meets Oetter Gaarroo. This latter follows nearly parallel to Mevagh shore and easting the channel till it passes Mevagh Point, and thence it norths the navigable channel past the north east point of Inishfar, occupying all the space between it and Oetters Cluig and westing the east channel.

Oetteroona commences off Fanny's Hole and terminates on the south west extremity of the west shore of Islandreagh. Oetter Cluig dries with low ebbing spring tides only. Oetter Gaarroo sometimes bares with low ebbing neap tides but, except with very bad ebbs, its south east, south and south west parts are seen. Oetter Oona seldom all uncovers but with spring tides. The southmost part, the north west point and a spot or two towards the middle often bare with neap tides. These Oetters or beds are formed of various materials: mud, sand, gravel or small stones.

I have not heard of a bed of shells in Mulroy. The Bradden Point of Inishfar is a bed that runs out pretty far north easterly from it and then southward to, and a little south east of, the north east point of Illanaviaie and is a part of the strand that dries south of Inishfar and Islandreagh, and from the south of Oetter Oona within west and south of Illanaviaie, and south west of it to Carrigart, Roughan and Rosapenna <Roseapena>.

In proceeding up Mulroy from Coolaward or Teerluaghan, the navigable channel keeps pretty close round the point of Ballyboe, Rawries and opposite the ferry trends over towards Leahid (it is deep into Bulloyfeam) to rather nearest Bulloyfeam and mid channel, thence until you are in the middle between Denniston's rock and Ummeracaam. Here wind between 2 large rocks up the Hassans towards and near the Glassen rocks, close to Devlin shore, near to which and between it and the Scraps, keep until above the big Scraap.

Carrick

At Carrick, three-quarters of a mile above Rawrus on the south shore, there is a good sheltry creek for boats that does not altogether dry; and near three-quarters more above it, the Naggles in Devlin, a pretty deep but partly narrow inlet, runs a little east of south about a mile within sand. It is quite sheltered and deep enough for boats.

Other Anchorages

Bulloyfeam on the opposite or Fanad shore has deep water as 2 and 3 fathoms to its entrance.

Pullnaplughog anchorage at Ummeracaam is about half a mile below the Narrows of the Hassans and on the Fanad shore. Here vessels detained below the Hassans by either contrary winds or strong stream of tide in the Narrows anchor while delayed.

The Hassans

The Hassans or Upper Narrows are rendered still narrower by groups of rocks that lie in and near the channel. For about half a mile above and as much below it the navigable channel lies between 2 of these, hardly a ship's length, as under in the Hassans. The stream of tide runs with greater force and velocity than at any other narrows on these shores (see tides) and has a considerable fall in the Hassans near the lower part of the rocks.

The channel is but a rocky ford of only a fathom deep. Above this, in the Hassans, it is 2 and 3 fathoms and within the Scraaps 1 fathom and even less on a rocky bed (strong bottom). Scraaps are beds of gravel and distinct stones of various sizes, eastward of the Hassans where we enter the broad water or Upper Mulroy, in which there is above this place almost everywhere deep water.

When vessels descending Mulroy are detained above the Hassans they anchor under the bank Drumnaskeie of Devlin until it is a proper time to proceed, or, if ascending, the anchorage is equally safe and convenient.

Having ascended to Drumnaskeie, steer only as far off the land as that shore and off Cranfwer Park Point as will ensure safety. You may keep within or without the rock off Cranfwer Park Point, but the best course is east of it and thence near Greencastle Island, west of it and on either side (the most convenient) of the rock next south east of Greencastle and so to within 2 or 3 ship's lengths of Ranee Point; and from Ranee Point keeping west of Teerhernin Island and the rocks and isles west and south of it, sail east and south of Inishweal or Watts Island and westward south of Rossgarrow Island near the middle point of Rossgarrow, and thence direct to Hay's store near Milford.

Anchorages near Mevagh

Continued stormy weather hindered me to take the soundings of Upper Mulroy, but I have described the track by which vessels navigate it with much exactness as it was described to me by William McCauley of Ranee, Charles Williams of Drumbear, pilot and [blank] Graham of Devlinreagh, who all know it perfectly.

William McCauley asserts that he fished in every part of it and that he knows it from his infancy (about 40 years), and that there is water sufficiently deep for large sloops and brigs up to 400 tons burthen in every part of the above-described tract; and Charles Williams, who is a pilot of Mulroy, and his son agree with him that it is the proper, best and deepest route for vessels, and that by which they always conduct them up Mulroy. The broad water or Upper Mulroy from the Keady and Ross to Ranee Point was in times of herring fishing accounted very fortunate fishing ground.

New Town

Dr Stokes is anxious to know where on Mulroy and where on Lough Swilly he should propose to build a new town, so as to have a good communicating road between them. On Lough Swilly the foot of Glenvar river is a very good situation and on Mulroy, Kerrykeel, in which fairs are already established, might answer very well yet. Ballymagowan (a mile further north) on the Fanad road, and close upon the shore with deep water, and a good site for a quay in a fishing bay close in front, might answer full as well. A very useful ferry would be easily established between Ranee Point and Drumbear.

Charles Williams of the latter place, pilot, has a good boat and finds that on account of Kerrykeel fairs and many of the Presbyterian congregation crossing Mulroy there to Gorteally meeting house, his boat could be employed. 2 small landing-quays one on each side would make it very convenient. I saw very great inconvenience at Rawrus ferry when, at full sea with a brisk wind on the frosty morning of Carrigart <Carrygart> winter fair, boatfuls and many of them females, were, for want of quays, obliged to wade to and from the boat.

Lough Fanad

Lough Fanad enters Fanad by a narrow sound wested by Melnaharda Point of Ummeracaam and easted by the Ross Point of Rossnakill, and, dividing the eastern from the western Fanad, it terminates at Kindrum about 3 miles north of the Ross and within less than a mile of Ballyhernan bay on the north coast of Fanad. Mr Patton of Fanad supposes this branch to be the deepest part of Mulroy and by much the largest proportion of the land along its shores including the peninsula. Moress is very fertile.

Manure and Seaweed

Mulroy produces abundance of the lesser seaweeds for manure (slatt marah grows in very deep water only) and limestone is conveniently distributed along its shores. The fish caught in Mulroy are herrings, glasson or greylords, codling, whitings, flatfish, but few cod, scallops and shrimps.

Traenaross

The Mulroy, Rosguill shore is described with Mulroy. Melmore, of which Mellgoim is the north point, and southward to Traenagin and Traenaross south of Crucknasleiga mountain, although bounded by a deeply indented and very irregular shore, does not without Mulroy present the fisheries with a single creek wherein a boat could be secured for a night, even in fine weather.

Traenaross bay is about half a mile over and terminates half a mile inland in a surfy sandy beach formed by a mound of sand, pebbles and small round stones within half a mile of Traenagin <Franagin>. In the south west side of Traenaross a salt pan was once worked on a very small creek in which very light vessels discharged cargoes of rock-salt, but this entire north west coast of the peninsula of Rosguill is so closely invested with formidable rocks of all descriptions and classes that even a good harbour should hardly induce mariners to frequent it.

The shore itself is, except the short sandy beach of Dooey, extremely rocky, round eastward to Doonans mostly high and partly very high rocky cliffs and altogether inaccessible to ships or boats for about 9 miles and an half, notwithstanding that just beyond the rocks and breakers, of which few are much more than a mile off shore, it is reckoned excellent fishing ground.

All the inhabitants keep curraghs or skin boats, in which they venture off in fine weather from 1 to 3 leagues or further to fish but bring their fish to Doonans for sale. One of these assured me that he would manage his curragh among waves that would overwhelm any ordinary boat. Curraghs are very buoyant. A Rosguillite will carry his carriage to the shore, descend with it by any footpath to the water and shove off to sea through a surf that would terrify any stranger to the shore, and will, on his return, take it up and carry it home.

I saw a petition written for the Doonanites by the master of a Howth <Houth> wherry at Doonans, wherein they state that want of shelter or a quay at Doonans and the dread of losing their boats on that account hinders them to keep boats; that Doonans and Rosguill could muster from 200 to 300 expert fishermen more; that they frequently have shoals of herrings to be off the shore without possessing the means of taking them; and that if they had a shelter on the Point of Illan-cranny at Doonans, they would in future keep boats and nets in readiness to fish whenever fish appear to be fished for.

The petition was to be given to Captain Cochran, to be by him transmitted to Earl Leitrim or to the Fishing Board.

Doonans

Doonans is a very celebrated fishing station at which Scotch, Manx and Irish from Rush, Howth, Skerries, Dublin, Balbriggan and from every fish port assemble annually in their vessels to take and cure every species of fish found on our coast, while unfortunate Doonans exhibits but 1 solitary boat hauled up and almost rotten on shore. These adventurers always bring their necessaries along with them: boats, nets, men, salt, provisions, everything; and, of course, have no necessity to leave a ready tenpenny among the unfortunate and frequently starving inhabitants of the shore that they thus invade and rifle of the abundance that the bounteous providence conferred upon it, and in the enjoyment of which these poor inhabitants have not the means of participating even in a moderate degree.

This probably is one principal source of the poverty so visible on the north coast of Donegal: in districts the rocky soil of which the plough is not calculated to furrow nor the narrow spade-filled deal to feed the hands that till and reap it or where the craggy pastures or the stunted heath produce no pampered animals for show or any produce for which premiums could be claimed, such districts can hope but little from agriculture or husbandry performed on deals; and along these shores, where few hold 3 or 4 acres of tillage, who can hope to become rich.

Probability presents nothing so likely to relieve the distress of the district along the coast as to enable them by any profitable means to engage industriously in the calling to which they are all brought up, fishing. But for this purpose they want everything, boats, oars and nets: but how they can be provided, I know not.

But there is a particular source of poverty peculiar to the inhabitants of these shores. They gather annually as much seaweed as manures near half their tillage for potatoes, and of this article they generally have a plentiful crop; but neither flax nor oats raised off land often manured with sea vegetables proves productive, and all the inhabitants of Fanad, Rosguill, Doe and [blank] concur in that assertion and affirm that barley alone is productive of potatoe land but that, as the excise laws now stand, barley is not worth cultivating.

They dare not distil it. That prevents sale for it at home and the price is too low to encourage them to take it to a distant market, any possible remedy for this. In Rosguill, as in Fanad, large quantities of kelp are manufactured, but even this article is less, much less, in demand than formerly.

Kelp Manufacture

I do not understand the process of kelp burning, but it must be very simple if what I see performed be the most effectual method of manufacturing kelp: 1, a small trench is dug in any dry spot near the shore and in this they begin to burn the dried weed with common fuel, adding, I am informed, weed and fuel successively until all is consumed. From this process I suspect much of the substance of the weed may evaporate and which might be prevented by using something like a lime-kiln for the purpose. There is good limestone in Umeracaam shore, Doonans.

Sheep Haven

The mouth of Sheep Haven is easted by Rosguill and wested by the high promontory of Horn Head, and comprises Doonans anchorage or road, Ards harbour, Pullinoer bay, Traichorbet or Marblehill bay and Dunfanaghy harbour.

Doonans anchorage or harbour is the south west or nearly the south shore of the peninsula of Rosguill and is easted by the isthmus of Rosapenna, where it is not three-quarters of a mile over from Traebeg, Doonans to Fanny's Hole on Mulroy, Lignahuller. Spring tides rise here (in Sheep Haven) in settled weather perpendicularly from 18 to 20 feet, according to the seasons and winds (sea tides). Tides in this bay rise highest with north west or northerly winds, but north easterly winds cause the lowest or greatest ebbs with southerly winds and frost. It ebbs least on this coast.

In tranquil weather, and with winds from north by west, north, north east, east and south east, vessels may lie safely across the mouth of Pullcamae and Traebeg sandy bay towards the middle of Mossluace high shore. The anchorage is on clean sand and roomy and the depth of water from 2 to 6 fathoms. This anchorage is too open to wind from north by west, north west [by] west, south west, south and south east. When any of these winds prevail, vessels immediately run for Ards House. The bar of Ards is seldom without surf but, unless it is greatly agitated, it is not dangerous.

The breakers east of the bar towards Traemore rise high and have obtained the title of the "champions," varies but little in depth from you enter by the east of the bar rock until you pass the Luace Pullinabucean or flag, but at going in as soon as you have passed the bar rock, bring the outer extreme of the Luace to bear on Ards old lime-kiln until you are near it (the Luace), pass it above on your starboard hand and then keep mid channel parallel to the shore until you anchor and I return to Doonans.

Doonans is by many supposed to be a village of more than ordinary importance. Every vessel from the eastward sailing westward or from the westward sailing towards east for Greenoc[k], the Clyde, the Irish Sea, Belfast or Liverpool, if overtaken by adverse winds and forced into shelter, runs for and stops at Doonans. Every vessel, sloop or wherry that fishes on the coast anchors first at Doonans. If vessels attacked by adverse winds at Doonans must run from it, Ards is about 2 miles nearly south of it and Dunfanaghy a little west of south about 5 miles.

Yet Doonans, however celebrated and frequented by mariners, consists of only 2 little scattered villages not a quarter of a mile asunder, and peopled by persons who, although hardy, skilful, expert fishermen and striving to subsist their numerous families by fishing, follow it with hand-lines in their skin boats, not being of ability to provide better craft or fearful lest better craft should be destroyed because boats have no place of shelter there.

Anchorages near Doonans

Doonans is easted by Traebeg smooth strand, half a mile over to Mossluace and within the anchorage; Illanceannog, the proposed site for a shelter pier, wests the entrance to Traebeg. Pullcormac rocky creek lies a furlong and a half west of it and is wested by the rocky point Ruinaskeagh, which is the south east point of the very rocky bays Claddaghluaghan and Ummeracaam; these extend about half a mile north west from it. The east shore of Claddaghluaghan is high rock. It and Ummeracaam are northed by low rocks and loose stones, on which the Rush and Howth fishers dry their fish in summer and keep watchmen living there in sod huts to attend them.

Ummeracaam is north wested by a very rich limestone rock of different strata and having deep beds of other rock between them; the last or lowest under the sea mark is kelp coloured. This meets the already more generally described west shore of Rosguill (which see).

Anchorages East of Doonans

Mossluace south east[s] Doonans anchorage. It is about half a mile of pretty high rocky shore with some detached low rocks under it, and extraordinary low ebbs sometimes bare the strand from Traebeg round its low rocky south point and connects it with Traemore.

Traemore from the east side of Mossluace Point takes a south westerly direction for about a mile and a quarter, then west about three-quarters of a mile to the channel and bar of Ards. The south part of this is the broad strand or point of sand (Rhuinaworgan) opposite to Ards that easts and norths the channel for about a mile south eastward to the foot of Glaanry or Black river, and from that westward and southing Ards. It is 2 miles' strand from Ards to Magheroerty and Cloone, and nearly as far as Drimluackagh bridge and Umerafadd in Doagh or Doe, except the channels of freshwater streams that meander through it.

Little (if any) more than 50 perches of bank from Rhuinaslegga Point of Ards to Rhuinarispie of Doe would embank about 420 plantation or something more than 525 Cunningham acres off the upper part of this inlet and of which about a third would belong to Lieutenant-General Hart. The freshwater stream could be easily confined to the new mearing. Another tract at Cashel, and between it and Doe, could be embanked but is hardly of value to remunerate the trouble and expense of embanking it.

Traemore is almost continually covered by a high breaking surf. It and Rhuinawingan are easted by sand-hills almost without verdure and forsaken of rabbits.

Doe

Doe or Doagh channel from the harbour at Ards up to Doe Castle and Luackagh bridge follows a very winding course but is deep enough for vessels of 300 tons burthen, even on Doe Castle ford, with good tides; but at Rhuinawargan high tides attended with storm alters it so often and so much that no stranger to it should even attempt it without a pilot. This inlet is pretty broad and with winds from north is subject to very heavy surges. Large shoals of herrings often frequent it.

The channel is conveniently wide for a mile above Ards but the bay affords no other creek for boats in distress but Baarnanroan south of the channel in Aghadhachor; it opens to a little east of north. A bed of partly high rocks lie before it over which, with high water and north wind, the sea breaks furiously into it and then destroys any boat not hauled up out of the reach of its fury. Herring boats can enter it from a little before half-flood of tide and the entrance would secure it. It should be cleaned of small rocks and loose stones from within it. A few good boats lie here.

Drimluackagh quarry is about a quarter of a mile long, of very rich limestone. It burns into lime of the best quality and rises in blocks and slates of large dimensions fit for tombstones, doorcases, hearthstones, cills, and it takes a beautiful polish and is easily worked. Boats come to the quarry, which is part of the shore, on from 10 to 12 feet water in spring tides. It is not a quarter of a mile below Luackagh bridge, at which there is a valuable salmon fishery and at which, and in every part of this channel and bay, large quantities of herrings has been taken.

Moress Hole

Moress Hole is a creek in the north east point of Ards opposite Doonans, in which herrings are sometimes taken. The beach is sand. It is an open surfy creek, the entrance to which is but a little north west of the bar rock.

Pullanore

Pullanore or the back strand of Ards opens immediately west of Killycoole, the north point of Moress Hole, and the rocks off Killycoole are called the Benhagorms and reach a little out into Pullanore in the mouth. There usually was a good take of herrings. The bar is sand shallows and breaks greatly with north east wind and often a swell from the north through the sound of Clonmess rolls dangerously upon it. All ebbs dry above the bar and is a little used by boats and never by heavy craft.

Clonmess Islands and Point with cliffy high shores north west the entrance of Pullanore and south east that of Roughan bay or, as it is called, Traecharbet. Traecharbet is open and quite exposed to north and north east and not much frequented by any description of vessels. It is pretty deep and clean to near the beach, which is sand under Marblehill House. Herrings are sometimes taken in Traecharbet and there is a quarry of coarse slates a little north west from it; and Modfen, a rocky creek on the north side, could, by a little shelter on the north east point of the entrance and clearing it within, be made very useful to the fishing boats of Sheep Haven.

Breaghy Head

Breaghy Head norths and north wests Traecharbet and is high and cliffy round to near Portnablagh in Dunfanaghy bay, and having a low rocky point about half a mile below Marblehill House and the remarkable high rocks Carralea and Skibbalh and more northward of Breaghy Head. The Skibbalh is a high rock connected with a cliffy point of the shore (Punteenskibbalh) under which there is a high, wide, irregular archedway through which one sees from the west shore of Rosguill.

Dunfanaghy Bay

Dunfanaghy bay is altogether exposed to every wind from east to north. The anchorage without the bar is from three-quarters to half a mile south eastward from it, or half a mile east or a little south of east from Catharine's Island in the most exposed part of the outer harbour. The bar is sandy and liable to alter its place; at some times it dries altogether, at others not at all. It has within 30 years occupied every foot of the bay from the side of Catharine's Island to the opposite shore of Horn Head. It almost always appears up or breaking, but is not dangerous to a well-managed vessel brought fair upon it with a leading wind to carry her over it; but fishing boats dare not attempt it at all but with moderate wind and weather, and must at other times take shelter in Portnablagh or Killyhoey.

Portnablagh

Portnablagh or Portnablaighea lies about a quarter of a mile a little south east of the outer anchorage and Killyhoey about as much south west of it. They are both sandy creeks. The former enters between rocky points. Portnablagh opens to north, has 6 fathoms at the entrance and capable of being sheltered at either side a little within it. It nearly dries with low ebbs.

Killyhoey dries from its north east point to Dunfanaghy bar by the north of Catharine's Island. It is open to north and north west. The beach is sand but the entrance and shore are rocky. Boats shelter in the north east part. But Horn Head shore, the north east side of the harbour without the bar, is shelterless, but about a mile and half down Horn Head, and just within Doongaup or Bhudacrappan north of it, boat crews have saved their lives in Pullinrighey. It is the south east extreme of the Skate bay which is that under the awfully high, cliffy north east shore of Horn Head from Doongaup to the north west point of the peninsula or the Horn. Here skates are taken in from 13 to 17 fathoms.

Catharine's Island

Catharine's Island is now so highly surrounded with sand that only very high spring tides flow between it and the land, and that not to any considerable depth. The ships' channel that formerly crossed the bar (when that bar dried with spring tides) close by it now flows over it almost in the middle, between the island and the opposite shore, with but from 3 to 6 feet water upon it at low water spring tides. It is now nearer Dunfanaghy than it heretofore was and has at high water spring tides, when highest, not above 16 feet upon it. From the bar the channel curves towards the Red rock and so close along the north side of the Black rocks, thence to a little [rock] without the green island off the bawn and pretty close by the town point, and so over to near the opposite low small point on Horn Head side and up to the bridge.

When a vessel has arrived safe within the bar, she is then in a dry harbour. She may anchor either on the north side of the Black rock in the channel, with one anchor on the rocks, or within, between it and the town, the bottom being clean or above the bawn in Frank's Hole. It is the safest berth for a light vessel and a very desirable place for a small landing-quay a little in front of the street. Here the harbour is not half a mile wide, so that small craft need fear but little from wind anywhere to the bridge or above the bridge in the creeks of Strachan to miles above the town, if the[y] run up on the flowing tide.

Dunfanaghy

Dunfanaghy is the last post town on this coast. Some well-attended fairs held at it, some cargoes of heavy goods, timber and are imported to it. Slates quarried at [?] Purt near it are shipped from it and, in fishing times, herrings.

Horn Head

Horn Head is by many said to be the highest promontory on the Irish coast. The bawn of Dunfanaghy, Horn Head House and the Horn or extreme north cape are almost in the same meridian. The peninsula of Horn Head norths the harbour of Dunfanaghy and wests the entrance of Sheep Haven. The east shore is mostly high rocky cliffs, but the north east, north and north west are stupendously high.

The south eastmost head or first remarkable rocky shore is Doonbwee. The higher north eastmost extreme is the Little Head. Carnabaartan rock, always above water near the shore, is less than a quarter of a mile northward of Doonbwee. Illanatawee high island lies somewhat south of the Little Head and is connected to the shore by rocks that bare at low water. Pullfeegus lies a little south of Illanatawee. Doongaup or Bhudacrappan lies about as far north of it and Pullanrighey just west of or behind Doongaup.

The access to this is most difficult. The connection between it and the main shore is much lower than the doon, and the doon perhaps not above half as high as the main coast behind it. Here, however, boat crews have in a few instances saved their lives and their boats from total wreck.

Between this, Pullanrighey and the Horn (about a mile and an half) is called the Skate bay. From the Horn or north cape to the north west cape or MacSwine's Head the coast lowers and the west shore ceases to be high cliffs. About a quarter of a mile south of it there is a rocky bay between MacSwine's Head and Claggin Point, and another south of that point and of MacSwine's Gun to Murravagh, and the shore of Murravagh to Traemore is all rocky without any very safe harbours.

Traemore, Corgannive is perfectly open to every wind from north to west. It is a low sandy beach a mile long, almost east and west, and southed by blowing sands and sand-hills, and altogether shelterless.

Caarnaharwee

Caarnaharwee rocks begin north west of MacSwine's Head. These are large, black and irregular. They cover and uncover with every tide and, keeping nearly parallel to the shore, extend a little southward of the west point of Murravagh. The bottom near them, and between them and the shore, is foul and breaks exceedingly with but little wind.

The description of the shore westward of Horn Head is taken from a boat sailing in view of it, assisted by information obtained from the crew, who were fishermen, from Captain Smyth of Rathmullan and from James Meenan and 2 other natives of Tory Island, round which I sail, and I described the shore south westward from the Bloody Foreland Point to the Gweedore <Goodoer> on land.

Murravagh Point

Murravagh Point, on the south west of the peninsula of Horn Head, runs a little south of west about a quarter of a mile from where it bends off north of Traemore strand and forms a roomy rocky bay south of it, and in which the Sheep Haven fishermen believe a good safe landing-place for fishing boats could be made with secure shelter from all winds but from south to west, and that it would be most useful on that exposed and shelterless coast, of which the shore west of Traemore is high, rocky and partly cliffs to Errarooey.

Cirarooy and Ballyness

Cirarooy river, the narrow and barred, admits small boats at about half-flood and when in affords them good shelter from almost every wind, and westward of Errarooey to Ballyness about 2 miles the shore is low and sandy and without harbour.

Ballyness bar is shallow. It breaks with a very high surf and lies about a quarter of a mile north east from the entrance of the channel within the range or line of the shore. Ballyness inlet is more than 2 miles from the shore or entrance at north to either Gortahork at south or Ards mill west of it. The bottom is mostly sand or mud and is in several places three-quarters of a mile broad, and has within it several large creeks. It is north wested by a mostly narrow sandy point about a mile and a half long.

Inishbofin, Inishdooh and Inishbeg islands lie off that point, the outside of which also is a sandy beach.

MacSwine's Bay

MacSwine's bay from Traemore, Corgannive westward to Inishbofin is 4 Irish miles wide, in navigating which (or rather by not navigating it) McKenzie's soundings show upon his chart that he sounded but on one course directly from a quarter of a mile north of Horn Head to Inishbofin Island, and that in that course he was for half the way nearly 2 miles from the shore and not within less than half a mile off Ballyness bar, and could not of course have formed a very correct notion of the coast between Horn Head and Ballyness, north for 2 miles, west of Ballyness bar in the bay south of Inishbofin and of Magheroarty.

Portmush in Bunininver creek lies about 2 miles east of Bloody Foreland Point and is a very productive of seaweed. It is said that want of convenient landing-places east or west of it near it causes most of the weed gathered along shore to be collected to it and carried from it for manure by a road leading through or into the county. My informants say that, although it is rocky, it is improvable, that a ledge of rocks that runs eastward from the north west point of the entrance would, with very little addition, shelter it from north west and north. It is naturally sheltered from west and south and nearly to east. Should not anything to assist poor farmers to collect and land sea manure in safety be an object of public interest?

Fishing is practised extensively off Bunininver or Portmush and boats often run to it for shelter, having no other harbour near on either side of it.

Shore West of Bloody Foreland

The shore westward from Bunininver to the Bloody Foreland or Rhuinarooey Point is a moderate height, rocky under the shore without cliffs and said to be without any creek capable of being sheltered.

Rhuinardallagh Point lies about half a mile south west from Bloody Foreland Point and as much west of the signal tower on Wheecruick. It north easts Aaltaiinoe bay, which is south wested for half a mile by Rhiunassnapiel Point.

The shore from the Farland to Aaltawinnae and Rhuinasnahid, and a mile southward to Bunininver, Glashagh, is low with a border of low rocks that covers with every tide (at least with spring tides) and exhibits an almost incessant surf upon it, that shore being exposed to all winds but east. However, when there is fishing near it with wind from north east and nearly from south, boats find shelter in Aaltawinnae in settled or summer weather.

Shore South of Bloody Foreland

Bunininver, Glashagh, about 3 miles and an half southward along the coast from Bloody Foreland, is an irregular rocky-shored creek with rocks close off the middle of the entrance which open to north east but which leave room enough for boats to enter or depart either north or south of them. The inside is mostly clean. It is tolerably well sheltered and has a short stony beach at least, on which boats are hauled up close below Glashagh houses in time of storm or swell upon the shore.

South of Glashagh for a little more than a mile and an half to Goeenkoeggal the shore is mostly sandy, with here and there a lump of rocks along the high water mark of Carrick and Luinniagh shore, which I take to be what was the old natural shore before the sand was blown away or off it and by which the present waste there became extensive.

Goeenkoeggal, east of Gola Island, is a shallow sandy inlet about a quarter of a mile broad from the main entrance. It runs half a mile east to low small islands and as far south east from the island to Shanacoskragh near the great road from Gortahork, and a third branch ascends three-quarters of a mile from the 2 islands by the east of Magheragaalin which souths the entrance and bar which are sand and ebb almost dry at low water.

However, fishing boats could find shelter in it from wind from every point of the compass when once within it, and the situation of the group of islands before it should afford the entrance to it much shelter.

Islands

The islands: what I have learned respecting the islands from the persons I have mentioned I must, in respect of situations, bearing and distance, refer to McKenzie's chart, not having any better map to refer to.

Inishbofin is about an Irish mile long from north to south and about three-quarters of a mile broad where broadest, and is inhabited. The south point lies about a mile north west from the bar of Ballyness and the strand from the bar to that point dries with the low ebb of spring tides, and a bed of rocks at the east side of the strand at the south of the island dries then also. Off this the water is shallow but deepens north west towards a small harbour on the north east of the island and which opens directly towards the south west point of Inishdooh Island, about half a mile north eastward of it.

Inishdooh is [?] inhabited. It is but narrow and little more than a quarter of a mile long. Inishbeg is but small and not inhabited and is less than a quarter of a mile north of Inishdooh. The west side of Inishbofin is openly exposed to all the fury of the west, but the little harbour on the north east is sheltered from north west, west and south by the land of Inishbofin, and from north east by Inishdooh, and disturbed materially only by winds from south east and north or a little east of north.

There are no harbours in Inishdooh or Inishbeg. The shores of Inishbofin, Inishdooh and Inishbeg are, except about a furlong of the middle of the east side of Inishdooh, low and weedy.

A large cluster of rocks lies off the north west of Inishdooh and reaches near a quarter of a mile from the shore, and about a third of its length from its north point a similar cluster lies about as far east of its south point. These both dry at about half-ebb of tides and should be avoided by any vessel going to Inishbofin harbour, either from north or east.

This harbour is embraced by sandy shores, has 3 fathoms inside on a clean sandy bottom and right in the sound between it and Inishdooh, third way over, 4 fathoms, and 2 fathoms at two-thirds over the water round Inishdooh, and Inishbeg is 5, 6, 9 and [more] fathoms.

There is, in the sound between them, about quarter way over from Inishdooh, a rock that does not altogether cover with spring tides, and midway between that rock and Inishbeg there is from 2 to 3 fathoms on a rocky bottom. Captain Smyth says it is unsafe unless with a smooth sea and calm weather. Rock cod are taken off the west of this sound and off the north and west of Inishbeg, and greylords to 2 miles east of it.

It is less than 3 miles from the north of Inishbeg to the nearest land under the East Town of Tory. It is little more than 5 Irish miles from the bar of Ballyness and hardly 6 miles and a quarter from Portmush.

McKenzie shows the deepest water in crossing the sound of Tory from Inishbofin to Tory Island 17 fathoms, but fishermen say that in some places in the sound it exceeds 20 fathoms.

Tory Island

Tory <Torry> Island, according to McKenzie, is from the doon at east to Skreggagh Point at west little more than 2 Irish miles long and of variable breadth from Buillig Point northward to Luacnaluannan, where broadest. It is but half a mile broad and where narrowest, at the West Town, north of Cammusmore, it is only about a quarter of a mile over.

The east end or doon of Tory (like all doonans on the coast) is appended to it by a very narrow short isthmus. It projects a little east of north of the range of the island about half a mile and is, with the north shore to the extreme west point, with scarcely an exception, inaccessible high cliffs.

The southmost shore is almost low but very rocky, most of which rocks I sketched by view and may remark that in good ebbs they uncover rather further from shore than I would have expected on a shore to which the deep water approaches so very near.

McKenzie states that on the shore of Tory on the full and change days of the moon it is high water at half past 4 o'clock but on the main coast not until three-quarters past 5, and that spring tides rise perpendicularly only 12 feet and neap tides only 6 or 7; that the stream of tide sets eastward from the sound of Tory to the sound of Inishtuahull and that it runs but a mile and an half an hour when stronger.

Notwithstanding that McKenzie's delineation of the figure of Tory is very unlike it, I have written the proper names of the most remarkable points and creeks at least very nearly in their true places, according as they were described and shown to me.

Purtadoon and Portduillig

Purtadoon is a creek between the south east point of the doon and the east end of Tory. It harbours craft under 36 tons on a white sandy bottom, holds securely, runs inland a quarter of a mile and has shelter from every wind but from south to south by west.

Portduillig souths the East Town of Tory between 2 rocky points. Small boats enter or leave it at about half-tide and if to remain, they must be hauled up, it being very open.

A turf bog that wests the East Town in a northerly direction from Portduillig is said to be very deep, close to the shore. The islanders say from 20 to 30 feet deep and that for small wages they would excavate a basin in that bog capable of harbouring 20 or 30 boats, that there is but 3 or 4 perches of beach to cut through between the tide and the bog and no fear of it being choked by sand, the bottom of it being rock.

Cammusmore harbour souths the ruined steeple in the West Town. The principal bay is formed by 2 rocky points about three-quarters of a mile asunder and the harbour in the middle of it between 2 other inner points of rocks near the town.

Principal Points on Tory

Boats from the eastward can enter the bay by a passage through the Buillig that does not dry. There are 13 fathoms in the south east entrance, 6 in the middle and 3 in the north west entrance near the Buillig Hoanawaesh, which is a large body of rock that runs out from the west point of the bay and affords it much shelter. Vessels on the fishery, cruising armed vessels and vessels taking in kelp anchor here in settled weather or with moderate north west north, north east or east winds, but never stay long in it because it is so much exposed to south east, south and south west. From 60 to 70 tons leave the inner harbour at or after half-flood of tide or could enter until half-ebb.

Skreggagh is the north west point or westward point of Tory and Buillig-Skreggagh; a sunken rock breaks close under it.

Portnaglash lies near half a mile east from Skreggagh, under the high north shore. It is accessible from land by a very steep path when boats or small vessels that fish north of Tory anchor there in calm weather or with southerly winds on gravel and weed in 4 and 5 fathoms. A high rock near the shore and always above water stands but a little east of it, and within the east side of that rock Scalt Shoersha, a lofty cave, enters the almost perpendicular rocky shore and runs, it is supposed, under half the breadth of the island, being accessible by a very difficult way down the precipice.

Toroohnagallaman are 2 small high-shored islands in the angle formed by the north shore of Tory and the north or north east doon, and the passage between them leads into Portachalh creek within them, under the isthmus of the doon and in which boats harbour for a night or two in fine weather only, with southerly or easterly winds and when employed fishing northward of Tory. Vessels of the largest description may anchor off the north of Tory, within half a mile of the shore, when the wind is south or in calm weather.

Aspect of Tory

Tory lies from north west by north to south east by south, in an aspect that gives it the enjoyment of every hour of sunshine; and the height to which the north and north east parts rise above the southern covers it naturally from storms coming from the northward. Hardly any shore affords large[r] quantities of weed than Tory. Of this, the inhabitants use a necessary quantity for manure and make kelp of the residue, of which the[y] ship off many large cargoes annually.

The sound of Tory is proverbially celebrated for its cod fishery. Herrings are taken in and [around the?] rock off the entrance of Cammusmore and glassen, whitings and between Tory and MacSwine's bay, in which haddock and whitings are found in great plenty, each in the proper season, and what are called great ling are found in great plenty to 4 or 5 leagues north and north west of Tory and sometimes east of it. Wherrymen meet with them when fishing for cod and also west of Tory at that distance from land, until they are north of Ooey in Rosses.

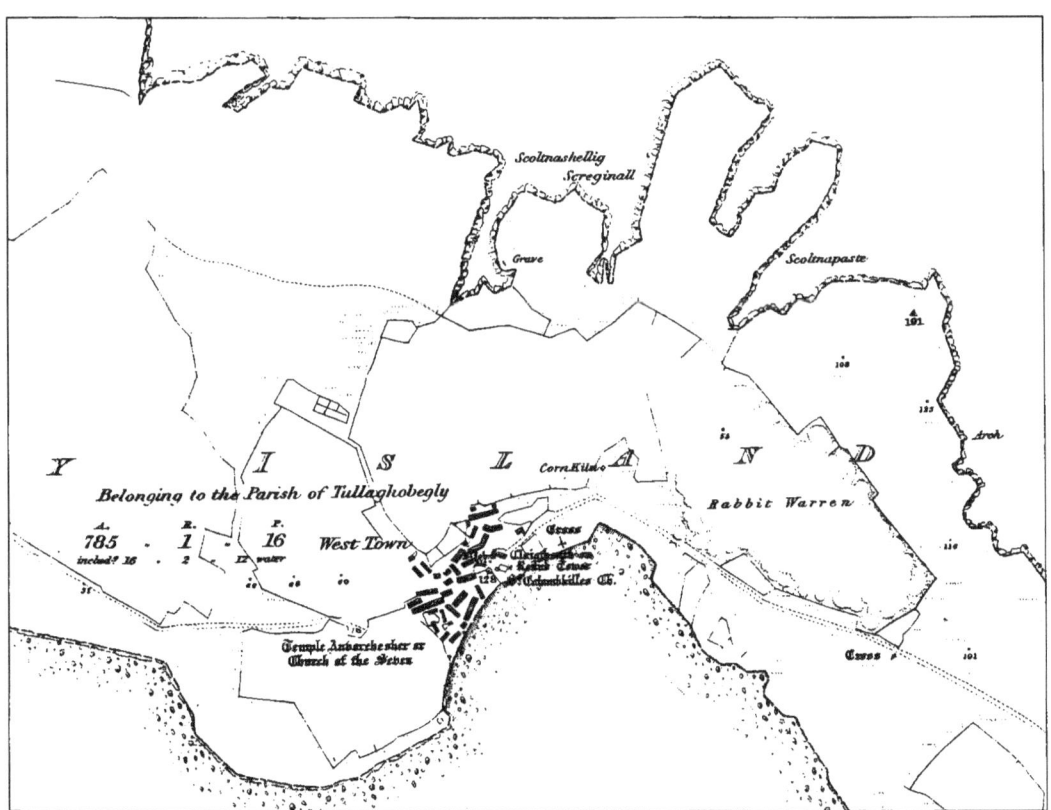

Map of West Town, Tory Island, from the first 6″ O.S. maps, 1830s

Other Islands

Of Gola Island and the island[s] near it off Gweedore, my information is probably less minute and less perfect. When shoals of herrings come on this coast, they are taken in Inishfree bay south of Gola, in the mouth of Gweedore, in the sound between Gola and Inishonaer, and towards the mouth of Goeenkoeggal inlet in the main shore.

Inishhunny lies a quarter of a mile off the north east point of Rosses and off the entrance of Gweedore. The east end is sandy. A small island lies south, one west and one north east of it. It is inhabited and the strand between it and the main shore dries at low water.

Gola is inhabited at south east and south. The north and west shores are high and cliffy. 3 small islands lies south of it and Umpin, [a] small high island, with 2 others close together lie off its north position and 3 boats belong to it. The south east point is sandy and some large rocks lie a little north of it on the east side. There are 2 creeks in Gola in which boats are harboured. The south point of this [is] about half a mile off the main shore.

Inishmaan is half a mile east of Gola and about 3 furlongs off shore. The nearest to land or east point is sand that extends round to a small bay in the middle of the south shore, which altogether is half a mile. This island is small and not always inhabited. Light vessels anchor in good shelter south of the west side of Inishmaan, about third way between it and Magheragaalin Point, in from 2 to 3 fathoms on clean sand.

Inish-hirrer lies a quarter of a mile off the shore of Buninver Glashagh. It is a low island and shore bound, with a broad border of low rocks. It is about three-quarters of a mile long and uninhabited, it and Inishmaan being pasture-island. The sound between Inishmaan is very rocky. These for the first three-quarters of a mile cover and uncover with every tide and so to about half a mile south of Umpin, but among these a sunken rock breaks with dreadful agitation.

The Builligchonnels are the north westmost in this bed and are only seen with the low ebbs of spring tides. A similar rock lies close off the north west point of Inishmaan. I only viewed this island from Inish-hirrer, Magheragaalin and Carrick.

Curraghs

Skin-covered boats or curraghs are much used. Among them I measured one 10 feet long at Carrick Point and saw embarked in it the paddle man, another man, his wife and child, a little girl, a ewe that had been on shore, with a tup and a goose held by a little girl in her lap. The sheep was tied by the 4 legs together and was held by the man, who sat with his legs extended with it between them. The ferry was about a mile and a quarter to Gola. The paddler had the whole management of the curragh. The wind was rather fresh and a little athwart the course, yet she performed well and landed safe beyond in 43 minutes.

McKenzie sounded only the usual navigable ships' road between these islands (altogether 13 in number and rocks unnumbered) and the land. Yet the inhabitants say that outside of Gola and Inish-hirrer, and 10 or 12 miles north and north west of them, is very good fishing ground, and that the wherries fish it for each species in the proper seasons annually. The whole group with the channel beds and banks among them, when viewed from Inish-hirrer and the main shore, appear to be altogether out of their relative places and order on the chart. I regret not having got them surveyed and mapped.

PRODUCTIVE AND SOCIAL ECONOMY

Shells

It is observable that whenever shells abound or mud makes a convenient and useful manure, sea vegetables of every kind is scarce on that shore. Experience has taught that mud or shells or weeds, however proper for a particular soil, may not be a suitable manure for every soil or for every park of the same farm, and the same may be observed of lime or marble where applied to lands remote from the coast.

To remedy this inconvenience, the inhabitants of the shore propagate the growth of seaweed by planting stones drawn from the sand in the mud beds or by laying stones or strands or anywhere that the tide will cover them. They will in that situation in a season or two generate the weed femnagh in great plenty and it is asserted that the nearer they are planted to the mingling of fresh and salt water, the sooner and the more abundantly they will produce weed.

Along the Upper Lough Swilly and as far northward as Rathmullan and Killygarvan on the west shore, and to the northward of Buncrana on the east and as far into the country as shells can profitably be carried, shell manure is very much used and particularly upon land about to be laid down in grass, and it is believed that the good effect of shells upon land, at least where it is naturally moist and cannot be sufficiently drained, is of longer duration than lime.

In the neighbourhood of Ramelton shells are

applied from 8 to 20 tons per Cunningham acre, according as the state of the soil or as the proposed crop may require. A boat-load of shells is 4 tons, a ton 450 bushels, but good boat-loads frequently measure 2,000 bushels or 500 bushels per ton; and I was informed at Ramelton that good boat-loads were sold last year from 6s to 8s per load. Sound sea shells make excellent white lime fit for every purpose for which lime is used, and particularly in medicine.

Manures

Sea mud or glar is very much used for manure where shells are not convenient. It suits new obstinate soil best and is best applied on the surface in autumn at about 3 inches deep, and living mussels make the best manure of all the marine productions; but weed is less used where shells are plenty.

On the south east and east side of Upper Lough Swilly in the Isle of Burt, Isle of Inch and in Fahan opposite to and below Inch, the use of shells for manure is every way similar to the practice on the western shore and lime is very little used for manure where sufficiency of sea manure, shells or weed can be conveniently supplied.

On Lower Lough Swilly and Lough Mulroy, which may comprise between them the parishes of Tully and Killygarvan, Fanad the peninsula and most of the south of Rosguill, indeed everywhere near the coast where shells are not convenient, seaweed is depended upon for the ensuing potato crop and to assist the continuance of other crops where the soil requires or permits it to be used. Weed ranks among the first manures for kitchen gardens, particularly for cabbages, onions, turnips and carrots, but I cannot find that it is applied by any fixed rule for quantity, either on the garden or the field.

In all the maritime districts or parishes the population is numerous beyond the extent and capability of the tillable land to produce food for their support.

Fisheries

Some years ago the fisheries on these shores were very prosperous and productive. That circumstance induced adventurers from various parts of the country to flock thither for employment. Many of these married and got, with their coast-bred wives, small holdings of land divided to them off the original farms occupied by the fathers or brothers of their wives, and at proportional parts of the original rent; and these again were subdivided among succeeding heirs until farms are reduced to mere deals of land.

I know an instance in Captain Babington's estate where the tenant's proportion of what was originally his grandfather-in-law's holding entitled him to graze only a year-old calf, so that his spouse and her 3 sisters (co-heiresses) graze but 1 cow annually among the 4; but into what portions shall this inheritance of the prolific dames be subdivided among their numerous progeny in future generations?

I know another instance of a farm of 37 acres, of which a full third is bog, that was in 1781 occupied by 1 man. He divided it off in equal shares to his 6 children. It is now (1823) in 13 holdings supporting 91 persons. These and similar cases certainly produce much poverty and misery in almost every part of Ireland.

Rights to Seaweed

In the vicinity of the coast proprietors of estates that extend to or border on the sea are generally as cautious to apportion the weed-producing shores among their tenants as they are in allotting them turbary, and many who have shore to spare let it at very high rent.

Nothing is looked after with more eagerness or attended to with more diligence than the weed. The moment of high water is strictly watched for and every accessible point of the shore is crowded with gatherers of every age and sex to collect the precious vegetable as soon as it touches land, and when gathered they share it among them by established rules that must not be violated, as no property is held more sacred than this, even when forced on shore by the fury of the waves.

When any portion of the coast is rocky and what is called wrack shore (shore productive of weed), or the rocks off or belonging to it, the persons, whose privilege the weed of that shore is, divide it once every year among them in lots or shares, the better to give to each his due and equitable quantity of the weed; but when rocks lie pretty far from land their produce is commonly gathered by whoever succeeds in availing himself of the first calm low water in spring that uncovers it.

It was by venturing first in the season on Swilly rocks to Shear Leahagh or Lucagh that Harry Deeny and Ned Kelly happened to find the mooring chain of the unfortunate *Saldanha* frigate entangled in its cliffs.

Seaweed for Manure

The privilege of sea manure enables the farmers

who enjoy it to raise very large crops of potatoes and this is the reason why the potato crop is always abundant near the sea-shore. In all the maritime districts, from 3 to 4 acres of tillage is accounted a pretty large farm to crop and in most instances about the third or half of the tillage is planted with potatoes and the remainder according as it is or is not mossy. Black land is cropped with barley, oats or flax.

But I find from the concurring accounts of the inhabitants of east or west Fanad, Rosguill, Doe and [blank] that crops of oats or flax after potatoes off land that has been often manured with seaweed are not profitable and that, however largely they may bulk, they both prove deficient in every other respect. They account barley alone the only sure crop off potato-land, but they say that under the existing excise laws barley is not worth the growing.

In winter and in the spring months cows feed upon the seaweed, femnagh or any tender seed vegetable with much apparent eagerness and relish.

In the bottoms (the north shores of Fanad and Rosguill), as soon as the land for the proposed potato crop is manured or a sufficiency of manure provided for it, all that the sea and the summer produces afterwards is manufactured into kelp.

The statmaara is the largest or grossest sea vegetable found on these shores. It grows only in deep water and, when driven ashore, its stems are most commonly piled up in heaps to dry preparatory to their being burned with other materials into kelp, but the leaves or tender parts make the best vegetable manure.

Ballymastoker Sand

Ballymastoker <Ballymastoken> sand, a rich mixture of sand and powdered shells, taken from where it is regularly overflowed by the tide, is a good productive manure that, from the extent of the strand from which it may be had, never can be exhausted or become scarce while the tide flows in Lough Swilly to collect it there. Mr Joshua Foster of Lower Drumfad (about a mile and a quarter from the strand) uses it at 40 wheel car loads to the Cunningham acre on every part of his farm, lay or lea stubble land, on land that never was tilled, and finds it good manure for each.

No known manure reduces obstinate new land so soon to mould, but it should be cautiously applied because too much of it at once exhausts the soil as powerfully (perhaps more so) as too much lime or marle. It is carried several miles into the country and would be used much more if the road to it through Carren was finished.

Portbaan Sand

Portbaan, a creek of Anny, the estate of Henry Irwin Esquire, produces a fine sand, of which a large portion consists of particles of broken shells. It can be had in large quantities at low water and is an excellent manure, particularly for reclaimable moory or mossy lands. I have mislaid the memorandum I took from Mr Irwin concerning it and cannot from my recollection give a more accurate account of it.

There is also good manure sand at Dundoan on Lower Mulroy, of which large [quantities], from 18 to 20 loads, on an acre prepared for flax is sufficient applied on the prepared ground before the seed is sown. Quantities are in every summer boated up to Milford and to other places on Mulroy, and sold to farmers who carry it into the country for use. It is said to be the best substitute for shells where shells are not convenient and is used to promote the growth of grass on ground prepared for a flax crop, on leas or lays and on moor or moss about to be reclaimed, and in preference to lime even where limestone and fuel are convenient, and is probably of the same nature and composition as the sands of Ballymastoker and Portbaan.

Limestone

I have ascertained that limestone is pretty convenient to most parts of the parishes of the east, middle and north of the barony of Kilmacrenan. In Aghanunshin there is good limestone, in Magheryennan, in Tullyaughnish coarse limestone, in Drummonaghan, in several parts of Glen, in both Cairns and in Gortnavernnear, Kerrykeel on Mulroy.

In Killygarvan quarries of excellent limestone cross the parish from Killygarvan bridge to Glenalla near 4 miles in a westerly direction, and of which much lime is burned for sale and supplied to Inishowen and many other parts where water carriage makes it convenient.

In Kilmacrenan a vein of rich limestone crosses from the neighbourhood of Gardenina, north easterly direction to Cranfwer on Mulroy, and from Mulroy westward and south westward across the south of Rosguill or Mevagh through the mountains to the village of Glen.

There is limestone on the shore of Lough Salt and in the rivulet a quarter of a mile below it in Meenformil, about a mile below it and at the road from Lough Salt to Glen near the village half a mile south east of Glen, in a valley southed by a high precipice and a mountain and at Glen mill. This vein is a branch of that mentioned above at Cranfwer and it may reasonably be conjectured that it makes a submarine passage under Mulroy to Gortnavein, and that it possibly is the same that crosses the country from Glenalla to Killygarvan bridge (for which see Killygarvan) and runs with respect to Cranfwer in a south easterly direction.

In east Fanad there is a good limestone 2 miles north of Kerrykeel, in Ballymagowan, and very good limestone quarries in the Ross of Rosnakill, in many parts of the peninsula of Moress, a mile north west of it in Croaghan and Springfield, about a mile and a half north of Rosnakill and in Ballyhernan. These lie along Mulroy, on the west shore of this Fanad, and there are on the east shore also very good limestone quarries in Caarreen and Magherawarden on Ballymastoker bay.

In west Fanad there are several good limestone quarries but those in Ballyheeran and its subdenominations are esteemed the best. Limestone at Ummeracaam, of Doonans in Rosguill and at Drumluackagh have been already mentioned, and also in Trachar strand above Horn Head bridge.

I had not any opportunity of ascertaining whether there are limestone quarries in the other parts of this barony or not, or what other manures it affords. Lime when used as a manure is applied to land from 200 bushels to 260 bushels upon the Cunningham acre.

Cattle

Of cattle I have not learned that any trials of consequence have been made in these neighbourhoods to improve or at all change the old Irish breed, because the prevalent opinion is that any better heavier or larger cattle would not live upon their mountains; nor do I find that these, like the mountaineers of Bannagh, go to distant fairs to purchase even a few good lambs for either stock or breed.

Fairs and Markets for Linen

Since the establishment of monthly fairs and yarn markets at Milford, Kerrykeel, Rosnakill, Carrigart and Glen, much improvement has been made in spinning linen yarn. I have been assured by buyers that Fanad and Rosguill produce good linen yarn as any other districts of Donegal.

There are a great many good linen weavers in the north and east of the barony of Kilmacrenan who make, I am assured, very good linen of various grists and breadths when for country customers but whose industry is materially discouraged by the want of an established certain linen market at Letterkenny or Ramelton, at which they could hope to receive the full and fair value of their webs. For although linen buyers do attend Ramelton market, the weavers say they are not established linen merchants but jobbers who will not purchase webs but on terms very disadvantageous to the seller and by which they secure to themselves in other markets, by reselling these, the profits by which the poor weavers should live.

Several linen weavers of the parish of Tullyaughnish and the parishes near it seem to entertain a strong opinion that a properly established linen market at Ramelton would, in a very short time, invite a multitude of weavers to settle in the country and create to itself a large and certain supply of good brown linen and introduce prosperity into that neighbourhood.

Woollen Trade

In Fanad very good country woollen cloth and flannel were manufactured and dressed at a tuck mill there at Kindrum, but farms are become so small that sheep cannot be kept to produce wool for these purposes beyond a small quantity which is manufactured by a few country families for their own use; nor do they knit woollen stockings for market in these neighbourhoods but children and young persons of both sexes in Fanad, Rosguill and Doe manufacture large parcels of neat bent hats.

Woods and Plantations

In every neighbourhood of Ireland into which we travel the ancient wooded state of the country is strongly expressed by the still visible remains and vestiges of extensive woods. Very gross stems or trunks of oak and fir trees are yet frequently found in our bogs and of these the timber is generally sound and fit for use in building.

We cannot now conjecture how many species of timber were indigenous to the Irish soil, but we have no reason to doubt that every species now visible in our stunted undergrowth, mountains, glens, brows of rivers and in moist, mossy and marshy plains and valleys and in the islands of large lakes all flourished in the Irish woods and thronged that portion of the soil most genial to their growth and nature: whether on the summit of the lofty cliff upon the mountain's elevated side, in the deep ravine or the mossy plain. But, however this may have been, I have seen only oak, fir and yew raised in a sound state from underground and a small tough species that, when newly raised, appeared of rather a reddish or crimson colour, but I never heard it called by any name nor did I see it of more than at most 6 inches in diameter.

The wild box is very hard clean wood. It grew pretty gross and in tolerable plenty in the woods along Lough Erne and in its islands in days of yore (and is still plenty there but of small growth). Yet I never saw or heard of box being found underground.

In almost every parish of the county of Donegal woodsteads are visible almost to the brink of the sea and in many instances natural woods and plantations prosper on the shore of the ocean, particularly in eastern and southern aspects. What pity when that the growth of timber is so greatly neglected in our country, to the prosperity of which timber is so very necessary and to which every succeeding year will increase that necessity.

The want of timber for country use for roofing farmhouses and offices, and for all necessary farming purposes, is already much complained of and it is certainly calculated that more than a year rent in every 4 or 5 years must be expended by many farmers in the purchase of timber for their various purposes, and the price of which had in too many instances to be drawn from money raised by the sale of various articles towards the payment of rent.

If I ask a farmer why he or his predecessor did not plant trees, he replies, as the law is, we dare not use the trees we plant. The[re] are the landlords and why should we trouble ourselves to plant trees and encumber our land with them, to only ensnare ourselves or our children when they are [old]?

This is understood almost the same in every part of Ulster and it is my opinion that few landlords ever get much value for timber growing on country farms, whereas if the right of planting and using the timber when fit for use belonged to tenantries, the whole country would again bloom with quicksets, hedgerows and plantations. Landlords would not lose much, if anything, by it: the farmers' timber would protect the natural woods and when every man possessed his own timber he had no temptation to steal from his landlord or his neighbour, and this will apply to the propagation of willows also.

Fuel

The visibly approaching scarcity of fuel should awaken farmers to another use they will in many places very shortly find for timber, and to the utility and necessity of immediately planting a supply for that day of necessity before it arrives. Many districts of Ireland, both upon the coast and in the interior, have almost entirely exhausted their turbaries, have been long stripped naked of wood and have no prospect whatever of a future supply by the discovery of collieries in convenient situations with respect to them.

The inhabitants of the coast may be supplied with imported fuel but that supply must unavoidably come at a price much beyond what their old Irish peats used to cost them and perhaps very much beyond their means; but the same supply delivered at the port to inhabitants residing remotely in the interior will, by reason of land carriage, cost them still considerably more or higher. The loss of a single cargo of coals bound to a particular port or its detention by storm or other casualty might, at the approach of a vigorous winter, involve a populous tract of country into very great distress.

Need it be asked how valuable would the branches and prunings of a few full-grown trees be at such a time to a remotely situated country family? All who remember the eventful winter of 1816 will recollect that many, very many, families were saved from its perishing effects by the lopping and prunings of but a few trees.

Whins

Furze or whins afford, when properly prepared for burning, a ready and valuable substitute for fuel, and where properly cultivated and managed, they prove fully as valuable and substitute for fodder. In some parts of England, of Scotland, Wales and the Isle of Man gorse or whins are cultivated for these uses.

The hardy Galloway, Raghery and Manx ponies are all reared upon gorse or goss, for hay is very scarce in their native soils. Every small farmer there sows a deal of whins according to the number of his stock. On a good soil at from 2 to 3 years' growth, they cut whin and stack them for fodder, and in many instances they bind them in small showes. They are, I imagine, less prickly than our common Irish whins. What are intended for firing are bound into small compact faggots and very tightly tied, to hinder them to burn too rapidly or to flame dangerously while burning.

Many districts in Ireland have very little meadow. Many have no turf bog and others are without turbary or meadow. Any farmer so circumstanced would find a lot of whins a very profitable crop. Whins sowed on a rich soil and pretty thick, grown to a good length in 2 years and will at that age be juicy and not too prickly to be handled and eaten unbruised by cattle. I saw in a large field of newly planted potatoes, when the manure ran scarce, 2 ridges planted upon green whins gathered from an adjoining common and the produce was fully as good as the principal crop of burned land on the adjoining ridges.

NATURAL FEATURES

Inishowen Shoreline: Doony-ougherty

From Doony-ougherty, the north west point of Crummy's bay, the shore trends a little east of north. It is formed by the high south west and west of Cronkurris mountain that terminates upon it there in high, rugged and very irregular cliffs. Here the shore is wholly inaccessible from sea, and on land is very dangerous to cattle that graze near it, for at least 2 miles and a half to the low beach of Lienankeel (Lienankoeel).

Lienan beach consists of gravel and paving stones formed into a ridge-like mound and bounding the eastern shore of Lienan bay which runs out sandy and shallow from the beach seaward and is northed by the cliffy south shore of Lienan Point or Lienan Head, and in which shore and about a third of the way from the south west extremity of the point towards the beach is Portevlin or Port-tevlin, a small creek but the only shelter boats find in Lienan bay. It ebbs dry but can be entered with or a little before half-flood of tide. It receives but a few fishing boats but these, when once within it, are in perfect safety except from a direct south gale, and from the danger of even that, the beach permits them to be hauled up.

The only constant impediment to the entrance into Portevlin is a rock directly in front of that entrance which the fishers are most anxious to have removed; but perhaps the amount that would be employed in blowing and removing it would be more usefully employed in connecting that offensive rock and the westmost point of the creek by strong work and in ridding the east entrance. That effectually done, Portevlin would, with almost all winds, lie as secure and as tranquil as a mill-pond.

From Portevlin west and north round Lienan Head into Dunnaff bay the shore is high, cliffy and inaccessible, but the east shore of Dunnaff bay is low and mostly very rocky for about a mile, but the south westmost creek towards Lienan, with southerly and easterly winds, and the north eastmost creek called Portvagh, with east and north winds or during calms, permitted small vessels to discharge cargoes of rock-salt for the use of a saltwork that stood about midway between them on the shore.

A good road communicated between these landings and the Salt Pan, and between it and the great road in Urris, but the saltwork does not now exist there; nor do vessels anchor in Dunaff bay with other winds than those last mentioned and never longer than to wait a wind or a tide to carry them forward.

Dunnaff shore from Portvagh round Dunnaff Head to Sluddanmore and Carrigatuimpeal is very high and cliffy, particularly to the south west and north of Dunnaff hill, and is not approached by boats but in calms in April and May when, at low ebb of tide, they anchor to cut luagh off rocks that uncover under the shore for manure or to make kelp.

Sluddanmore

Sluddanmore pool or port lies between Bwelloore or Dunnaff north east shore and Carrigatuimpeal low rocky island, the whole shore of which is bordered round with rocks, most of them much higher than the island and that never cover with the highest spring tides. A little more than half a mile north west of the mouth of Sluddanmore a sunken rock breaks in foam in stormy weather, and a furlong and a half nearer Sluddan a rock uncovers only with very low ebbs.

There are, along Dunnaff north shore and pretty near it, several rocks that always stand high above water and some of them within less than a quarter of a mile of the mouth of Sluddan, and but a very little north of west from it; and a small cluster of rocks that cover and uncover with every tide lies between the road in and Carrigatuimpeal, and but a little without the entrance, but the worst impediment to this entrance is the rock (O'Dougherty's rock) in it and nearest to Carri-gatuimpeal that covers it about half-flood and is dangerous to craft coming in. All the others are more easily avoided than this, but the removal of it would leave Sluddan a commodious safe boat-port, with deep water in and shelter for a numerous fleet of fishing craft.

The inner beach is a pretty high or raised mound of paving stones and pebbles, along which the tide very soon deepens. It already harbours several boats that must in rough weather be hauled on shore.

Carrigatuimpeal

Carrigatuimpeal is partly described above. It is

connected with the beach of Bwelloore by a narrow ridge of stones and gravel, and only with spring tides a few perches of that ridge covers a little before high water. The island is but an irregular connection of rocky and stony points not regularly covered with herbage, but having here and there spots tufted with herbage of various kinds and of which some bear very beautiful flowers. It produces weed sufficient to make a very large quantity of kelp annually and a few tons of dillisk or dulse.

Kinnea Bay

Kinnea bay, east of Carrigatuimpeal, is accounted deep, having from 3 to 4 fathoms in the entrance and from 5 to 5 and a half fathoms farther in above the rocks that form the extreme north east of Carrigatuimpeal and from 3 and a half to 2 fathoms within half a cable's length of the beach, where the boat of the preventive waterguards that quarter at Roxton House lies in the south east part of the bay.

But notwithstanding that, it appears to be covered from east and north east by Tullagh Point. The rocks that west that point extend far across the entrance and the sunken rocks to the north west of Sluddanmore lie too much in the entrance of this bay also or in the approach to it. It is very open to north and north west and, as I am informed by the naval officers stationed at Roxton, so frequently troubled with surf and swell of the sea that vessels never enter it all.

From Sluddanmore for about a mile eastward of this place the beach and shore are entirely formed of paving stones, but mostly of the smallest size, and the soil immediately behind this is sandy.

Peninsula of Tullagh

The point or peninsula of Tullagh may comprise the lower or northmost parts of Kinnea, Tullagh and Crossconnell to the mouth of Binnian or Clonmany river, which is at the sea the eastmost limit of Urris, and will comprehend about 2 miles and three-quarters of sea-shore which, although low, is on the west, north and east so rocky and shallow near shore and so sandy on the south east and south that it does not afford a port or any shelter for boats in any emergency whatever (see Binnian port adjoining this).

The blowing away of large extents of sandy soil has done very considerable damage to the whole shore of this peninsula, but particularly in the south east and south of Tullagh and north shore of Crossconnell. The devastation has been excessive, and Binnian, that meets the sea next east and north east of Crossconnell, although suffering but comparatively little, has lost still something by the blowing sand. And although not of Urris, yet because the north shore of Binnian easts Tullagh bay and encloses Binnian port, I here take leave to describe it with Tullagh bay.

The west point of Binnian, called Sooilabinnian, is a narrow, high, rocky peninsula and connected with Binnian mountain by sand-hills.

The Sooil is about 50 perches long and in nearly the direction of north and south. Eastwards of the north end of the Sooil, and between it and the Bhinns or high cliffy north shore of Binnian, lies a small sandy creek called Portluaghan, in front of which, northward and westward to beyond the Sooil, lies an extended bed of rugged rocks that produce annually in April and May an inconceivable quantity of seaweed which alone brings Portluaghan into notice, its situation and difficulty of access leaving it in all other respects useless.

The south point or precipice of the Sooil is surrounded 4 or 5 perches without it by lower rocks to the channel from Binnian river which separates it from Crossconnell strand and in which, near to these lower rocks, a little without them, is 7 fathoms, and Binnian port is entered from this.

It is situate close under the east side of the Sooil, from the south high point of which northward to high water mark is 12 or 13 perches of high rock. The bottom is clean and, considering the narrowness of the water before it towards south, to which alone it is open, it may be pronounced secure from wind in any direction. Boats may reach shelter within the Sooil with the first quarter of flood of tide and may run higher up as the tide deepens.

This is the haven of safety to which all the fishing boats from Fanad to the north of Malin run for security, when forced off their fishing stations or kept from their proper ports by adverse winds or sudden squalls coming upon them at sea; or when the bar of Strabreagagh is up and too much agitated to be ventured over, which it too frequently is. And Binnian port requires but a landing-quay to give it every necessary convenience that such a port can have occasion for; but here a quay would be easily erected on a rock situate about 10 perches east of the Sooil, parallel to it and inclined to or sloping towards the deep water, and materials for the work are at hand.

The Binnian salmon fishery is but a furlong above this and Clonmany bridge about a mile and a quarter up Clonmany river, from which I return to Urris.

Urris

From Oanirk bridge at south, the celebrated valley of Urris is entered northward by a steep, difficult and partly narrow road through Maammore glen, the only passage through which a road could lead, over the continued ridge of Cronk Urris and the Raghties that runs from Lough Swilly at south west near Dunree, north eastwards near 5 Irish miles along the ridge of these mountains to the road from Clonmany to Urris, which lies west and north west of the bridge.

From Maammore glen the road descends northward to Urrismanagh where, dividing into 2 branches that continue one north eastwards and the other north westwards a couple of miles, until this last, by turning eastward from Bwelloore in Dunaff, meets the eastmost branch near Roxton, and from that junction the road continues to Clonmany bridge either directly by Straed or by Tullagh through the ford by Binnian.

Urris has in a few bygone years very much increased its quantity of tillage and still possesses very great capability with ample means for further improvement. Its shore abounds with very rich manures. The sands of Lienan and Tullagh are not inferior manures compared with the sands of Lisfannon, Ballymastocker or Portbaan. They possess the same qualities and effervesce as strongly in acid and, when applied with judgment to cold, mossy or heathy land sufficiently drained, prove to be excellent continuing manures. Every rock too along the shore, and that the tide covers, produces abundance of weeds wherewith to manure the more improved soils.

Drainage

Draining is still very necessary to several parts of Urris, but particularly to the low parts of Urrismanagh and Lienan, Tullagh and Crossconnell (not long ago bogs). The drain that meres between Urrismanagh and Lienan should be widened and deepened, and continued so through the low mossy tillage of Lienan and Lienankoeel into the sea, say in all about 180 perches. It is evident that the present drain, insufficient as it is, is choked at high water mark by sand forced into it from the sea by the surf that frequently bursts into it and it does not appear that it was ever deepened towards the sea beyond that limit, but it appeared to me at low water that it could be deepened 2 or 3 feet through sand and gravel and that it could be easily kept open.

And it is most certain that the large tract of valuable lowland above it would, by that means, be completely drained and rendered tillable in future at any season of the year. And about the same length of drain, if well made, across the partly reclaimed bog and lowland of Tullagh and Crossconnell into Clonmany river, would immediately bring that large plain under the dominion of the spade.

Shore near Binnian

From Sooilabinnian and Portluaghan eastward round Binnian mountain, Annagh and Ardagh the shore is a continued high cliffy face to Pullins lower rocks where, by riddling [ridding] away about 13 perches through rocks already partly hollowed by nature, a necessary, useful and, in such a place, very convenient landing could be made for the boats of Pullins bay; the want of which, on account of the almost ceaseless surf that attends it, often detains them on shore unemployed when they could be profitably employed upon the water.

Pullins

From Pullins north easterly to the westmost point of Carrigabraghey is about 2 miles and a quarter of low, sandy, surfy beach called Pullins strand. This west point of Carrigabraghey is the extreme west point of the Isle of Doagh and but a little south west of the ruined castle. Here is a pretty large pool separated from the land by an almost steep pebbly shore and from the sea by rocks that cover only with very high tides. The communication between the pool and the sea is a narrow, rocky, crooked canal through these rocks and never dries but with low ebbs.

Fishers assert that there is no harbour for boats but this on the west or north of the Isle of Doagh, but that it cannot now be entered or sailed from but in calm weather. But I have no doubt that if two or three ends of rocks that narrow the passage in and one or two that lie in it were removed, it would then be accessible in ordinary weather.

And if we consider the number of active trained fishermen that inhabit the parishes of Clonmany and Donagh, and that they are often for long periods unemployed because they have not ports or boat harbours that they can enter or sail from in ordinary weather, or in which their craft can find continual safety, and farther, when we really know that they so frequently cannot venture out to fish, we cannot consider the circumstance without regret; when it is obvious that a few small improvements of their boat harbours would prepare them to give full scope to all their enterprise and industry in fishing and to give to the surrounding country a very large and welcome supply of wholesome food.

For were there safe harbours without the bar of Strabreagagh (which see) at Carrigabraghey or Pullins, where boats could pass safely out and in and be hauled up for safety, there is not a man residing along Strabreagagh, in the Isle of Doagh, Clonmany or Donagh that could provide a boat and fishing tackle that would not keep one in constant fishing order in such a harbour.

Strabreagagh

The mouth of Strabreagagh opens westward. It is northed by the high head or point Bhinns and cliffs of Dunargus and Knocknamengagh or Knocknameny, north easted by the sand-hills of Lagg, and southed by the Bhins and precipices of the north shore of the Isle of Doagh, eastward to Bwellindhawoa and Legachurry.

The breadth of this entrance between Dunargus Head and the nearest opposite point of Carrigabraghey is about three-quarters of a mile, and above this, on both sides of the new channel, except a rocky border along shore, the bottom is sand to Doonmore and Rhuin-awaed, above which Strabreagagh is at low water a continued bed of sandy and shelly mud or shells.

Area near Strabreagagh

The channel into Strabreagagh is now considerably north and eastward of its former course, beginning near the Dutchman's rock and winding from it somewhat east and south easterly. It crosses the dangerous and frequently impassable bar and passes almost mid-channel up the narrowest strait between Lagg sands and the Isle of Doagh in a new course, but above this the channel remains unaltered.

The channel of Strabreagagh on the bar at low water is not 3 feet deep. [Insert footnote: The preventive waterguards' boat upset here and drowned 2 men 19th last July 1823]. It is very liable to alterations in respect both of situation and depth of water, and subject to heavy surfy breakings upon it that too often hinder fishers that keep boats in Strabreagagh to venture out; and it as often hinders such as venture out to return, so that Strabreagagh can hardly be reckoned a harbour. However, light vessels sometimes go up and anchor at Doaghmore Point or Gorey.

Considerable portions of the Isle of Doagh shore are rocky and with its beds afford variety and large quantities of manure to the occupants of the surrounding country farms. The manures, as on other shores, consist of seaweed, sand, shells and mud, and possess such qualities as are ascribed to them in other bays.

Strabreagagh also offers about 1,030 Cunningham acres for embankment, exclusive of 100 to 120 acres of low green pasture now covered by every high tide. Of the 1,030 acres, 165 lie in the upper part of its westward arm and may be enclosed when the tides rise not perpendicularly above 6 or 7 feet by a line from the middle or north point of Cregamullin, directed perpendicularly to the opposite shore of Ballymageeghan in the Island of Doagh and but from 60 to 70 perches long and the bottom everywhere firm.

The remaining 865 acres may be enclosed by a line carried from the north east point of the same Cregamullin, directly towards the channel 9 or 10 perches and thence at a convenient distance along and down the channel until a point is found to range generally or nearly so in line with the east shore of [?] Figgert beyond the point. And a line directed from the point so determined towards Malin Hall will mark out the remaining portion of the bank to enclose it, and which may be about or near 400 perches long; and it is probable that high spring tides rise on the middle of this last line not more than from 11 to 12 feet perpendicularly and that depth diminishes towards each shore.

Rivers

The rivers and small streams that fall into this tract laid out to be enclosed can, on the level of the strand, by the shortest possible cuts be collected into a large drain and sluiced through the bank [insert footnote: see Cole bay below Castleford] and may, in the upper or westmost lot, become the continuation of a small canal proposed to be made from Cloghernagh at Pullins about a mile and three-quarters to Strabreagagh, for the purpose of drawing turf from the bogs of Donagh so far up the country and also sea manure.

PRODUCTIVE ECONOMY

Proposed Canal

The canal is proposed to be made by widening and deepening a drain already open all the way through nearly a perfect level; and that possibly may, by a little extra sinking, be made to fill to the necessary depth by the tides. And if the poor of the country are to be employed, the continuation of the above narrow, cheap canal is very practicable from Strabreagagh eastward. This is best seen when the tide has filled it. The level of nature is then applied to the ground and shows that from the Strand Head bridge eastward over flat bogs in Tullyarb and Maghera-ard to a mile east of Cashel or crossing the low bogs of Drumaville, Templemoyle and Muff to Culdaff, there does not appear to be any considerable rise above the level of high water.

A cheap, narrow canal in either of these directions would be of great service to the islanders of Doagh and the inhabitants of the north of Clonmany, who draw all their turf and lime from Donagh, Clonca and Culdaff. But how extremely valuable would the accession of 1,030 acres of rich crop-bearing land be to the neighbourhood of such a district as the Isle of Doagh, to which it is contiguous and of which above a third of the tillage and green pasture has suffered devastation and expulsion of its inhabitants from blowing sand.

General Description of Coast

The coast of Urris, Binnian, Ardagh, Pullins strand, the Isle of Doagh and the south shore of Strabreagagh eastward to and including Cregamullin belong to the parish of Clonmany, and thence eastward to Tullyard near Kintrae or Strand Head bridge (on the eastmost extreme of Strabreagagh) belongs to Carndonagh.

General Economy

Agricultural pursuits and habits in industry in Donagh and Clonmany are almost perfectly similar but their means of following these pursuits differ in these principal points, viz. Clonmany is destitute of limestone and scarce of fuel everywhere near the coast, but Donagh possesses abundance of both. Clonmany, including Urris, possesses upwards of 22 miles of sea-shore producing, season after season in eternal succession, a great variety of excellent fish.

In this, nature has been lavish to Clonmany, but has left her bays, creeks and fishing boat harbours in so unsafe and unfinished a condition that, unless art deigns to improve them, the Clonmanyites can but seldom avail themselves of her bounty; but so large an extent of shore affords such certain abundance and variety of manures that the farmer, whatever may be the nature of his soil or the crop he intends to cultivate, always finds on the beach a ready manure perfectly adapted to his purpose.

Donagh

Donagh, on the contrary, does not bound upon the sea for altogether 3 miles, and that towards the eastern shore or extreme of Strabreagagh where, producing very little weed, the only manure it affords is mud; but this, although very much mixed with shells, is but little used except on the borders of the extensive bogs that approach that portion of the shore; and notwithstanding that, Donagh abounds in excellent limestone quarries in Churchtown and down the river from it to Lower Milltown in Glennygannon and in Balloskey and Ballynaree. And in Gorttyarran quarry slabs of large dimensions and various scantlings fit for various uses in building are easily obtained, and Gorttyarran, the most distant of these famous quarries from Carn, is hardly 2 miles east of it; and with these quarries Donagh possesses turbaries not exhaustible for centuries to come.

Lime in Donagh

Yet in the whole parish very little lime is used for manure: the poorer farmers do burn a good deal of lime, but from the result of much enquiry I am led to believe that circumstances compel them to sell it when made. It sells now (July 1823) at the kiln for 10d per barrel and they drive it from different parts of Glenneely in Culdaff and from the neighbourhood of Carn, from 6 to 10 miles, for 15d the load of 1 barrel and a half, and to Bunnafubble and more distant parts of Moville. For that price I accounted these prices very moderate for good rich lime, but nevertheless the sellers thereof assured me that they could not afford a bushel of it for manure, so much stand they in want of the trifle it brings in ready cash.

Clonmany

Clonmany, on the other hand, although without the rich limestone quarries possessed by Donagh, finds the deficiency in a great measure supplied by the sea manures produced by her extended length of coast. It enables her to plant large crops of potatoes, to reclaim cut-out bogs and moors, to improve meadows and to cultivate cold coarse soils with greater certainty of good crops; and when her farmers have completed these manurings, they manufacture all the weed they can afterwards gather into kelp and which may sell annually for perhaps as much ready money as the lime disposed of by Donagh.

Economy in Clonmany

I have not observed industry pursued with more diligence than along the shore of Clonmany and the adjacent neighbourhood. Very large tracts of bog and moor have within a few years been brought into cultivation and some of these that I saw in a hopeless, swampy state do now exhibit very luxuriant crops. Convincing instances of this fact are met with in Urris, particularly in Lienan, Urrismanagh, Kinnea, Dunnaff, Tullagh and Crossconnell.

In Annagh, a mile from Clonmany bridge towards Carn, rank crops of potatoes, oats and rye wave on the brows of the banks, from the faces of which several turf deep were recently cut away. Also the fertile flat, not many years ago swamp and bog, from Pullins to Strabreaghagh, and part of which belongs to each of the townlands of Ballyliffin, Cloghernagh, Maghera-ard, Ballymacmurty, Ardascanlan and Claggin, and through which, at the suggestion of William Granny, I have recommended a navigable drain or narrow canal to be opened for the accommodation of the numerous groups of tenantries that inhabit these several townlands, and concerning which Mr Harvey of Meentaghs, on the 20th July 1823, wrote me as follows:

"The proposed canal from Strabreaghagh appears practicable and certainly useful; and I should be most willing to join Mr Montgomery, Sir A. Chichester, Mr Dougherty, Mr Marshall and other persons interested therein to have it completed." And I have no doubt that the present drain, if a lock could be dispensed with, could be completed into the proposed canal at a very small expense; and if it was completed, there is little doubt that the tenants of each townland along it would immediately cut branches from it through the low ground to the great road where it most nearly approaches their villages.

Means of Improvement

It is the opinion of well-informed persons that, if the Inishonians who live within from a mile to 2 miles from the sea had on the shore secure little boat harbours that they could use with ordinary convenience and hope of safety, they would prefer the employment of fishing to illicit distillation and risk making a legal and encouraged livelihood in that way on the water, rather than follow smuggling at the risk of incurring the penalties attached to it.

Many of them expressed this sentiment to me. Perhaps it should be communicated to the Irish government as a measure worth trying for the suppression of private distillation in districts near the fishing shores.

Illicit distillation is far from being suppressed. The continual presence of an active, armed excise police has proved insufficient to put it down even partially, and does not that circumstance recommend the trial of any other probable system, particularly one that they would adopt willingly?

Other Improvements

What would, under other circumstances, be a great benefit and an inestimable favour is, in too many instances, the greatest evil to the inhabitants of the Irish coast. They are in general hardy, resolute and often full of enterprise, but all these high natural qualities are [less?] frequently employed in nobler pursuits than in manufacturing contraband malt and whiskey and in opposing the excise man when, in the execution of his duty, he disturbs their trade.

Say one of these occupies 3 or 4 acres, perhaps not so much land; he employs every opportunity that the seasons afford him in gathering sea manure, to plant as much as he possibly can of that few acres with potatoes. On this he founds his future hope and fortune. The succeeding crop must be barley. This, when reaped, is soon turned into malt distillation; is attempted immediately afterwards. But in how many instances do the gaugers and the police overtake the operation, surprise and arrest the unfortunate individual that conducts it when, perhaps big with hope of final success, and who, after destroying all his hopes and all his means together, hurry him and his assistants off to prison.

Crops

Of almost every parcel of tillage in the vicinity of the coast, about a third part is planted with potatoes, in a third part barley succeeds the potato crop of last year, and the remaining third is frequently sowed with flax, but often part in oats and part flax. But in mossy soils barley or flax are not sown, and when an upland tillage farm is very small, potatoes and barley generally succeed each other continually.

Flax

The inhabitants of the parish of Clonmany do not cultivate more flax than is necessary for their domestic uses and to employ their females in spinning. They live far from good markets and do not account it profitable to grow flax for sale; nor do they save flax seed. They never store grain for any purpose other than to malt it or to sell it for that use, nor does a farmer there make more oaten meal than he thinks a sufficiency for the consumption of his house through the season.

Mossy land produces good crops of rye (sown in March), but I understand it is of greater value made into whiskey than into meal. Some of the crops no doubt would bear good wheat but, being open in winter and barley a more favourable crop, wheat is neglected.

Livestock

Here the old Irish breed of cattle continues unchanged, being considered the best suited to the pastures. Sheep are kept in greater numbers in Clonmany for the last 3 or 4 years than for many years before that time, and the wool is spun at home on the little wheel and manufactured into grey cloth, flannel, drugget, blankets and stockings by each family for its own use. Any overplus is disposed of to such neighbours as need to buy.

Manufacture of Cloth

I saw some fine, good substantial grey or blue cloth that was dressed at Carn cloth mill and that did great credit to every hand employed in the manufacture of it. There were, however, shades of inequality of colour for which I taught several a remedy by showing them how wool is mixed with perfect equality of colour in the south and west of Ireland, and I have the satisfaction of seeing a few of them succeed well in their first essays in practical mixing. And it may be hoped that the male population of this parish will shortly appear clothed in cheap, strong, comfortable home manufacture, such as [no further text].

NATURAL FEATURES

Other Ports

Carnashamer creek receives the stream that separates the 11 ballyboes from Carryhul and Silver hill. It is southed by the east point of the ballyboes called the Warrens, wested and northed by Carryhul or Silver hill, and open seaward towards east. It is shallow, at low water a strand and not frequented as a landing-place. It lies nearly west of the south part of the Tun bank.

Portnagaarley in the mouth of the river that souths and south wests Corratrasna is a small but safe good port and exposed to winds materially from south east and east only.

Portsallagh

Portsallagh lies about 2 miles below Greencastle without the mouth of Lough Foyle. It is entered in deep water and is formed or enclosed between points of Corratrasna and Shroove at the foot of Essabuck rivulet that meres between them. It is accounted a very safe boat-port, very well sheltered from the north, north east and to nearly from east by the rocky east point of Shroove, and from west and south west by the north east rocky point of Corratrasna, and consequently it is open only to winds from south.

It is a noted place of security or retreat for fishing boats when either proceeding to sea to fish without the heads or towards Inishtuahull or Hempton's bank [insert footnote: Hempton's bank on Lough Swilly and Fanad], or when returning from any of these stations into Lough Foyle with fish. They are compelled by either adverse winds or tides to put into port. But Portsallagh is too small, too confined, too narrow a space to afford shelter to many boats at once. It is nevertheless capable of being enlarged and of receiving artificial shelter.

Creation formed and placed it where it is, in its present rude but useful state, to rescue fishing boats with their distressed crews and valuable cargoes from perhaps utter destruction, and should not men who possess the means and power set about its immediate completion contemplate, but for a moment, the situation of a boat's crew abreast of this little port?

The tide ebbing irresistibly from Lough Foyle, a strong north easterly gale meeting that tide and rolling the ocean against it in fearful commotion; the billows bursting against the Moville shore with terrific fury, at, as it were, but a little distance off on the one side; and the Tun bank foaming and surging in the most awful confusion within as short a distance on the other; no possibility of standing out again to sea and no port westward on the north of Inishowen that could be proceeded for with the existing gale, and easterly all things equally inauspicious; the north shore of Magilligan and Dunboe, ever covered with surf and bursting foam, ever inaccessible to mariners, dare not be approached; the bar of the Bann, up, breaking and impassable; Portrush, 9 miles east of Shroove, hardly to be thought of under present circumstances; and the Skerries road, the last, the farthest hoped-for haven, 3 or 4 miles eastward beyond Portrush and no circumstance to favour escape of the little bank even thither: no attempting to thwart the storm, no possibility of stemming the tide.

In such a critical situation, and such is not impossible, nay it might occur even at the still more to be dreaded hour of approaching night, consider then how great a deliverance must such a little haven as Portsallagh frequently be to boats and their crews, when batted by adverse and distressing circumstances in the sound of Magilligan, and of how great and how much importance its improvement would be to the fisheries and to the country.

Productive Economy

Abundance of Fish

It may be unnecessary to inform the North West Society and the inhabitants of interior Ireland of every rank and class how astonishingly productive our circumfluent waters are of cheap, wholesome, nutritious food, consisting of so great a variety of fishes, whose distinct natures direct them through all the seasons in continual succession to our shores, where these industrious, hardy, enterprising fishermen, for whose protection, preservation and deliverance the improvement of Portsallagh is recommended, take and bring them on land for our use, and at no smaller risk than that of their lives.

I trust that the bare mention of it will stir every Irishman to join his fellow Irishmen in offering unanimous and irresistible solicitations for the means of accomplishing so very desirable an object.

Fishers from Lough Foyle would then approach it with confidence. They would, from the remotest corners of the lough, assemble and harbour there at night, in readiness to proceed with the dawn of the approaching morning to their destined stations, which would enable them in the shortest winter day to follow every species to most frequented or most distant haunts, and too oftener pursue the cod and glasson to several miles beyond the heads of Inishowen and Malin.

Cod are taken everywhere off the heads and often very near to the shore, and from Inishowen eastward to and around Inishtuahull Island and to Hempton's bank above 10 miles east or north eastward from it.

Rock cods are frequently taken along the west of the Garrive Islands (Gaarro Illans) in very great plenty. Turbot are caught everywhere from Malin Well to Stackaruddan and sheelogs, which are lythe or whiting pollock, off these shores and in Lough Swilly in summer.

Lough Foyle

Within Lough Foyle, according to all information of which I could avail myself, the changes or variations of the tides are in all respects the very same as in Lough Swilly and Mulroy, and need not be redescribed here.

I have not a map from which I could, with any tolerable degree of accuracy, determine the area of Lough Foyle. I have, however, taken the whole content of that inlet, according to the maps of the barony of Inishowen and of the county of Londonderry, at 64,600 plantation acres. Of this, I reckon a navigable portion of the lough that does not dry with ebb of spring tides 16,180 acres, and the beds that cover and uncover with spring tides 48,420 acres. Of this content, the great bed or Foyle bed lies in the navigable tract and will be more particularly noticed by and by, but by much the greatest part lies east of the navigable part and fills all the shores of the lough to Magilligan and Myroe.

Some parts of this wide extent are beds of sand and sandy mud, some parts are rich beds of sea mud; many parts of it are deep beds of such mud covered with sea grass or sweet grass; and off Faughanvale and Ballykelly lie very large beds of rich shells, so that these beds may be said to contain manure suited to every description of soil.

Lough Foyle Fisheries

The fishery commences in Lough Foyle towards the beginning of August annually. Herrings are generally taken in it about that time and commonly continue to be taken to the end of the following December. The best herrings, and in the largest quantities or numbers, are most frequently taken near the Inishowen shore and particularly off Drumskellen, Aght, Three Trees and Trumaty, but often too on the flats off Kilderry and Killmore.

Cod are looked for in Lough Foyle immediately after the arrival of the herrings in it. They are always met with about that time in large bodies pursuing the shoals of herrings, which they continually follow until they evacuate the lough towards the end of the ensuing winter, and even then from the disappearing of the cod about the time the herrings take leave. It is supposed that they pursue them to the ocean.

Flatfish, viz. sole, plaice etc., are every year taken in very great abundance from June to the following February among the back strands of Magilligan and south eastward to the mouth of the River Roe. These flatfish, rays or skates and herrings retire, it is believed, in immense shoals, each species in its proper season, to deposit their spawn in the mud beds that are covered with sweet grass, and that their spawn quickens towards the end of April or the beginning of May and leaves the beds in that season in shoals of very small fry; but no one tells us where they go to.

Nature would hardly direct them in that tender helpless state to proceed directly to the deep, to be devoured in millions by the voracious inhabitants of that element: and notwithstanding that in that season we meet with shoals of very small fishes in every little quiet pool and creek along the shore, yet the aggregate of all these amounts to nothing compared with the idea we must form of the myriads of herrings alone that come annually upon our shores.

Observation of Fisheries

During the spring tides in April and May 1823 I employed every method I could devise to discover spawn in the beds of the Isle of Inch and off Lisfannan in Upper Fahan, but did not discover any substance that any way resembled what might ever have been spawn in any possible state, between the time of having been shed by the parent fish and a quickened state.

It is, however, asserted by fishers who pretend to know the circumstance with certainty that these species deposit their spawn in the sweet grass beds, that pulling or shearing that vegetable before the departure of the fry from among it destroys the spawn by dislodging it in an immature state, and consequently the fry to an incalculable extent.

That shearing and pulling the sweet grass has contributed exceedingly to the scarcity of fish; and they suggest that a statute should prevent this evil by prohibiting the removal of the sweet grass from the beds any year until after the period by which the fry shall be known to have quitted them, which they probably do early in April; because, from the close examination made by me of the sweet grass beds on, and subsequent to, the 24th of last April, I am convinced that spawn or fry did not then exist in these beds among the sweet grass or within 18 or 20 inches of the surface of the mud in which it grows, on either side of the Isle of Inch or at Lisfannon, in a known, visible state (no embryo substance whatever).

I afterwards through the summer could very frequently distinguish the fry of flatfish on muddy bottoms, in still or very smooth water; but notwithstanding that I frequently saw shoals of small active round fish, I could not find any native of the coast that could certainly distinguish the fry of herrings from the other infant inhabitants of the seas; at least not to my satisfaction.

For while one asserts that the sprat is really the young herring, another with as much probability in his favour declares that the piccagh or some other small fish of similar conformation is the infant of that species. But, however these matters are, the destruction of the fry of every species should be prevented and I do not conceive that farmers could be materially inconvenienced by being hindered to strip the sweet grass off the beds before the latter end of April, because few plant any considerable quantity of potatoes on seaweed at an earlier season.

Had I been apprised of the matter earlier in last spring, I would have searched for the spawn sooner and perhaps with greater certainty; and I may remark that the poor fishers who bring the complaint are rather dependent upon the farmers against whose interests they exhibit it too readily, disclose all they know or believe of the destruction of the herring fry. But they blame the trawlers in Lough Swilly exceedingly for the destruction of embryo fish.

Water-Fowl

It has been long observed that innumerable flocks of water-fowl frequent sweet grass beds in winter and particularly late in that season, and that they flock to them more numerously by night than by day; and this flocking is offered and urged as an incontrovertible argument in favour of the opinion that herrings do spawn in these beds and that sea birds flock thither to feed on their spawn, and that it is by searching for that delicate food they pull up, break and send afloat the large quantities of that weed that are found upon the beaches after every tide; and it is urged further that nature or instinct directs them to the beds always at the very season when the spawn is most certainly to be found on them.

Fishing Practices

The fishermen who met me at the request of Mr Montgomery at his house at Moville informed him and me that the use of long lines in fishing for cod and other whitefish is very injurious to the fishery in Lough Foyle, and say that the great length of such a line, the number of hooks suspended to it and the quantity of bait they exhibit collect the fish to it and make them negligent of the common hand-lines which they will not then follow; and that such numbers of them are wounded by being but slightly caught by the hooks of the long lines, from which, having escaped, they will not afterwards take bait.

That the use or introduction of these long lines has ruined the cod fishing in the lough and that it is not now worth following by the poor hardy fishers, who use only the hand-line and who always supplied the country with cheap fish, and who are not of ability to mount or fit up long lines; and that comparatively only a few fishermen belonging to the lough are able to fit up such lines; and that they employ them to the exclusion of all the poorer of their class who hope relief, by the prevention in future of this injurious mode of fishing.

Being rather unacquainted with fishing, and not having a really disinterested opinion of this matter, I may not be competent to give a correct opinion about it; but as I now view it, I cannot imagine why one of the many hooks of a long line, and when all are concealed within their baits, should be more liable to wound a fish attempting to seize it than a singly-baited hook hung to a hand-line, when attempted to be seized by that or any other fish.

Fishing: Long Line

A long line consists of 12 lines of 40 fathoms each, which makes the whole length 480 fathoms (or 2 marine cables' length), equal to 960 yards. Each short line or 12 part carries 25 hooks, so that to the whole long line 300 hooks are suspended and baited with wilks, which are also called coohorns, or with slices of fresh herrings, sliced for the purpose, or with lug, a large worm dug from sand-beds just uncovered by the ebb of tide.

An anchor or sink is fastened to each end of the line to hold it in its place in the water, and a bow head or buoy to float over each anchor to mark its place. A long line so mounted and baited is set or shot across some part of the channel or un-ebbing part of Lough Foyle for cod or skate etc. Seldom fewer than from 30 to 40 fish are found upon it, however often it may be examined or fished.

The best ground to set or shoot a line upon in winter within Lough Foyle is right off Cregbwee under Bunafubble or, without the lough mouth in the sound, between the Tun bank and Shroove shore. Fish caught in or brought up Lough Foyle are generally sold in Derry, but frequently boats land their fish towards Ballykelly and Newtownlimavady to supply their neighbourhoods; and now and then, when circumstances encourage it, a boat with cod proceeds up the Foyle and so by the canal to Strabane.

A long line fitted up or mounted completely costs from 3 pounds 10s to 4 pounds.

Trawling

Trawling is not practised in Lough Foyle. Such is the account I have learned of Lough Foyle and I have from the same sources of information elicited the following particulars respecting that portion of Inishowen that bounds upon or lies most contiguous to it, in the parishes of Upper and Lower Moville. In these parishes the habits of the people, their employments, modes of industry and means of following it may be accounted altogether similar.

Farmers and Fishing

Farmers and their undertenants who reside conveniently near the shore are continually employed in farming and fishing, and in disposing of the produce of their industry at market.

Upper Moville has no town that holds a weekly market, but in Carricknaquigley 3 winter or rather spring markets held on the first Friday old style in the months February, March and April with 4 fairs patented for Redcastle but held here on the 1st January, 1st June, 12th August and 12th November; and such persons as cannot postpone the sale of yarn, fish, butter, cattle or such articles as they must necessarily dispose of to those fairs and markets must either sell them at the weekly Thursday market of Bunafubble, only 3 miles below Carricknaquigley, or attend Derry weekly market on Wednesdays, nearly 12 miles above it.

Moville Market

In Lower Moville weekly markets held all the year on Thursdays in Bunafubble, with 4 fairs in the year [insert footnote: without patent] and 4 at Greencastle; and at these fairs and markets are sold all things that the industry of the country prepares for market, viz. linen, yarn, coarse linen, drugget, country flannel, cattle, fish and butter.

Potatoes

The potato crop leads here as in other parishes. Scotch Downs and Scotch reds are most productive and, when well managed in the usual way on good soil, and with the usual course of manure and labour, the Cunningham acre commonly yields in favourable seasons from 120 to 160 measures. But if the soil be stiff or cold, and has been ploughed early in winter, break it in with a course or two of a coarse harrow and give it in the proportion of about 20 wheel car-loads of manure sea-sand to a Cunningham acre, equally spread over it in February.

Let it lie so until late in April, then plough it lightly down. Harrow, manure and finish in the usual way and the produce will be very much increased, not only of that crop of potatoes but in the succeeding crops of barley, flax and oats.

Barley

In crofts or uplands, barley always succeeds potatoes. It is sown as early as the oats in almost every part of Inishowen and is generally sooner ripe. But notwithstanding that barley is the customary and favourable crop in Inishowen, wheat would, if the lands were enclosed, probably do well in the same soil. Mr Montgomery raises good crops of wheat in Moville.

When potato land was but sparingly manured and the succeeding barley crop but light, that barley leave is prepared for a flax crop by ploughing it early and sanding it in February with 18 or 20 wheel cars of sea-sand manure to an acre, and letting it lie spread so to sowing time. Then plough, sow and finish in the common or customary way and a very good crop of flax is certain, and the succeeding crops of oats will also be very much benefited by the sand.

Flax Seed

Farmers in Moville do not save flax seed or raise flax to sell in flax, but every inland farmer grows sufficient to employ the females of his family at home, and it generally is of good quality; but the custom here is to prepare and spin both the lint and tow together (or as it is termed) "through-other," to only 2 hank yarn, which sold all last winter at 1s 10d per spangle and in spring and summer up to August 1823 for 2s 3d per spangle.

Weaving

There are about 40 weavers in Lower Moville and they all have machinery for weaving both linen and woollen in the same loom when necessary, at the common rate to regular employers of 3d per yard for either, but no linen finer than shirting is woven there for sale. And although pure water is very abundant and kelp etc. cheap and easily procured, there is very little bleached at Moville, either in yarn or in linen (see Clonroanny).

Manures

The Movilles have no limestone, but from all that I can learn here, sea-sand manure is better understood and more employed in Inishowen than in any other district of Donegal. The Inishowenians seem to study the nature and, as it were, the constitution of the land on which they intend to employ it and to adjust the quantity of sand sufficient for any lot of land, according to its condition, by the number of wheel car loads that should sufficiently manure a Cunningham acre of equal quality, and in the same condition, allowing that the same lot of land will not require so much sand taken from 1 creek or bay as it will of sand from a different bay, where it is less nutritive.

The best manure sand on the north coast is found in the creeks of Teermoan, which comprehends from 5 to 6 miles of shore on the north of the parishes of Culdaff and Lower Moville, and comprising mossy glen and Glenaguivna, but which has not been surveyed and to the figure of which the delineation on the barony of Inishowen map bears no resemblance.

Sand intended for manure should be dug at low water from a bed that covers with every tide and should be left above the reach of tides, to discharge itself of salt from 6 to 8 weeks previous to its being laid on the land; and sand raised during spring tides is accounted much better manure than sand dug from the same bed at neap tides.

Sand

Farmers who reside along Lough Foyle take sand from beds opposite to their farms that uncover only with spring tides and lay it on shore to drip and purge itself, as directed above, before they use it; and I have imagined heaps of sand so left on shore to have undergone something like fermentation: at least the smells sometimes emitted by such heaps are symptomatic of such an effect, if fermentation will happen in masses so free of vegetable matter.

Sand for manure is carried into the country, and particularly towards the mountains, as far as the advantages it offers promise to compensate the labour and expense attending it. Sands taken from different bays are applied to the Cunningham acre in different quantities, according to the nutritive qualities it possesses. The following are the proportions in which I learn they are most commonly applied, supposing the land to be the same and in the same state of preparation.

Sand from any of the ports or bays of Teermoan from 14 to 16 car loads to a Cunningham acre;

Lough Foyle sand taken from any creek or strand north of Greencastle, from 16 to 20 wheel carloads per acre; Lough Foyle sand taken from any creek or strand or dug from any sand bed south or west of Greencastle within Lough Foyle, and dried, from 25 to 30 wheel car loads per acre.

Shells

Shells brought from the beds of Faughanvale and Ballykelly to Moville are sometimes purchased by the country gentlemen and wealthiest farmers at 4d per barrel of 3 measures, and applied to land, and chiefly to land designed for meadow, or to be laid down in grass at from 40 to 60 such barrels to the Cunningham acre, but are most beneficial to lays or leas when laid on in the October next before the intended crop, and to cold or moist meadows after being sufficiently drained. But sea-sand is most useful to reclaimable and reclaimed bogs, mossy tillage and land reclaimed from moor and mountain.

Seaweed

Large quantities of seaweed come ashore in Moville and, in addition to it, very large quantities of luagh are boated in from without Shroove Head in April and May, so that at least a third of the potatoes raised in Moville are planted on seaweed; but very little is burned to kelp there or in the parishes of Culdaff or Clonca.

Moville: Economy

The Movillians manufacture a good coarse linen, good strong woollen cloth, blanketing, flannel, drugget and bent hats for domestic consumption, and some bent hats for sale [insert note: see Clonmany and Donagh]. They continue the old common country breed of Irish cattle, which they believe to be best suited to their soil and pasture.

NATURAL FEATURES

Water

Moville is well watered with small rivers, rivulets and good springs. I was not informed that any of the latter possessed medicinal virtues except one, near Bunafubble and within a few yards of the shore, that is celebrated for curing jaundice. Meadows and pastures have been materially improved by watering wherever it was fairly tried.

SOCIAL ECONOMY

Education

Mr Montgomery, rector of Lower Moville, superintends the Sunday school of his parish at his own house, where he causes it to be held every Sunday and considers that it is well attended, allowing for the great distance that many of the children travel to it.

Mrs Montgomery and the young ladies, her daughters, instruct the young females of the parish in sewing and other needlework every Monday. And besides these, there are 4 other schools taught in this parish and in situations tolerably convenient to the pupils. Tuition at these is, I understand, from 2s 6d to 3s per quarter.

NATURAL FEATURES

East Inishowen

East or Inishowen shore from Drimbwee Point to Dunnaff: the better to accurately ascertain the extent of the bays, beds, shoals and sands of this shore, the streams that enter it, the usual landing-places of boats and vessels, what quays or eligible improvements may be erected or made along it, what impediments to navigation should be removed, and to what extent enclosures off the sea may be made, I recommence my survey at Drimbwee Point, south of the mouth of Cole bay.

Cole Bay

Cole bay, or the bay of Cole Mackeltrean, dries entirely with good ebbs. It is south wested, wested and southed by Drimbwee, Monygregan, the Glaar and Moyle moss (of which the Glaar was embanked of it and the tide of Moyle moss by Sir Henry Hamilton about 60 years ago). It is south easted by Colehill, easted by Castleforward demesne, Tunnyhabbock and Bohullian, and northed and north wested by Castlehill grange and Ballymoney in the Isle of Burt.

4 small freshwater streams meander through the mud of this inlet; 2 of these enter it from Moyle and Newtown Cunningham through the rampart dyke and meet below the Coney Island. It stands in the bay in a central situation west of Colehill and containing from 10 to 12 acres of good tillage and pasture. The other 2, which are very small, flow, one from Castleforward and one from Bohullian. They meet north of the Coney Island and meet the confluent stream formed by the other 2 between Drimbwee and Grange; and below this confluence the channel runs pretty

near the Isle of Burt shore until, having passed the westmost part of Ballymoney, it takes a new direction towards the low hill between Mr Delap's house of Roy and the saltworks, until it meets the deep channel of Lough Swilly and is navigable but for small vessels.

Narrow Channel

The narrow that is between Drimbwee south eastmost point and Burt grange is about 150 perches over and is called the throat of Cole bay. Here, a little below the confluence already mentioned, there is a ford in the channel on a hard bottom that in dry weather dries almost entirely at low water, and here I proposed to build a rampart to enclose about 800 Cunningham acres off the head of this bay, of the richest soil in the world, composed of sea-mud or rotten shells in large beds, covering a deep, sandy, mossy subsoil in some parts and large deep beds of shells and covered in others.

The mud between the Coney Island and the rampart dyke is deep. It consists of little else than rotten shells covering very extensive beds of shells yet in an undecayed state. But north of the Coney Island, between it and the Isle of Burt, the shell-beds are less deeply covered with mud and shells are easily raised from them and carried on shore, the bottom being sufficiently hard to bear loaded carts in the absence of the tide.

However, shells are but little used for manure on the rich warm crofts of Burt, but in consequence of the scarcity of limestone, large quantities are burned into lime for building because they are easily procured and because very little fuel burns them, for fuel is rather scarce in the Isle of Burt. To make good clean lime of shells they are drawn on shore and spread on smooth grassy ground close to water, which is thrown upon them until they are washed clean of sand and mud, and when cleansed and dry, they are burned in the same manner. Broken limestone is burned into lime.

But finding that shells and all the marine manures are used pretty nearly in the same manner in the Blanket Nook or Nuke, Burt, Isle of Inch and Upper Fahan, it may be best to narrate the practice of these several districts in the use of these manures together, next after the description of their respective shores, soils and situations, which will follow next after the statistical solutions respecting Inch and Burt.

Isle of Burt

The Isle of Burt is from the south east part of Mulleeny about a mile and nearly three-quarters in a direct line to the north west point of Ballymoney, and a mile and three-quarters from the south point of Castlehill directly to the Farland Point, and contains about [blank] Cunningham acres [insert footnote: the blanks will be filled up as soon as the calculation of the acres is completed], of which only about [blank] acres are bog, and that nearly exhausted of fuel of the tillage and green pasture comparatively, but little is steep, rocky and bad and none is mountain.

The tillage is accounted extremely good naturally and can, in the hands of industrious skilful farmers, be kept in perpetual fruitfulness by the abundance of manure left by every tide upon its shore and deposited by creation in every bed and strand around it.

The Isle of Burt was, and is still, so called, although a natural peninsula, because the sea surrounds it to nearly three-fourths of its circumference, and of the isthmus part the one-half was in early times a deep bog and the other half a marsh that the tide probably then overflowed and which, although now the course of a small stream, still overflows at least with spring tides.

The isle is well accommodated with roads that branch through it from the south east side, so as to afford convenience to the whole and also to the Isle of Inch by leading to the ferry from the Farland Point into that island. Brigs of from 200 to 300 tons discharge cargoes of coal at the Farland Point for Mr Latham's public distillery at Bohullian; but a very good and a more convenient landing-place could be made at the entrance of the road into Cole bay or strand near the old church of Burt or Grange. Most of the boats belonging to the isle are kept at the Farland Point.

About a mile and a quarter of the shore of the Isle of Burt, on the north and west, is clay banks of but moderate height. All the rest of the shores of the isle and of the mainland is low and muddy, but most of the mud bed along shore, particularly along the south west, west and north of the isle, is planted with stones to encourage the growth of the weed femnagh for manure. Femnagh grows near shore on rocks and stones that uncover or nearly uncover with ebb of tide and should be cut or gathered only every third year, by which the quantity is greatly increased and the quality of the plant is greatly improved.

The whole length of main shore, including the Isle of Burt, from Drimbwee to the point of Buinaraa, at which the Rathmullan ferry-boat lands below Fahan Churchtown, is about 17 and a half miles, viz. from Drimbwee to the Burnfoot 12 and three-quarter miles and thence to the point of Ruinara 4 and three-quarter miles; almost all low muddy shore or such planted to propagate weed and of which the most remarkable points are Tredy, a point of Speanog in Burt, and Tooban and Magherabeg or Magherabueg, between the Burn Foot and Fahan.

Magherabueg Point is frequently called Quigley's Point because one Quigley keeps the ferryboat that plies from it to Carrickanee in the Isle of Inch. Roads lead to and from this ferry.

Isle of Inch

The Isle of Inch lies directly north of the Isle of Burt and the north of Inch lies beyond Fahan channel nearly west of Fahan Churchtown. It is about 8 and a half miles in circumference, about 2 and a half from the south east extreme of Carrickanee, north westward to the point of Binnault or Bheinaalt at the Hawk's Nest; and but little more than 2 miles from the ruins of Inch Castle at south to Carrignahaa Point in middle Grange at north.

The Isle of Inch comprises 8 quarterlands and contains about [blank] Cunningham acres, of which [blank] acres are under tillage, meadows and green pasture, [blank] acres are heathy and steep rocky mountain and exhausted turbaries. [Insert footnote: The blanks cannot be filled up correctly until the map is constructed which, from the fieldwork already [done?], will employ from 6 to 8 months]. These last are so wholly stripped of moss and bared to the subsoil rock or sterile till that the parts of the island that afforded any kind of peat or substitute for fuel are so wasted in this way that they must remain irrecoverably or irreclaimably useless.

Soil on Inch

The tillage soil of Inch is in general good, warm and productive, and is, like Burt, easily kept in very good condition by sea manure, with which every part of its shores are ever plentifully supplied. The meadows are manured with seaweed, shells, mud, sand and by watering. Irrigation very much improves both meadows and pastures and lay or lea tillage, if a good deal watered through the season next before it is to be ploughed for a crop of oats, and it is very beneficial to succeeding crop of flax.

The island produces excellent crops of potatoes, barley, flax and oats, and from a small trial of wheat, there is not a doubt but it would be equally good if the farms were parked so as to protect it sufficiently in winter.

Replies [by G. Montgomery?] to Queries on Burt and Inch from North West Farming Society

NATURAL STATE

Situation

With the assistance of Thomas Anderson of Cloghglass, I collected the following answers to as many of the North West Society's statistical queries, as far as they are applicable to the Isle of Inch and to the chapelry of Burt.

   1st. Burt and Inch are in the county of Donegal.

   2nd. In the barony of Inishowen and diocese of Derry.

   3rd. In the parish of Templemore and curacy or chapelry of Burt and Inch, and deanery of Derry. Burt has a Protestant chapel in Churchtown and Inch has the like in Moress <Moruss>. The cure is supplied alternately or every second Sunday at each. The Roman Catholic priest attends Burt and Inch in the same manner. The Presbyterians of the island attend sermon, some at Burt and some at Fahan.

Proprietors

The proprietor of Burt, the Earl of Wicklow by lease from the Marquis of Donegal. The proprietors of Inch: the heirs of Mr Darcus, Thomas Woore Esquire and others. Mr Woore resides in the family mansion in Moress mostly in summer and the Earl of Wicklow part of each summer in Castleforward in the parish of All Saints. All the temporal lands of Inishowen are Lord Donegall's.

Subdivisions of Inch

The Isle of Inch comprehends the following quarterlands; their contents are in Cunningham measure as under: 1st, Grange; 2nd, Moress; 3rd, Carrickanee; 4th, Byletts; 5th, Ballymakernaghan; 6th, Castle Quarter; 7th, Bohullian; 8th, Ballynakillue.

Townlands of Inch Island

In Grange, which norths the island, are comprised the townlands of Greddy, Grange, Strachack and Fergans.

   Moress has no subdenominations, lies north east.

Carrickanee comprises near or north Carrickanee and far or south Carrickanee at east.

Byletts has no subdenominations, at south east.

Ballymakernaghan, Upper and Lower, in the interior of the island.

Castle Quarter, no subdenominations, lies at south.

Bohullian comprises Bohullian, Glaak and the Milltown of Inch.

Ballynakillue is the westmost quarterland and comprises Bhinaalt, Drum, Mullnadee, Cloghglass and Boarran.

Quarterlands of Burt

Burt comprehends 9 quarterlands which are, with their contents in Cunningham measure, as under: 1st, Castlecooly and Milltown; 2nd, Kairnamuaddy; 3rd, Bohullian, part of which is enclosed in Castleforward deerpark; 4th, Speenog; 5th, Moress; 6th, Mulleeny; 7th, Carrowan and Drumgowan; 8th, Ballymoney; 9th, Grange and Castlehill. [Insert note: [Last 4] the Isle of Burt].

PRODUCTIVE ECONOMY AND NATURAL FEATURES

Size of Farms

5th. Farms are of various sizes. Some are 40 or 50 Cunningham acres but many are smaller, being from 10 or 12 to 16 or 20 acres each, of tillage and green pasturage. They are enclosed partly with clay ditches, some of which are quicked with thorn and some with whins, and partly with stone fences. The spade and the plough are both employed in tilling.

Every kind of manure from the farmyard, the sea and burned soil is made use of in Burt and Inch, and the succession of crops after land has lain lay is: potatoes, barley, oats, flax and oats; but if the land be not very good, flax must succeed barley.

Few farms in Burt or Inch offer at this time much maiden land for improvement beyond what is already reclaimed. New manure is the most expeditious reducer of obstinate or moory soils.

Pasture-Lands

6th. This applied to in no.5. Very little pasture remains untilled. Such lots as are not reclaimed are either very rocky, too steep or otherwise unpromising.

Hills and Mountains

7th. Inch has but one hill of considerable height. It is situate near the north western part of the island, is covered with stunted heath or partly rock, having been long since bared of moss by digging peat or peat sods for fuel, and does not offer anything of consequence for improvement. Burt is southed by a ridge of high land, of which the top or several tops are partly heathy and lie too high to be good subjects for improvement.

Bogs and Moors

8th. The bogs of Inch and mostly of Burt, except a lot of turf bog in the former reserved for the use of the mansion, were long since exhausted of moss, bared to the subsoil, and without bog timber for many years.

Woods

9th. There are no woods, orchards, plantations or nurseries of consequence in Burt or Inch. The appearance of such trees as have been permitted to grow shows that timber would grow prosperously in either. I saw large trees in Moress in Inch.

10th. Ash and sycamore, of which a few grow about the gardens in Burt and Inch, appear to thrive. Larch and fir in moderately low situations in Mr Ferguson's demesne appear to do well but do not seem to prosper in high situations.

Rents

11th. Good arable and meadow, let some time ago, pays from 23s to 28s per Cunningham acre. Ordinary arable from 18s to 20s per ditto. Bad [arable?] and green pasture from 8s to 12s per ditto. Moory pasture per query 8th, of little value.

12th. [Rent for bogs] Answered in query 8th.

13th. [Agricultural implements]: the introduction of one or two (but few) English and Scotch ploughs only.

Fencing and Walling

14th. Stone fences and ditches with clay banks; probably clay banks sowed with whins may be the best fence among ordinary farmers. Such, if well made, are pretty permanent and not expensive. The whins afford very good green winter feeding for horses, cows and sheep.

Provision for Poor

15th. In the present depressed state of agriculture, the farmers, particularly of Inch, cannot afford to employ one-half of the labouring poor. They get little to do in winter, which comprehends the months of December, January, February and the beginning of March, and the fisheries do not give them much hope of winter employment.

Wages

16th. Along Lough Swilly few hire servants throughout the year; but for spring labour labourers get from 8d to 10d with diet or from 1s 1d to 1s 8d cosnant or cosnet, and for the harvest from the beginning of August to the end of November good labourers get from 2 pounds 10s to 2 pounds 16s 6d. Jobs are not worked here to the piece. Female servants who hire for all works, spinning harvest etc., get from 1 guinea to 25s half-yearly.

Grazing and Draining

17th. [Grazing]: none here.

18th. Clover and grasses of each kind do as well in Burt and Inch as in any such soils, but, except in gardens, farmers have not enclosures to keep clover at any time from sheep.

19th. Both surface and underdraining are practised in Burt and Inch very profitably.

Manures

20th. Stable and sea manures, chiefly weed, to warm soils; but for cold soils moss, moor or clay, in tillage or in lay or to be reclaimed, manure with sea mud, shells or sand; weed will give good crops off either when once thoroughly reclaimed. In Burt mossy soils are burned, and in some instances near the shore, where mud and shells were both convenient, but in Inch the soil has too little moss to bear burning.

Irrigation

21st. In Burt and Inch farmers water meadows with profitable effect, and lay or lea through the summer before it is to be cropped with oats, by which both that crop and a succeeding crop of flax are very much benefited. Burt and Inch have numerous springs and small streams of good water flowing from high situations. Few tracts could be more readily watered than these.

Dairies and Oxen

22nd. Dairies do not exist here but several persons send milk, some once and some twice a week, to Derry in summer but from Burt only.

23rd. Oxen are not used here in husbandry.

Spade Tillage

24th. Spade tillage is practised on wet, rocky soils where the plough cannot be conveniently employed. Ground so tilled always yields good crops. Good practical farmers hardly doubt but any land would bear better crops after spade tillage than after being ploughed, nor have I a doubt that were the Glenawley laye used in the mountain glens of Donegal, it would soon be preferred to either plough or spade.

Crops and Rotation

25th. Course of crops: potatoes, barley, oats, flax and oats.

In Burt and Inch, in June 1823, potatoes sold for 2d per stone, oaten meal 1s 1d per peck, barley from 1s 4d to 1s 6d per stone, oats from 8d to 10d per stone and butter from 5d to 6d per lb. of 16 oz.

26th. The measure of land here is computed by the Cunningham acre.

Livestock

27th. Inch always rears the old Irish breed of cows; Burt in some instances feeds larger.

28th. Horses, cows and sheep in Burt and Inch graze the pastures in common. Inch produces good small mutton and fine wool. The island, considered under all its circumstances, capabilities and localities, would probably appear admirably calculated for a sheep-walk.

29th. The common Irish sheep only are reared in Burt and Inch, and with very few exceptions in all Inishowen. The inhabitants think them more than all others adapted to the soil and climate.

30th. Extensive farmers require and keep large horses to perform their labour but the smaller class of farmers commonly use ponies.

31st. The common description of broad and small-eared swine seen in almost every village in Ulster are met with in Burt and Inch.

Flax Seed

32nd. To this query no probable reply was offered. It could not be pressed in a district where so few individuals would venture into conversation concerning flax seed.

Improvements in Livestock

33rd. No material improvement has taken place within the last 20 years in Burt or Inch, nor do its

Lough Swilly

best-informed inhabitants expect any immediate improvement in their livestock while farms continue so generally small, the produce of the tillage insufficient for the maintenance of the occupying families and the pastures so much overstocked and bare as we every day see them, and mostly of bad quality and very unproductive. We cannot hope for much improvement among the cattle that graze upon it.

Fishing and Coast

34th. A great many small rivulets descend from the high grounds of Burt and Inch to the sea but nothing worthy the name of river or lough. In Burt the Farland Point only is used as a harbour; see the Isle of Burt. The strand around the point is broad at low water and clean, and is landed upon with very little inconvenience on either side according as the wind permits. But in Inch, Keady creek in the north of the Mill bay is the chief harbour in the south of Inch; several boats, however, are kept hauled up near the mill in Mill bay, which is situate but a little westward from Inch Castle. And the large bed before it norths the entrance to Farland channel.

The outer edge of the Mill bay bed from the north entrance of Farland channel takes the direction from the outer north point of Ballymoney of Burt, towards the outside of Drum of Inch, or of the rock Cregmacconnack for near three-quarters of a mile, leaving a space that does not ebb dry north of it between it and Dunleeny old fort towards Drum Point.

That space is Keady port, where boats and light vessels may for a quarter of a mile lie sheltered from north west, north, north east and east winds; but the cleanest ground to anchor on is along pretty close to the large bed which comprises several beds of sweet grass, mud and shells. The Keady would be rendered very secure by a small shelter built in a south easterly direction from Dunleeny upper point to cover boats between it and the head of the Keady, where the road descends into it a little north west of the mill. Very large plants of Carduus benedictus grow near this shore of the Mill bay.

Seafood

Skates and flukes are speared among the sweet grass. The shell-beds consist of the shells of oysters, cockles, aghens, cockspurs, periwinkles etc., every species that are natives of Lough Swilly. The best Irish oysters are obtained by dredging Farland channel from Ballymoney up past the point to between Ardnancel Point and Tredy; and when herrings are in Lough Swilly, the take is generally good in Farland channel.

Coastline

From the Mill bay, Duncrotagh and Inch Castle (which a solitary old woman inhabits) round eastward to Farland ferry, the shore is bounded by mostly sloping clay banks under which the shore is stony and rocky. The Castle port or creek east of the old castle is cleared of stones and rocks for a boat-port at which turf for the village of Castle Quarter and others near it are landed and drawn to their owners by a road from it through the island.

The bottom of Bylett's bay in the south of Inch or north shore of Burt bay, and 5 or 6 furlongs eastward of the Castle port, is generally gravelly and the beach low here. Several boats lie hauled up as well as on Farland Point.

Ardnancel Point of Byletts is the south east point of Inch and hardly 2 furlongs east from Byletts bay, and from 2 to 3 furlongs farther down the shore. The new road through the strand into Inch enters it about the easternmost part of the island. Half a mile (by the shore) northward of the new road we meet Magherabeg or Quigley's ferry from Fahan into Inch, and from which roads lead to both Inch and Fahan; and at nearly half a mile further the Caaslagh muddy creek separates Carrickanee from the point of Moress along which, and a mile below it, the shore is gravelly. But without that gravelly border to the channel (here called Fahan channel) is deep mud beds, partly overgrown with sweet grass.

From Moress House, Mr Woore's, to Moress Point is nearly half a mile, but directly under the house the beach winds to within less than a furlong of the road and a neat walk communicates between them. This place is a kind of dry bay with a quarry of coarse or heavy bluish slate in a point of Moress that north wests it. In this bay boats can be easily hauled on shore but cannot cross the mud bed to it without a good depth of tide to carry them over it.

The foot of Strachack brook, Luackan Point, Carrignahaa creek, Doon Lower or East bay and Doon Upper or West bay are landing-places used by boats while employed fishing in Fahan channel, and herring boats may also land and may be, if necessary, hauled up within the Scaart rock in Maltman's bay, in Bhinaalt. From Strachack to Doon the north shore of Inch or of Grange is beached with altogether dry shells. The shore-banks are partly rocky and partly clay, and northward from it the large bed that wests the mouth of Fahan channel extends half a mile and westward from the channel to the doon, which is a peninsula point of Grange.

The outer shore of Doon is moderately high, upright rock on the east, north and west, nor is the isthmus quite low; and the land immediately south of it is high and craggy and the Doon is now a fort with a strong tower.

The creeks of Inch afford sea-sand, shells, mud and weed, all rich good manures. Farland channel is celebrated for the famous Burt and Inch oysters and this, with the other creeks and shores of Burt and Inch, afford their poor a very large proportion of their food in cockles, mussels, barnaghs or limpets, wilks, periwinkles, in summer sand-eels and some dillisk.

Quarries and Minerals

35th. Metallic ores have not been found in Burt or Inch, but the appearance of a spa in Byletts indicates that it flows through a strong iron mine.

36th. A slate quarry in Moress in the eastern shore of Inch, on Fahan channel, produces strong, heavy, bluish slate. It has not been sufficiently opened or worked to a sufficient depth to enable one to form an opinion of how it may answer expectation.

A quarry of coarse blue limestone in Castle Quarter produces kiln ribs; see query 37th.

Quarries of common, hard building stone may be had in many parts of Inch and Burt but none has been so effectually opened and worked as that in Grange, from which the port and tower of the Doon were built. It is convenient to Upper Doon bay but exportation of such stone from Inch is improbable.

37th. A vein of blue and grey limestone crosses Inch from north west to south east and may be quarried in Bhinaalt, Boarran, Ballymakernaghan and Carrickanee at the south east and in Castle Quarter towards the south west part of the island, but scarcity of native fuel hinders Inch to burn any more lime than barely what is necessary for building and repairing their houses, and a superabundance of the sea manures renders any more unnecessary. A lime-kiln in Inch worked with coal would probably be worth consideration.

There is now a road from Inch to Burt. The latter has no limestone nor is lime burned any nearer to it than Cloghglass near Derry.

Coal

38th. Coal has not been found in Burt or Inch, but John Hagan of Bhinaalt says that an engineer and others, military officers and seamen, challenged 2 places, one in Bhinaalt and one in Moress, where they said the indications of coal were such as should not disappoint any who would take the trouble to search for them. Hagan was not at hand when I wished to see him on that subject.

Springs

39th. There is a strong, copious chalybeate spa in a high situation in Bylett. It cures pains in the stomach and heartburn, besides possessing the other medicinal qualities and virtues commonly ascribed to chalybeates; see query 35th.

Geology

40th. White and probably calcareous marle is found in a bog a little above the corn mill in Inch. It is visible in the surface of the bog and, from causing a shovel shaft of from 4 to 5 feet long to be thrust down directly into it without feeling any change of substance, it may be supposed to be of considerable depth.

What I saw at the pit resembled newly slaked lime in a wet state. It was, however, lifted out of the pit when overflowed with water and not from a depth of more than 10 or 12 inches under the surface. It is used by the islanders for whitewash and has as good an immediate effect as ill-coloured lime, but not being naturally adhesive and being untempered by any substance necessary to give it adhesion, it soon crumbles off. It was tried upon land but produced no visible effect.

Upon enquiry, I was informed that the water was not overturned off the pit and that none has ever been raised from any greater depth under the surface than can be had by a common shovel from the upper strata thereof. May not the marle so lifted have been much affected or changed in quality by having lain long in water?

Condition of Inhabitants

41st. The condition of the islanders of Inch most generally resembles that of their neighbouring district of Burt and Fahan. Here, as there, some possess more comfort than others, even when equal diligence in industry is visible. Want of the convenience of turbary in Inch produces other inconveniences and diminishes such domestic comforts as good warm fires and fire light affords to country families in the spinning or winter season.

The Inchites are strongly disposed to industry on their farms and on the water when the presence of the fishery invites them to it, but when the latter fails money must be earned by rearing flax, by spinning and selling linen yarn, or by weaving and selling linen; and in the prosecution of these pursuits, and the purchase and sale of sheep, they commonly employ the little money they earn.

The greatest number of the islanders are Roman Catholics, who are the poorest. Presbyterians occupy the largest portion of the island and are the wealthiest. The Church Protestants of Inch, although few, are nevertheless in circumstances somewhat comfortable.

Houses

42nd. In Inch the farms are generally small and of course the farmhouses upon them are small also, and too many of them but indifferent, in but bad repair. However, a few farmhouses are of decent appearance and are internally comfortable, both in regard to cleanliness and good repair.

Fuel

43rd. Inch is wholly exhausted of native fuel except a small lot of turf bog belonging to the proprietor of the island. The islanders get turf from both sides of Lough Swilly, some from Buncrana and some from Teeroddy in the parish of Tully, and from both they are drawn by water.

Diet

44th. Farmers in Inch, from the circumstances of their farms not being sufficiently parked, cannot conveniently fatten cows. Some buy beef and almost all fatten hogs (some for food and some for sale). These and a due proportion of fish, butter, eggs and milk with potatoes, oaten bread, oaten meal, water [comprise their diet].

Letter from W. Stokes to James Sinclair, April 1823

MEMOIR WRITING

Letter from W. Stokes to J. Sinclair

My Dear Sir,

I have read Mr Montgomery's account of Lough Swilly and Mulroy. I have not had leisure to examine it minutely since I received it on the 4th of March.

I cannot rely on the judgement of the gentleman in the country whether the points he selects for small harbours are the best. I suppose it would be quite advisable that he should continue his survey of the remaining parts of the coasts of your district.

I wish he would add to the new surveys an estimate of the bulk of each proposed pier, distinguishing the number of cubic feet of loose stonework and squared stonework. I suppose similar estimates would be added to what he has already surveyed, if he knows the length of his proposed piers and the soundings of the shore. I suppose his surveys will be much more accurate than any hitherto published.

Mr Montgomery desired me in his last letter to determine the size and scale of the extracts from his map which I should publish. I cannot do so as yet: I must ascertain from the London booksellers what support can be got for the work. I think it likely I shall find it my interest to have the maps done by lithographic printing, which is now executed neatly, and the expense is moderate. I don't think Mr Montgomery should be troubled to collect specimens.

The principal object to the eastern extremity of your district would be to improve the communication between Coleraine and the sea. Might not the whole country be served by regular ferries at Magilligan, between the 2 batteries at Lough Swilly, across Mulroy in any present ferry sites, and further along the coast in whatever is the best direction?

With respect to a railway to connect Lough Foyle and Lough Erne, Mr Robinson's general judgement on the subject is excellent. Railways are much less than half the expense of moderate canals. I suppose a horse cannot do on a railway more than the fifth of what he can do on a canal. There would be 2 shiftings of the cargo on quitting or resuming the water communication.

There would be no difficulty in getting persons sufficiently qualified to give lectures on botany, chemistry and mineralogy in your principal towns, the lectures on botany or chemistry to go so far only as to assist the farmer or linen manufacturer. All this would be done for a very moderate allowance to the lecturer, but you must be at the expense of a cheap portable apparatus. If you add to it the making collections of plants and minerals for a statistical report, you will more enhance the expense than benefit the public. Whatever you determine on with respect to lecturing, I will be happy to choose a lecturer for you, if you will entrust me, and sketch an outline for him to fill up.

Mr Kirk has cut a head in basse relief on the Dunloughey marble. He would be glad to have a block 18 inches in one direction and 12 inches in the two other. If such a block was delivered to him free of expense, he would cut a head of Anacreon Moore on it [continued in a different hand] for a society in London which, as he says, would give it a name in the market. A block for a full length statue, 7 foot long, of the best Carrara marble would cost, during the war, 600 pounds. This subject requires a letter by itself.

I am, Dear Sir, your obliged and faithful, honourable servant, [signed] W. Stokes, 17th April 1823.

[To] James Sinclair, Holyhill, Strabane.

Miscellaneous Papers, County Donegal

List of Birds with Latin and Common Names

NATURAL HISTORY

Names of Birds

Gallinadae. Tarsus feathered: Lagopus, grouse <grous>; Lagopus scoticus, red grouse; Lagopus vulgaris, ptarmigan; Ictras [Icterus]; Ictras ictrix, black cock.

Tarsus naked: Perdix, partridge; Perdix cinerea, common partridge; Perdix rufa, Guernsey partridge; coturnix, quail; Coturnix vulgaris, common quail.

Domesticated Gallinadae: Pavo cristatus, crested peacock; Mealeagris gallopavo, turkey; Gallus domesticus, common fowl; Numidia mealeagris, pintado or Guinea-hen; Phasianus colchicus, pheasant.

Extirpated Gallinae: Urogallus vulgaris, cock of the woods or capercaillie.

Stragglers: Coturnix marilanda, American quail.

Columbadae. Columba, pigeon; Columba palumbus, ring dove; Columba oenas, rock dove; Columba turtur, turtle dove.

Accipitres. Rapacious birds: Diurna, hawks; Nocturna, owls.

Diurnal rapacious birds: Falco, falcon; Falco lanarius, lanner; Falco subbuteo, hobby; Falco tinnunculus, kestrel; Falco avalon, merlin; Gyrfalco, jerfalcon; Gyrfalco candicans; Balbusardus, osprey; Balbusardus haliaetus; Milvus, kite; Milvus vulgaris; Pernis, honey-buzzard; Pernis apivorus; Aquila, eagle; Aquila chrysaetos, golden eagle; Aquila albicilla, the erne; Circus, hen-harrier; Circus cyaneus; Buteo, buzzard; Buteo vulgaris, common buzzard; Buteo lagopus, rough-legged buzzard; Buteo palumanbarius, goshawk; Buteo nisus, sparrow-hawk; Buteo ceruginosus, moor buzzard; Buteo cincraccus, ash-coloured buzzard.

Nocturnal rapacious birds: Otus, horn-owl; Otus vulgaris, long horn-owl; Otus brachyotis, short horn-owl; Aluco, barn-owl; Bubo, eagle-owl; Scops aldrovandi, Scops strix; Scops stridula, ivy-owl; Scops myctea, snowy owl; Scops passerina, little owl; Hirundo, swallow; Hirundo rustica, the swallow; Hirundo urbica, the martin; Hirundo riparia, sand-martin; Cypselus, swift; Cypselus apus, common swift; Cypselus caprimulgus, goatsucker; Cypselus europeus, European goatsucker; Lanius, shrike; Lanius excubitor, cinereous shrike; Lanius colluria, red-backed shrike; Muscicapa, flycatcher; Muscicapa atricafrilla, red flycatcher; Muscicapa grisola, spotted flycatcher; Bombycilla, chatterer; Bombycilla garrula, Bohemian chatterer; Turdus, thrush; Turdus viscivorus, missel [sic] thrush; Turdus musicus, common thrush; Turdus iliacus, redwing thrush; Turdus pilaris, fieldfare thrush; Turdus [blank], ground colour of the plumage black; Turdus merula, blackbird; Turdus torquatus, ring thrush.

Pastor roseus, rose-coloured ousel; Oriolus, oriole; Oriolus galbula, golden oriole; Cinclus, dipper; Cinclus aquaticus; Saxicola, chat; Saxicola oenanthe, fallow-chat; Saxicola rubetra, whinchat; Saxicola rubicola, stone chat; Sylvia rubecula, redbreast; Sylvia phoenicurus, redstart; Curruca, warbler; Curruca locustella, grasshopper warbler; Curruca salicarica, sedge warbler; Curruca arundinacea, reed warbler; Curruca luscinia, nightingale; Curruca hortensis, pettychaps; Curruca sibillatrix, wood wren; Curruca atricapilla, blackcap; Curruca provincialis, Dartford warbler; Curruca sylvia, whitethroat; Curruca sylviella, lesser whitethroat; Accentor modularis, hedgesparrow; Regulus cristatus, golden-crowned wren; Regulus trochilus, yellow wren; Regulus hippolais, lesser pettychaps; Troglodytes, wren; Troglodytes vulgaris, common wren; Motacilla, wagtail; Motacilla alba, white wagtail; Motacilla boarula, grey wagtail; Motacilla flava, yellow wagtail.

Anthus, titling; Anthus petrorsus, sea titling; Anthus pratensis, meadow titling; Anthus trivialis, field titling; Loxia curvirostra, crossbill; Corythus, hawfinch; Corythus enucleator, common hawk; Emberiza, bunting; Emberiza cirlus, cirl bunting; Emberiza miliaria, common bunting; Emberiza schoeniculus, reed bunting; Emberiza nivalis, snow bunting; Alauda, lark; Alauda arvensis, field lark; Alauda rubra, red lark; Alauda arborea, wood lark; Parus, titmouse; Parus major, great titmouse or ox-eaze; Parus ater, colemouse; Parus palustris, marsh-titmouse; Parus caeruleus, blue titmouse; Parus cristatus, crested titmouse; Parus caudatus, long-tailed titmouse; Parus biarmicus, bearded titmouse; Sitta, nuthatch; Sitta europaea, common nuthatch; Pyrrhula, bullfinch; Pyrrhula vulgaris, common bullfinch; Coccothraustes, grosbeak; Coccothraustes vulgaris, common grosbeak; Coccothraustes chloris, green grosbeak; Pyrgita, sparrow; Pyrgita montana, tree-sparrow.

Fringilla, finch; Fringilla coelebs, chaffinch; Fringilla montifringilla, mountain-finch; Fringilla cannabina, brown linnet; Fringilla montium, mountain linnet; Fringilla linaria, rose linnet; Fringilla spinus, siskin; Fringilla carduelis, goldfinch; Sturnus, starling; Sturnus vulgaris, common starling; Garrulus glandarius, jay; Pica, magpie; Pica caudata, common magpie; Corvus, crow; Corvus corax, raven; Corvus corone, carrion crow; Corvus cornix, hooded crow; Corvus monedula, jackdaw; Corvus frugilegus, rook; Corvus certhia, creeper; Corvus familiaris, common creeper; Pyrrhocorax, chough; Pyrrhocorax graculus, Cornish chough; Upupa, hoopoe; Upupa epops, common hoopoe; Alcedo, kingfisher; Alcedo ispida, common kingfisher.

Scansores: Cuculus, cuckoo; Cuculus canorus, common cuckoo; Picus, woodpecker; Picus viridis, green woodpecker; Picus major, greater spotted woodpecker; Picus minor, lesser spotted woodpecker; Picus martius, great black woodpecker; Picus villosus, hairy woodpecker; Yunx [Jynx], wryneck; Yunx torquilla, common wryneck; Grallae, waders; Glareola torquata, Austrian pontincole; Platea leucorodia, common spoonbill.

Cultrirostres: Ardea, heron; Aardea cinerea, common heron; Ardea stellaris, bittern; Ardea egretta, Ardea garzetta, Ardea purpurea; Ardea nycticorax, night heron; Ardea ralloides, squacco heron; Ardea minuta, little bittern; Ardea aquinoctialis, Ardea cayanensis; Ciconia alba, white stork; Ciconia nigra, black stork; Psophia crepitans.

Pressirostres: Rallus, rail; Rallus aquaticus, water-rail; Oortygometra, crake; Ortygometra crex, corncrake; Gallinula, gallinule; Gallinula chloropus, common gallinule or water-hen; Gallinula porzana, spotted gallinule; Gallinula pusilla; Gallinula foljambei, olivaceous gallinule; Fulica, coot; Fulica atra, common coot; Phalaropus, phalarope; Phalaropus lobatus, grey phalarope; Lobipes, cootfoot; Lobipes huperboreus, red cootfoot; Recurvirostra, avocet; Numenius, curlew; Numenius arquata, common curlew; Numenius pheopus, whimbrel curlew; Ibis falcinellus, glossy ibis; Totanus fuscus; Totanus calidris, redshank; Totanus ochropus, green sandpiper; Totanus glareola, wood sandpiper; Totanus macularia, spotted sandpiper; Totanus hypoleucos, common sandpiper; Totanus glottis, greenshank; Scolopax, snipe; Scolopax rusticola, woodcock; Scolopax major, great snipe; Scolopax sabini; Scolopax gallinago, common snipe; Scolopax gallinula, jack snipe; Scolopax grisea, brown snipe.

Limosa, godwit; Limosa aeocephala, black-tailed godwit; Limosa rufa, bar-tailed godwit; Tringa, sandpiper; Tringa subarquata, Tringa alpina, Tringa pusilla, Tringa minuta; Tringa canutus, knot; Tringa striata, purple sandpiper; Tringa pugnax; Strepsilas, turnstone; Vanellus, lapwing; Vanellus cristatus, common lapwing; Squatarola; Cursorius isabellinus, cream-coloured courser; Himantopus plinii, long legs; Calidris, sanderling; Calidris arenaria, common sanderling; Charadrius, plover; Charadrius pluvialis, green plover; Charadrius morinellus, dottrel; Charadrius hiaticula, ringed plover; Oid- ienomus, thick knee; Oidienomus bellonii, common thick knee; Haematopus, oyster-catcher; Haemotopus ostralegus, common oyster-catcher; Otis, bustard; Otis tarda, great bustard; Otis tetrax, little bustard; Phalacrocorax, comorant; Phalacrocorax carbo, common cormorant; Phalacrocorax graculus, common shag; Phalacrocorax cristatus, crested shag.

Sula, gannet; Sula bassana, common gannet; Oidemia, scoter; Oidemia fusca, velvet scoter; Oidemia nigra, black scoter; Oidemia leucocephala, white-throated duck; Somateria, eider; Somateria mollissima, common eider; Somateria spectabilis, king eider; Clangula vulgaris, golden eye; Clangula histrionica, harlequin duck; Clangula glacialis, long-tailed duck; Nyroca leucopthalmos, white eye; Nyroca ferina, pochard; Nyroca marila, scaup; Nyroca fuligula, tufted duck; Tadorna, sheldrake; Tadorna vulpanser, common sheldrake; Spathulea, shoveler; Spathulea clypeata, common shoveler; Anas, duck; Anas boschas, common duck; Anas strepera, gadwall; Anas acuta, cracker; Anas penelope, wigeon; Anas querqedula, garganey; Anas crecca, teal; Anas glocitans, bimaculated duck; Cygnus, swan; Cygnus ferus, wild swan; Anser, goose; Anser apustris, grey goose; Anser ferus, wild goose; Anser erythropus, laughing goose; Anser bernicla, bernacle or claikis; Anser brenta, brent goose; Anser gambensis, Egyptian, ganser or gambo goose; Anser canadiensis, Canada goose; Anser hispanicus, Chinese, Spanish, Guinea or swan goose.

Mergeus, goosander; Mergeus merganser, green-headed goosander; Mergeus serrator, red-breasted goosander; Mergeus albellus, white-headed goosander; Alca, auk; Alca impennis, great auk; Alca torda, razorbill; Tratercula, coulterneb; Tratercula arctiae, common coulterneb; Podiceps, grebe; Podiceps cristatus, crested grebe; Podiceps rubricollis, red-necked grebe;

Podiceps cornutus, horned grebe; Podiceps auritus, eared grebe; Podiceps minor, little grebe; Colymbus, diver; Colymbus glacialis, northern diver; Colymbus arcticus, black-throated diver; Colymbus septentrionalis, red-throated diver; Uria, guillemot; Uria troil, foolish guillemot; Cephus, scraber; Cephus grylle, common scraber; Mergulus, rotche; Mergulus melanoleucos, common rotche.

Procellaria, petrel; Procellaria glacialis, fulmar petrel; Procellaria pelagica, stormy petrel; Procellaria bullockii, fork-tailed petrel; Puffinus, puffin; Puffinus anglorum, Manks [Manx ?] puffin; Cataractes, skua; Cataractes vulgaris, common skua; Cataractes parasiticus, Arctic skua; Larus, gull; Larus glaucus, burgomaster; Larus islandicus, Iceland gull; Larus marinus, black-backed gull; Larus fuscus, yellow-legged gull; Larus argentatus, herring-gull; Larus canus, common gull; Larus rissa, kittiwake; Larus capistratus; Larus atricilla, laughing gull; Larus minutus, little gull; Larus candidus, snow bird; Sterna, tern; Sterna boysii, sandwich tern; Sterna anglica, gull-billed tern; Sterna hirundo, common tern; Sterna nigra, black tern; Sterna minuta, lesser tern.

www.ingramcontent.com/pod-product-compliance
Lightning Source LLC
Chambersburg PA
CBHW082337300426
44109CB00045B/2414